At the Elbow of Another

Studies in the
Postmodern Theory of Education

Joe L. Kincheloe and Shirley R. Steinberg
General Editors

Vol. 204

PETER LANG
New York • Washington, D.C./Baltimore • Bern
Frankfurt am Main • Berlin • Brussels • Vienna • Oxford

Wolff-Michael Roth
and Kenneth Tobin

At the Elbow of Another

Learning to Teach
by Coteaching

PETER LANG
New York • Washington, D.C./Baltimore • Bern
Frankfurt am Main • Berlin • Brussels • Vienna • Oxford

Library of Congress Cataloging-in-Publication Data

Roth, Wolff-Michael.
At the elbow of another: learning to teach by coteaching /
Wolff-Michael Roth and Kenneth Tobin.
p. cm. — (Counterpoints; vol. 204)
Includes bibliographical references (p.) and index.
1. Teachers—In-service training. 2. Teaching teams. 3. Education, Urban.
I. Title: Learning to teach by coteaching. II. Tobin, Kenneth George.
III. Title. IV. Counterpoints (New York, N.Y.); vol. 204.
LB1731 .R65   371.14'8—dc21   2001029274
ISBN 0-8204-5567-9
ISSN 1058-1634

Die Deutsche Bibliothek-CIP-Einheitsaufnahme

Roth, Wolff-Michael:
At the elbow of another: learning to teach by coteaching /
Wolff-Michael Roth and Kenneth Tobin.
−New York; Washington, D.C./Baltimore; Bern;
Frankfurt am Main; Berlin; Brussels; Vienna; Oxford: Lang.
(Counterpoints; Vol. 204)
ISBN 0-8204-5567-9

Cover drawing by Wolff-Michael Roth
Cover design by Lisa Dillon

The paper in this book meets the guidelines for permanence and durability
of the Committee on Production Guidelines for Book Longevity
of the Council of Library Resources.

Printed in the United States of America

ACKNOWLEDGMENTS

A project that leads to a book such as this is never possible without the help of many others, whose agency remains in the background.

We are grateful to the new teachers, Andy, Cam, Elwyn, Mark, Nadine, and Stephanie, who never hesitated to have us coteach with them in their classrooms, despite differences in experience and power that could have mediated our interactions. Of course, we extend our thanks to all those other new teachers who also allowed us to coteach with them, but who are not part of the cast of characters here. We thank the various teachers with regular positions who invited us to coteach with them, including Bert, Loretta, Mario, and all the other individuals not featured in this book. Our thanks also go to the superintendents and principals that encouraged us to work in their schools and thereby to assist some of the resident teachers to improve their praxis and learn about teaching. We are grateful to all of these individuals for allowing us to videotape coteaching lessons and cogenerative dialogue sessions, and for allowing us to use the materials in this book.

Our special thanks go to those individuals who, through their willingness to discuss our budding ideas with them, allowed us to recognize our shortcomings and, by attempting to overcome them, to learn about teaching. These individuals include our graduate students, Daniel Lawless, Judith McGonigal, and Gale Seiler. Others assisted us in videotaping and transcribing, including Sylvie Boutonné and Michael Bowen—we extend our thanks to these individuals.

Importantly, we thank our spouses Barbara and Sylvie, because, with seemingly infinite patience, they put up with our visiting each other and with the countless hours that we spent at the computer analyzing data, communicating with each other, and writing chapters.

Finally, grants from the Social Sciences and Humanities and Humanities Council of Canada (410-96-0681 & 410-99-0021) and the Spencer Foundations assisted in the data collection and writing of this work. All opinions are our own.

TABLE OF CONTENTS

Preface   ix

1. Teaching as Praxis   1

2. Re-learning to Teach   49

3. Becoming a Teacher at City High School   89

4. Historical Contexts of Coteaching in an Urban School   129

5. Learning to Teach Science in an Urban School   177

6. Researching as Coteaching and Colearning:
   Lessons from the Dihybrid Cross   213

7. Coteaching/Cogenerative Dialoguing:
   Research as Classroom Praxis   243

8. Coteaching/Cogenerative Dialoguing as
   Evaluation Methodology   271

   Epilogue: Looking Back—To the Future   295

   Glossary   315

   References   319

   Author Index   331

   Index   335

PREFACE

Teaching and learning are concepts that almost anyone seems to know a lot about. Every one of us has experienced teaching one way or another. At home, our parents, siblings, relatives, and neighbors teach us. At school, we had an array of teachers, some of whom we regard as good and others whom we regard less favorably. Accordingly, most of us have developed views about teachers and teaching based on our experiences of being learners and having been taught. For many of us, what we know is captured best in the stories we tell about the ways we were taught, the ways we prefer to be taught, and, on some occasions, the ways we taught others. Most people we have spoken to are practiced, too, at evaluating teaching. 'Tell me about the best teacher you ever had' is a prompt often followed by a brief pause and a number of stories that are rich in detail. Even better is to ask about the worst teacher a person has ever had. What is salient here is that most people have had first-hand experiences of teaching and have stories to tell about it. They also know how to distinguish good and bad teaching. Often the most vivid and detailed stories are those that reflect the insider status of the teller, of lived experience through the eyes of those who experienced it. Such accounts rarely connect explicitly with theories or research on teaching and learning.

Within educational institutions, where decisions about teaching and learning are made for numerous purposes, the situation is frequently quite different. Stories about teaching and learning still get told but they are about what we heard from the corridor, what we saw as we peeked through a window, what we were told about Period 2 by our Period 3 class, or what we observed during a formal evaluation. Usually the stories are impersonal and the experiences are less direct and more vicarious. Less frequent are stories (from adults) about being taught or teaching with someone else.

When teaching and learning are dealt with formally it is unusual to tell stories unless the purpose is to write a letter recommending a colleague for a job or a promotion. In fact, the accounts used in evaluations and research tend to be impersonal and factual in an effort to make them appear detached, unemotional, objective, and fair. There is a conscious effort to be detached (or to appear so) by separating the report on teaching from the emotions and the rich examples that are essential features of many stories. In this process, the observed is separated from lived experience as the observer adopts a detached, *fly-on-the-wall* perspective. Evaluators and researchers observe teaching and learning from the side or the back of the room and tell their stories according to specified guidelines within pre-established categories. In evaluation and frequently in research, too, it is regarded as good practice to pre-specify the categories in which teaching is described or evaluated because it is considered unfair to compare different teachers on different aspects of teaching. Comparisons dictate a need to be fair and to employ public criteria. Furthermore, it is desirable in many contexts to move away from the storied ways of reporting about teaching and learning. Instead, procedures are advocated that involve checking off observable phenomena, rating the frequency of occurrence of specified events, or using rating scales to make judgments about the quality of specified aspects of teaching. Check marks and ratings lend themselves to quantification and quantification to statistics.

Over the past 40 years the tendency to quantify evaluation has increased, a trend that has enabled decisions about teachers and learners to become even more distant and detached from persons. Decisions now can be made on the basis of numbers and statistics. Performance, expressed as a numeral, can be compared to pre-established benchmarks, perhaps based on normative data from thousands of teachers and teaching episodes. It is considered possible to be quite objective in comparing a number that represents teaching quality to a number that represents a benchmark to be surpassed for purposes that might include the granting of tenure, certification, promotion, merit pay, or retention as a teacher. The stakes can be high when teachers are evaluated.

In research the stakes are of a different type but they can be just as significant. Numerals and statistics can be the basis for comparisons, estimating strengths of relationships, and examining trends. Research reports and presentations become resources for educational policymakers, teacher educators, teachers, and other researchers. We learn, plan, and decide what to do next based in part on what we learn from a burgeoning research literature, of which a great deal focuses on issues relating to teaching and learning.

In this book, we break with these traditions. We present a different way in which teaching and learning to teach can be studied and evaluated. At the same time, our approach, in which individuals teach and make sense collectively (*coteaching/cogenerative dialoguing*), has tremendous potential for addressing current problems faced by teachers and students of teaching.

About This Book

This book is about teaching and learning to teach, written from the perspectives and experiences of two educators who teach and, in so doing, learn to teach. Teaching and learning to teach at the elbows of other teachers (including each other) provide us with new and different understandings and allow us to describe a different epistemology of teaching. We adopt a first-person perspective on teaching, sometimes our own and at other times that of peers, but seen through the eyes of coparticipants engaged in an activity with the same primary intention of assisting students to learn.

Throughout the book we focus on teaching and learning to teach at different stages of the career ladder and explore different ways of conceiving the roles of researchers, supervisors, evaluators, cooperating teachers, and 'new teachers'. We use the term 'new teacher' in preference to 'student teacher' or 'prospective teacher' because these latter terms are inconsistent with coteaching, which is premised on the ideas that we learn to teach by teaching (as distinct from observing, studying, or reflecting on teaching) and that learning to teach is a continuous 'becoming-in-the-classroom'. Coteaching allows for *legitimate* peripheral participation, whereas 'student teachers' are often regarded as novice or even deficient teachers whose presence ruptures otherwise high-quality learning environments. The individuals whose teaching and learning to teach are featured in the book include new teachers (Cam, Elwyn, Nadine, and Stephanie) enrolled at the time of the studies in a teacher preparation program and doing their internship, a teacher at the beginning of his career (Mario), and experienced teachers (Bert, Ken, Loretta, and Michael).

We take seriously the idea that distanced perspectives on teaching and learning are likely to differ markedly from those of insiders. Also we are concerned that the different ways we think about teaching can make a difference in how we describe, judge, and decide. Insofar as there are distinctly different ways to conceptualize teaching, we may expect that there will be different ways to enact practices involving teaching. For example, how we think about teaching will shape decisions on how we learn to teach. Such decisions are at the heart of designing and enacting programs of study for new teachers in universities, for professional development activities for practicing teachers, and for the ongoing/lifelong learning of teachers. Accordingly, in this book we examine the nature of teaching and investigate fresh approaches to teacher preparation, professional development, research, and evaluation.

As a result of the failure to take teachers' ways of experiencing classroom events as a starting point for theorizing their activities, practicing teachers continue to experience and bemoan a gap between what they encounter and learn in university courses (knowledge, theories) and their lived experiences as teachers. This gap is felt most intensively by new teachers engaged in field experiences. That is, despite normally having expended considerable time and effort in education courses, new teachers often feel that what they have learned is of minimal utility when they endeavor to teach their classes. Our conceptualization and application of coteaching was a response to these problems. As coteachers, we experience classroom events not as 'flies on the walls', outside observers, but from a similar perspective and under the same constraints as our fellow coteachers. Our own experience of the same then-and-there is in some senses shared with those with whom we coteach, resident teachers such as Mario and new teachers such as Cam. Co-teaching enables teachers to teach at one another's elbows and then, through collaboration in a professional discourse community, to formulate localized theories that accord with their shared experiences.

Overview of the Book

In the first chapter, we articulate our epistemology of teaching, which is grounded in practice (rather than focusing on 'knowledge', 'beliefs', and 'values' that are often considered to reside between the ears). Our epistemology highlights elements in the experience of teaching such as the fact that we always and already find ourselves *in* a world and *with* other people, who sometimes are the recipients of our actions, and that we are unreflective about a lot of the things we do in our daily work as teachers. From past experiences arise patterned dispositions that allow experienced practitioners to perceive and act in particular ways. We show how coteaching (accomplishing the task of teaching in a collective manner and, in this case, also learning to teach) provides a context in which teachers can develop and new teachers can learn to teach.

Chapter 2 is based on Ken's autobiographical account of having to learn *again* to teach when he moved to Philadelphia, where he eventually taught science on a daily basis in the lowest stream of an urban high school. Ken taught in Mario's class and, although they had talked about teaching the class together, Ken found himself often teaching on his own with an expectation that he would expertly deal with difficult situations. Ken's account allows us to understand that past experience may lead to forms of teaching that are not appropriate under all circumstances, especially when the teacher and students have markedly differing social and cultural histories. Ken's autobiographical account does not conclude on a happy note. In our conversation about the experience of (re-) learning to teach we address some of the particular difficulties that arise from teaching and learning to teach when there is a considerable gap between the social and cultural backgrounds of the teacher and the students.

Chapter 3 deals with Mario's experiences of teaching and learning to teach during his first 3 years in the same inner city school. As a recently certified teacher Mario has not had teaching experiences equivalent to those of Ken but he has more in common with the students in terms of age and interests and he understands more about the social and cultural dimensions of their lives. As a youth Mario had extensive experience of what Eli Anderson[1] described as the 'code of the street'. Consequently he is in a position to make sense of the ways of being that students bring with them from the street to the classroom. In this chapter we use an autobiographical narrative of Mario's 'becoming-in-the-classroom'[2] as the starting point for our conversation about important issues that arise from teaching and learning to teach. In particular, we focus on the dialectical tension that arises from teaching as a means to enhance students' opportunities in a world very different from the teacher's and the reproduction of inequities that arise from cultural differences.

Changing one's approach to teaching and teacher education does not come easily. Both personal and institutional contexts provide starting points for and constraints on how coteaching will evolve in a particular setting. In the first half of Chapter 4, we provide autobiographical narratives that describe the development of our own teaching and theories of teaching in the course of our careers and that ultimately led us to our coteaching/cogenerative-dialoguing model. In the second part of Chapter 4, we describe how coteaching/cogenerative dialoguing was implemented in the contexts of teacher education at the University of Pennsylvania and City High School (CHS). We describe how coteaching evolved in different ways for particular individuals and classroom settings. The background information in this chapter is of particular importance, as it sets up the context in which the stories of teaching featured in Chapters 5–8 occurred.

Urban schools with large proportions of students from an 'underclass' and largely of African American origin provide particular challenges for new and resident teachers and the students they teach. In Chapter 5, we articulate some of the issues faced in an urban school and subsequently show the potential of our coteach-

1   Anderson, 1999.
2   Roth, Masciotra, & Boyd, 1999.

ing/cogenerative dialoguing paradigm to assist the work of teachers. In this chapter, we particularly focus on how Stephanie, concurrently enrolled in a teacher education program and coteaching with Bert, learned to teach in an urban school in which coteaching/cogenerative dialoguing were used.

It is well known that in the course of their careers and with increasing experience, teachers deepen their understandings of subject matter and subject matter pedagogy. This is often a rather long and protracted process. In Chapter 6, we provide a case study in which a group of coteachers (Michael, Ken, Stephanie, and Bert) deepened their understandings of an aspect of genetics (from a grade-10 science course) and the pedagogy associated with it. Specifically, we focus on our own learning of genetics in the process of being researcher-teachers, an aspect seldom made thematic in educational research. Coteaching and cogenerative dialoguing turn out to be ideal contexts for learning to teach in implicit and explicit ways.

In their studies of teaching and learning, researchers traditionally look, as if through windows, from the outside into classrooms, to observe teachers and learners participating in an enacted curriculum. The outside view is frequently regarded as objective and too often is highly jaundiced and critical of teachers and students. Alternatively, teacher-researchers generally rely on their own experience to characterize a world they experience through rose-colored glasses, easily falling prey to the dangers of immediate understanding (since they are too close to the events). Our paradigm of coteaching/cogenerative dialoguing provides for a different way of doing research, because 'researchers' and 'teachers' engage in both activities. Soon after a shared coteaching experience, the participants, or representatives from the key stakeholders involved in coteaching, meet to discuss what happened, why it happened, and how learning might be afforded in the future. Differences in individuals' understandings of 'shared' events provide the starting points for critical hermeneutic analysis and a foundation for the development of a local theory or praxeology. In Chapter 7, we theorize coteaching/cogenerative dialoguing at a meta-level, using activity theory, and thereby articulate new roles for researchers with respect to classroom events. In this chapter, we also examine learning environments from the perspective of activity theory and thereby lay out a fresh approach to research in one of the rapidly growing areas of science education.

An important part of becoming a teacher resides in the evaluation of teaching performance. New teachers in the field are usually evaluated by their cooperating teachers and university supervisors. Similarly, during their first two years in a particular school system and before receiving a permanent contract, beginning teachers are evaluated by department heads, principals, or other evaluators appointed by the local school board. In each of these instances, the manner of performing evaluation has been to use people external to the process of teaching a particular class. In Chapter 8, we propose coteaching/cogenerative dialoguing as an alternative means of supervision and evaluation. We argue that our proposed evaluation process retains the focus on teaching students, while making evaluation of teaching more equitable.

In our epilogue, we look back at what we have written while looking forward to a thorny future of enacting what is a rosy vision for reform of teaching and learning. In so doing, we balance the optimism of our vision with the pessimism of social and cultural reproduction cycles that are all too common in social institutions such as schools. In considering the plausibility of revolution or evolution as bases for change we face the necessity for the reform to touch schools and universities in ways that alter traditional practices and ways of being. We acknowledge that unless institutional changes occur to remove contradictions in the salient activities of key stakeholders, it is unlikely that their efforts will receive the support that is essential for lasting improvements.

Making Sense as Practice

In coteaching/cogenerative dialoguing, a unity between research and teaching praxis is achieved because the members of a community are continuously engaged in transforming their praxis through critical analysis during debriefing sessions. These debriefing sessions are characterized by *cogenerative* dialogue in which all participants (including students, new teachers, cooperating teachers, supervisors, and researchers) are enacting an equitable approach

to making sense. These debriefing activities are designed to develop local theory beginning with the primary experience, the understanding of which is further developed through critical analysis. The purpose of cogenerative dialoguing is also to develop new
ways of enacting classroom life and therefore to bring about concrete change. In this way, we enact the precepts of hermeneutic
phenomenology[3] and critical psychology,[4] according to which immediate understanding has to be further developed so that new
practical action possibilities arise for all participants, and therefore possibilities to enact change. We also enact principles according to a neo-Marxist view that concretely achieved change is
more desirable than mere understanding.[5]

Hermeneutic phenomenology is grounded in the dialectic of explanation and understanding. In this context, understanding really
refers to immediate common-sense understanding, the way we experience ourselves in everyday situations at home or at work. This
understanding often remains unarticulated (many excellent cooks,
teachers, or craft workers do not have explicit theories about what
they are doing). Explanation, on the other hand, seeks to articulate the primary, immediate understanding by means of critical
analysis.

The work presented in this book is the result of a hermeneutic
phenomenological process. First, to construct formal explanations
of teaching events we enact a critical, analytical moment. Explanation develops understanding in an analytic way, and is grounded in the history of relevant research and theory. Second, explanation is enveloped (preceded, accompanied, and concluded) by
understanding, which arises from our practical engagement in the
world of teaching. That is, immediate practical understanding a-
rises from *being-in* the classroom and *being-with* others. According
to Peter Grimmett,[6] this movement from praxis to conscious ways
of knowing has to become the main approach if we have any aspi-
ration to understanding teaching. Grimmett's position is based on
the assumption that understanding associated with praxis and
lived experience is primary. But, if we are not to remain stuck in a

---

3   Ricœur, 1991.
4   Holzkamp, 1983a.
5   Grundy, 1987.
6   Grimmett, 1996.

stagnant understanding and therefore ideology, this understanding has to be developed through critical interrogation, itself informed by the historical understandings available in the domain. However, critical analysis itself is only possible because analysts already bring their primary understandings to the interpretive situation. Egon Guba and Yvonna Lincoln captured this approach in the notion of 'progressive subjectivity'.[7]

In actual praxis, we construct data sources for our analyses in the form of videotapes, recorded debriefings, videotapes of the analysis sessions, reflections in journals, face-to-face and email interactions designed to further develop a new understanding and local theory. All results of earlier analyses are subsequently incorporated in our analysis as resources, or as objects of inquiry on their own. In this way, our research results arise out of the recursive application of hermeneutic phenomenological analysis, beginning with primary understandings and data and moving on to subsequent understandings and results. Our analytical goals include the generation of local theory (or 'praxeology'), that is, theory that provides new action possibilities for the participants in the teaching-learning endeavor. Therefore, this form of research practice is authentic in the sense that it has instant application in our situation because outcomes can be immediately tested in the praxis of teaching.

We do not attempt to achieve a unique understanding by means of triangulation or negotiation of differences, particularly if the differences are outcomes of the different locations of individuals in the teaching-learning situation. For example, it may not make sense to achieve a consensus between a student and a university supervisor, or between a new teacher and a university researcher. It is more important for us to understand the emergent differences as the results of different positioning in the overall teaching-learning system and, therefore, to understand these differences as the results of more global institutional structures and personal histories.

A basic tenet of the hermeneutic phenomenological framework that underpins our research is the discursive/dialogic nature of understanding.[8] Thus, we favor talk about praxis as a way of

---

7   Guba & Lincoln, 1989.
8   Bakhtin, 1981.

coming to understand praxis (praxeology). Rather than developing 'theory', and thereby producing an irremediable (ontological) theory-praxis gap, we want understanding of praxis to arise out of the work of praxis. We are interested in generalizations that come from the inside and remain attached to it in a very practical sense rather than generalizations that come from the outside, based on common attributes. Acknowledging and accepting difference as legitimate (e.g., in the different voices of participants) is one of the salient aspects of our approach. In addition, the development of a sense of communal responsibility and agency is paramount in the unfolding conversations that constitute cogenerative dialogue. We do not condone critique focused on any one teacher, nor do we view it as reasonable that any one teacher will bear the brunt of promoting learning through lone (and heroic) efforts. Instead, the creation and maintenance of productive learning environments is regarded as a collective responsibility involving the coparticipation of all stakeholders.

Writing Research

In the social studies of science, making the process of construction explicit in the writing of the object has come to be known as 'reflexivity'.[9] These studies encouraged us to seek ways of writing research that are more consistent with our research topic and the epistemology that underpins our work. Over the past half-decade, we have therefore begun to take reflexivity seriously and we have employed a variety of 'w/ri(gh)ting'[10] techniques. These techniques have included the use of multiple voices, voice-over as in cinematography, metalogues, multi-leveled conversations, and auto/biography.

Our literary form of presenting our argument reflects the process by which we arrived at our understanding; this book embodies the very forms that led to its existence, thereby setting the construction of knowledge and its representation in a reflexive relationship. In contrast to much of educational research practice, we use a first-person methodology, that is, we use our own first-hand

9   Bourdieu & Wacquant, 1992; Woolgar, 1988.
10   Roth & McRobbie 1999.

experience of teaching in order to find out about teaching and learning to teach. Much of what we learned was developed in conversations with teachers and subsequent interactions through further face-to-face and email conversations. We practice reflexivity in the sense that we write our research from the same first-person perspective (auto/biography) and as conversations (dialogic nature of learning process). Much of what we, the two authors, present here has arisen from our own conversations while analyzing data in our offices, conversations that follow shared experiences in coteaching, and email exchanges between us, as well as those that we had with other coteaching partners. To make our book project reflexive, we choose to re-present our experiences using the various forms in which we interacted and developed our understandings.

One critical issue that distinguishes modernism from postmodernism involves the dispositions toward representation of objects and subjects. How we articulate the objects of our writing, things or people, matters because we do not simply and naively depict 'things as they really are', our writings are constitutive of these things. That is, our writing constructs as much as it depicts its object. Now, if our research and writing constructs the object as much as it describes it, then who we are also contributes to the writing of the object both in form and content. We can therefore reject the more formal, impersonal styles that delete the author.

On Auto/biography

Ken: Communicating what I learned from research on my teaching of science in an urban setting has involved me in writing and presenting numerous papers, some as sole author and others with co-authors (colleagues, coteachers, and students). Each of the papers emphasizes different themes and voices and is written in a different style. As I look back on the different ways of writing about research, I find this is a propitious moment to consider the relative merits of each.

Michael: Given that we are using auto/biography[11] in this book as re-presentations of events at City High School, let us talk about auto/biography and its potential for w/ri(gh)ting (science) education research.

Ken: Writing auto/biography was an emotional experience compared to writing in other genres in which affective state is relatively unimportant. I began to delve deeply into the troubled lives of some of the students I am teaching and explored their involvement in activities that included drug use and dealing, prostitution, crime, and violence. The prevalence of such issues cast a shadow over the transformative potential of science education. I wondered where social justice could fit into the curriculum and how it could intersect with science. Inevitably the focus returned to my own role and shortcomings as an urban science teacher. Influenced by my recent reading of the autobiography of a runaway street kid,[12] I began to see for the first time that I had failed to be a stable source of support for the learning of the students who needed me most. I realized that my middle-class life and value system saturated what I considered to be rational decisions.

Michael: How did writing auto/biography help you in coming to grips with your own learning or, perhaps, how did writing allow you to learn about your own development as a teacher?

Ken: As my auto/biography unfolded, the emerging story line focused on my learning to teach in urban settings. Ironically, when I began Chapter 2 I was not conscious of this as a goal, let alone as a focus for my writing. My purpose in doing the study in the first place was not to learn to teach science in urban settings but to find out how to teach science successfully in urban environments. There is a critical difference in these goal statements. I assumed I already knew how to teach science and it was just a question of adapting or applying what I knew to urban contexts. Doing the study and then writing it as auto/biography has deepened my sensitivity to the ontological differences between knowledge that can be spoken and written and knowledge that must be enacted. There is no doubt that my experiences at CHS were all about

---

11 We write 'auto/biography' with a slash, because in our writing, we feature biography and autobiography.
12 Lau, 1995.

learning to teach urban students and had little to do with adapting existing knowledge.

Michael: Following Fred Erickson's[13] method of interpretive research, we used to place a lot of emphasis on getting large amounts of information and subsequently on triangulating the (true?) state of affairs from the different data sources available. How did you deal with the issues of voice?

Ken: Initially I was constrained by the conventions of interpretive research and a commitment to the use of verbatim transcripts as thick description, particularly when I was examining issues about teaching and learning. However, with encouragement from you and Judith McGonigal, I focused on the genre of auto/biography and used my own words to tell a story that was consistent with the data. Once I had adjusted the voice to be consistent throughout the early drafts of the chapter, I gained a deeper appreciation of the significance of 'auto' in auto/biography.

Michael: Placing yourself in the center of the narrative must have made a considerable change in your position as interpretive researcher.

Ken: The writing of the chapter made a significant difference to the way I think about my roles as teacher, teacher educator, and writer. I believe that the best way to learn to teach in given circumstances is, with the assistance of others from whom to learn, to teach in those circumstances. The fallibility of knowledge of teaching as it is written and spoken was never more evident to me than when I tried to apply what I knew in urban settings. Now I cannot imagine teaching a science methods course without having an active classroom in which to show what can and cannot be accomplished, and associated field experiences in which new teachers can create their knowledge of teaching science by teaching science.

Michael: Recent publications that have used auto/biography show it as a powerful way to connect to others having an interest in science teaching and learning. Possibly because of the emotional involvement of the reader with unfolding events there is more of a connection with the issues expressed in auto/biography than in other forms of writing. The genre allows us to portray our perspec-

---

13   Erickson1986; Lau, 1995.

tives on those issues from the praxis that we regard as having most salience to the larger domain of science education.

Metalogues and the Voice of Participants

Metalogues are conversations that take previous texts or conversations and analyze them at a new, meta-level.[14] Metalogues therefore are a means to represent analyses that move through several levels of complexity (or logical order/type as Gregory Bateson called it). Metalogues appeal to us, because their presence enables previous analyses to become the topic of reflection and/or discussion. That is, metalogues constitute a practice of reflexivity.

Over the past several years, we have used metalogue to develop and explicate the perspective that knowledge of teaching is re-presented only while teaching. The context for this was the study that we had undertaken separately, in which we were teacher-researchers.[15] The interactions between the two of us were a significant resource for our own learning. From our respective studies we each prepared vignettes that were appropriate for writing Chapter 1 about coteaching as a vehicle for learning to teach. Then we identified several salient issues in the vignettes and took turns writing in a collaborative manner about each of them. In so doing we were able to explicate and elaborate our emerging theory through the contexts portrayed in our selected vignettes. We both learned from the process and communicated to readers our understanding of teaching as praxis in a variety of practice settings. Those insights were a foundation for the rationale of using auto/biography, conversations, and metalogues as means of writing research.

Ken: We have now used conversations and metalogues in a number of our collaborative writing projects. I remember you sent me copies of a manuscript that included conversations and metalogues as far back as 1996. What was so special about these forms of writing that you considered them for presenting research and theoretical arguments?

---

14   Bateson, 1980.
15   Roth, Tobin, & Ritchie, 2001.

Michael: One of my core concerns during the constructivist heydays was with the apparent contradiction between the claim that knowledge is individually and socially constructed, on the one hand, and the seemingly objectivist nature in which this constructivist research was presented in the literature. When I realized that the same concern was being raised in the sociology of scientific knowledge, I began to follow the debate. Now, by using alternative forms of writing, I pay attention to the fact that (a) there is an agreement between the content and form of my argument (use dialog if the claim is the dialogic nature of knowledge) and that (b) the text reflects its own nature as a constructed entity. Conversations also allow two or more authors to present their alternative perspectives on some issue rather than collapsing existing differences into one authorial voice.

Ken: Alternative voices as arguments unfold seem to me an important advantage of conversations and metalogues. This way of writing is a departure from the serial presentation of completely articulated viewpoints. In one of the collective writing projects in which I was involved,[16] we used metalogue to allow each of us to participate in a conversation that retained our discrete voices on issues we regarded as critical to learning to teach in inner city schools.

Michael: Bringing these differing perspectives into the foreground is vital in research in science education where, for too long, researchers have reported central tendencies and assertions built around the preponderance of evidence.

Ken: Our style of writing allowed us to include assertions about which we agreed and personal perspectives that reflected our different roles and experiences as educators. The presence of multiple authors and voices allowed us to learn from one another in the writing and to communicate with readers in ways that would not be possible using other forms. Another application of metalogue allowed me to highlight the student voice in an article that focused on student resistance in urban science classes.[17] One of the co-authors, Tyrone, was a student in two of my science classes at City High School. His candid perspectives and our associated discussions allowed us to learn much more about teach-

16   Tobin, Seiler, & Smith, 1999.
17   Tobin, Seiler, & Walls, 1999.

ing science to low-track students in an inner city high school than otherwise would have been possible. The inclusion of Tyrone as a researcher in the study allowed us to access and write about issues and perspectives that otherwise would have been beyond our reach.

How to Read This Book

This book does not need to be read in a linear fashion from beginning to end, although there are pieces of information or concepts that are introduced and explained in detail only once, in a specific chapter. For example, we introduce four central concepts with detailed examples in Chapter 1. We use these concepts throughout the book. To assist readers in beginning anywhere without stumbling across unknown concepts, we include a glossary at the end of the book, which readers may consult if they feel a term is unfamiliar. Furthermore, we provide detailed background information on the classroom in which Stephanie cotaught with Bert for the year during which she was enrolled in the teacher education program at the University of Pennsylvania. We use our coteaching experience in this classroom to exemplify different aspects of teaching, learning to teach, doing research, and evaluating teaching (Chapters 5–8). If a reader prefers to begin with one of these chapters, we strongly recommend her/him to read that part of Chapter 4 in which we present the context in which Stephanie and Bert cotaught. Finally, readers interested in consulting the sources that we credit for some of our ideas will find them at the end of each chapter. We provide citations in the footnotes to preserve the dialogic and autobiographic character in which much of the book has been written.

CHAPTER 1

Teaching as Praxis

The purpose of this chapter is to articulate and exemplify a different epistemology of science teaching and science teacher education, an epistemology that asserts the primacy of lived experience as the starting point for professional conversations from which new understandings emerge. Consistent with this epistemology, this chapter takes the form of professional conversations that arise from our own teaching experiences. We have introduced elsewhere the notion of *praxeology* (Gr. *praxis*, action, and *logos*, talk, speech) for understandings that arise from such conversations; such understandings therefore contrast with traditional theories of teaching produced by individuals who look at teaching from the outside.[1] Because a reliance on lived experience alone may lead to distorted visions, our professional conversations include critical and distancing analysis. In this, we enact the precepts of hermeneutic phenomenology, which is characterized by its dialectic of understanding, grounded in lived experience (phenomenology), and explanation-seeking hermeneutics, grounded in the intellectual history of the field. In our conversations, we draw on the phenomenological concepts of *habitus* and *being-in/with* to constitute our explanatory framework. *Coteaching*, grounded in our notion of *being-in/with*, is a practice that allows teachers to have shared teaching experiences (including planning, enacting, and reflecting on curriculum); these experiences then provide the ground

---

1   Roth, Lawless, & Tobin, 2000.

for meaningful professional conversations.[2] We propose praxeology as an alternative conceptual framework (rather than 'theory') of teaching and then present four vignettes from our own teaching, each accompanied by a critical conversation. We conclude with a reflection on coteaching as a different methodology for understanding teaching praxis.

Becoming-a-Teacher in an Urban Classroom

'I just improved so much in [teaching kids to think for themselves by asking productive questions]. I don't think three university courses could have given me what [coteaching] gave me in these 2 months'.[3] We have all heard new or recently graduated teachers talk in this way about the difference between what they learned in praxis and in university methods courses. These new teachers bemoan a lack of fit between their training and the nature of the job that they have been training for. Despite considerable research on teaching, this perceived gap persists. Accordingly, we should not lightly dismiss comments that imply a lack of relevance of university methods courses or explain them away in terms of teacher characteristics. Rather, we should endeavor to understand why some teachers believe that methods courses and teacher preparation programs lack relevance. In so doing we might identify the conditions and phenomena in schools that are not addressed and explore alternative approaches to minimize the gap between what is experienced in schools and what is advocated during teacher preparation programs. New teachers frequently experience another gap: when cooperating teachers in their field-experience programs teach in ways that are perceived as inconsistent with the exhortations of university teacher educators. Some of the problems experienced are exemplified in the following excerpts written by a prospective teacher in the master's-level urban teacher preparation program of a large U.S. university.

---

2   In this chapter, coteaching is a context that allows us to experience shared teaching experiences on the basis of which we develop praxeology. This chapter itself is the result of such conversations. We articulate coteaching and the associated cogenerative dialoguing in subsequent chapters.

3   Roth, 1998a, p. 358.

Initial Impressions!

My cooperating teacher (Mario) is a very nice guy and the kids seem to like him. He spends much of his time trying to keep the kids quiet and on task and they respond to him well. He doesn't teach at all the way we are being taught and I think that this might pose some problems later. He has minimal expectations of his kids and blatantly told me so. He basically gives them all of the answers to all of the problems at some point in time. Thinking is not fostered in the class at all. For example, in today's class, for the entire 54-minute period, the class had to answer five questions based on the lecture from yesterday. All of the answers were in their notes. If they didn't finish in class, they had to take them home and finish. But they aren't permitted to take a textbook home because they never bring them back. If the answers aren't in their notes, then they can find someone who knows the answer. The teacher walks around and helps students with the questions, keeping them quiet and working. (Cam, September 23, 1998)

I am beginning to realize that my kids like Mario because he expects nothing out of them. I want my kids to like me too, desperately, but more importantly, I want them to learn something—anything. Even if what they learn is how to tie their shoe, they will have learned something from me. I want them to want to learn how to write a sentence, discover that a plant needs light and water, and to relinquish their fear of critical thinking (lofty goals I know, but it's what I want). (Cam, October 21, 1998)

Ken: Cam's initial experiences in the school reveal that his cooperating teacher, Mario, holds depressingly low expectations of student participation and achievement. Cam provides examples of how these low expectations manifest themselves. Interestingly, I had almost the same experience when I began my teaching at the same school. The low expectations of the teacher are reflected in the low performance of the students and these catalyze a downward spiral in which plummeting expectations are matched by ever-decreasing levels of performance.

Michael: This is an interesting case where the value systems of cooperating teacher and student teacher seem to conflict. The cooperating teacher certainly had developed a set of practices that allowed him to deal with the situation in what he perceived as a safe environment. Low expectations were accompanied by students' (silent) approval shown in their appreciation for the cooperating teacher. Although this may be surprising, we encountered a similar case of collusion leading to minimal engagement in a school in a middle-class suburban high school in Australia. The school had many more resources than Cam or you had at your disposal.

Ken: The rule that students cannot take textbooks home makes little sense because the students have few resources in their home to support their learning. Because of this it is difficult for students to attempt homework or study what they have been taught during the day. In this instance Mario, the cooperating teacher, purchased a set of 10-year-old chemistry texts with his own money and was reluctant to allow the students to borrow them for fear of not getting them back. A question that needs to be addressed is why all students are not issued with a modern textbook to support their learning at school and at home.

Michael: The lack of resources is in fact constraining the kind of practices that can be enacted by any teacher. This lack of resources may be constraining Cam's development in two ways. On the one hand, he may develop a *habitus* (dispositions) for generating relevant teaching practices even in the absence of resources (my own teaching in a tiny school in the Canadian North allowed me to become resourceful). On the other hand, the lack may constrain Cam's development in the sense that he does not develop a teaching *habitus* that produces any interesting teaching practices and, instead, turns him into another Mario.

Ken: Just what do we expect Cam to learn from Mario and how do we expect him to learn it? Student teachers such as Cam are not told how to get the most from a young teacher like Mario who is struggling himself to find ways to reach students, all African American, who are from conditions of poverty and have histories of low academic attainment. It is difficult to imagine how any science methods course could prepare Cam for conditions like the ones he experienced from the outset and that I was to experience when I commenced my teaching assignment at the same school.

Michael: No doubt, the situation in which Cam finds himself *is* extreme, but a situation in which many teachers may find themselves. However, even students who find themselves in less extreme situations often experience fundamental gaps between what they hear in university methods courses, and what they live out in the schools as interns and beginning teachers. What they hear in university courses is generally declarative and procedural knowledge about teaching that has a timeless character; or they analyze and study cases and discuss issues with their peers. In their teaching, on the other hand, they have to cope with situations without having time out to reflect on their next move before doing something. In this case, the relentless unfolding of practice, different rules apply. Any conceptual framework that aspires to describe the experience of teaching will have to address this temporal nature of praxis. Most theories of practice simply neglect this temporal character and therefore fail to appropriately conceptualize the particularity of teaching as practice. These include the theories focused on pedagogical subject matter knowledge or reflection-on-action.

Bad Day

Today was by far the worst day of my short teaching career. I'm hoping that the weapons check had something to do with it, but I'm not quite so sure about that. My class started on time but nothing was accomplished.

I tried to introduce the lab, move the desks, get them into groups, and get them started on the lab. But no one would go with me. I had probably 5 or 6 kids out of the 25 in the class actually interested in doing what I wanted them to do. They were unruly. Totally disrespectful, loud and obnoxious!

Everything I wanted to do took about three times as long as I wanted it to. When I finally got around to handing out the materials and getting them started, it was 10:15, 19 minutes left in the period and they hadn't even started the experiments yet!!! I could tell that they weren't going to get anything done and so I told them to forget about it. I said if they didn't want to learn science by doing experiments and all they wanted to do was take notes, then that's how I could teach them. I collected all the materials and had them sit and do nothing for the last 10 minutes of class.

At this point, Mario got up and yelled at them, told them how disappointed in them he was, and explained that 'Mr. Riley spent a lot of time trying to plan a fun activity for you guys and all you did was disrespect him'. He then gave them a question to answer, sort of like my questions of the day, but different. The question is as follows: 'Explain why you acted like a 'knucklehead' in class today. If this statement doesn't pertain to you, then explain why it doesn't pertain to you'. The kids didn't really feel threatened or ashamed, to say the least!

I really appreciate Mario trying to stick up for me, but I feel like a little kid whose big brother comes around to kick the bully's butt for him. I feel as if any progress I've made with these kids has been lost and that now I'm back at square one, or even negative one, I don't know.

How do I get them to want to perform for me? Everyone says rapport, rapport, rapport and I understand it is important. But right now, the rapport that I am establishing is not the rapport between teacher and student BECAUSE I am not their teacher nor do I feel that I am qualified to be. Does anyone else feel this way? (November 4, 1998)

Ken: Cam's account of his teaching experiences brought back vivid memories of my own experiences with similar students from the same school. It is extremely difficult to get their attention and cooperation at the best of times. It is one thing for people like me, his methods instructor, to offer suggestions for Cam to try but it is quite another for him or anyone else to successfully enact well-intentioned advice. Even without the humiliation of a weapons check the students would be difficult to settle down and get started.

Michael: I believe that you have enacted an important move that few of our colleagues would dare to enact as supervisors of student teachers. Rather than talking about practice and what student teachers should do, you took a look at a classroom from the perspective of the teacher. Rather than sitting on the sidelines and checking off all the things Cam did not do, you looked at *this* classroom through the experience of a teacher dealing with *these* students at *this* time. I would have liked to see Mario enact coteaching with Cam in the way I do it with my own coteaching partners. Why did Mario not roll up his sleeves and stand right next to Cam to get the day's lesson done?

Ken: Mario's role is puzzling. When he and I taught together later in the year it was difficult to get him to participate actively when I was teaching. He was more likely to relinquish control to me and then watch what was going on. He would only get involved when asked specifically to do so. In Cam's lesson he jumped in and expressed his displeasure in a way that diminished Cam's self-esteem. Looking back at this event it is apparent that Cam should have a frank discussion with Mario about his role. I recognize the parallel situation that exists between me giving this advice here and my failure to have a similar discussion with Mario about his role in my class.

Michael: It almost seems as if Mario has developed a *habitus* that generates *interstitial* practices. He contributes to collusion where the students return low expectations on his part in terms of low cognitive involvement and acquiescence (sleeping). At the same time, his jumping in also constructed Cam in a particular way: as a beginning and perhaps incompetent teacher rather than as a coparticipant in the effort to get the day's work done: teach the kids some chemistry.

Ken: If an observer were to be assessing Cam's teaching performance using any of the beginning-teacher assessment instruments, it is unlikely that he would pass based on what is reported here and what I have experienced by observing him. To be just as honest, I am dubious about whether or not I would pass on such instruments while teaching these students. The issue that arises here and elsewhere in this book is whether or not any outside observer can assess teaching performance in a viable way without first teaching alongside the person whose performance is to be assessed. Cam speaks about being told to build rapport and to earn the respect and trust of students. I was one of those who gave such advice. I still maintain it is good advice but how to do it is a challenging issue. It can be accomplished one student at a time, with lots of effort and involving the parents or caregivers from home in a plan to provide support for their child.

Michael: You address an interesting issue, coteaching as a form of supervision and teacher assessment, which would have radical implications for the way we do teacher development, induction, and assessment.

Problematizing the Epistemology of Teaching

In the excerpts quoted above, we learn about the first experiences of a beginning teacher wrestling with the differences between a curriculum as planned and an enacted curriculum as it arises from an interaction of the teacher, students, activities, materials, and so forth. Almost every impression Cam shared with his peers shows how the contingencies of being-in-the-classroom can mediate and contravene any planned curriculum. Past theories of teaching have not paid enough heed to the fact that teaching is something that is done rather than being static sets of procedural and declarative knowledge waiting to be called up. Thus, when individuals speak about teaching they are speaking about re-constructions of teaching; and the knowledge of teaching is not the object of their discussions and reflective analyses. However, while teaching, a teacher enacts knowing in the presence of others within a community. The interactions that occur constrain the knowledge in action, and adaptations occur in ways that are reflexive and spontaneous—constrained by the actions of others in the community. As coparticipation occurs, the knowledge of teachers and students is adapted and mediated by the sets of interactions that occur.

In the excerpts, we see a new teacher who did not even experience himself as a teacher, for the others in the classroom did not construct him as a teacher, nor themselves as learners. At the same time, Cam constructed himself differently from his cooperating teacher and, at the time of his writing, there seemed little that he could learn from Mario. Thus, not only did Cam experience problems in interacting with the class environment, such as problems in making the curriculum unfold in the way his plan foresaw but he also found little help in the 'coop' teacher. Mario, perhaps because he has different values, is not interested in getting the students to do homework, enact higher level cognition, or take them to task when they do not participate in the ongoing activities.

Teachers rarely are provided with opportunities to work at each other's elbows despite the fact that in many domains it is very common that learning arises in praxis as part of getting the day's job done. Pilots, graduate students in science, banking employees, and others learn much of what they know by coparticipating on the job with colleagues who have different experiences and competencies. Furthermore, it has been suggested that 'the lack of opportunity for teachers to reflect, interact with each other, share, learn, develop on the job makes it unlikely that significant changes will occur'.[4] Yet teachers learn tremendously when they coteach, that is, when they work together with another teacher, at each other's elbows.

Here, we propose an epistemology of teaching as praxis as an alternative approach to understanding teaching and teacher development. Drawing on (sociological) phenomenology, we unfold a praxeology hinging on *habitus* and *being-in/with*, two notions that constitute the theoretical underpinnings of a new approach to research on, enculturation into, and supervision of teaching: *coteaching*. *Coteaching* is central to creating shared experiences that become the ground from which understanding of praxis is developed in professional conversations.

Understanding Praxis: Being-In/With and Habitus

Phenomenology is concerned with knowing and learning in everyday praxis. It has influenced much recent work in disciplines such as philosophy, cognitive science, artificial intelligence, anthropology, ethnomethodology, and sociology. Theories of knowing and learning grounded in phenomenology presuppose *being-in* the world (as body among bodies) as the fundamental condition of all knowing. Our bodies are open to the (social and material) world, and in this openness susceptible to be conditioned by the world, formed by the material and cultural conditions of existence in which they are placed from their very beginning. Through our bodily inclusion in the world (e.g., in classroom and school), we are therefore subjected to a process of socialization in which the for-

---

4   Fullan, 1993.

mation of a (teacher) Self is itself a product. The social is grasped as lived experience, through day-to-day praxis, and the singularity of the 'me' is worked out as an individual enacts and emerges from each social relationship.[5]

Being-in the world amounts to a non-thematic, unreflective, but concerned absorption in everyday activity.[6] The world is comprehensible, immediately endowed with meaning, because we have been exposed to its regularities since we entered the world at birth. We therefore acquire dispositions or systems of dispositions for perceiving and interacting with the world. Pierre Bourdieu termed these dispositions *habitus*.[7] *Habitus*, not accessible to our consciousness and therefore without reflection, generates the patterned ways we interact with the world, that is, our practices that em*body* actions, perceptions, and expectations. There exists a mutually constitutive and therefore reflexive relationship between the structures of the world and the structures of *habitus*. Being exposed to and formed by the world, *habitus* is structured by the world. But, because *habitus* generates our actions, perceptions, and expectations, the world is structured by *habitus*. *Habitus* therefore constitutes a system of structured dispositions in which the past is constituted in the present: our dispositions are always historical and biographical products. Because *habitus* is formed by the regularities of the world, it is enabled to anticipate these regularities in its conduct. This assures a *practical* comprehension of the world entirely different from the intentional and conscious decoding acts normally called comprehension. *Habitus* therefore temporizes itself in praxis through a practical mobilization of the past in the very moment that it anticipates the future.

Habitus cannot be described in the abstract. Central to the notion of *habitus* is that it only reveals itself in reference to the particular, that is, in definite situations. Thus, what has to be done cannot be pre-specified in the abstract (e.g., in the form of advice to Cam for building rapport), but emerges from the contingencies and temporalities of each situation. For example, even though it is highly desirable for teachers to plan thoroughly for enacting a curriculum in classes like those in which Cam is teaching, it must be

---

5   Giddens, 1991.
6   Dreyfus, 1991.
7   Bourdieu, 1990, 1997.

remembered that the most appropriate course of action will unfold in the enactment and cannot be pre-specified. Similarly, it is
not possible to sit at the side watching a teacher and his/her class
and specify a correct course of action to adopt. Thus, *habitus* produces given discursive and material (perceptual, classificatory)
practices only in relation to the specifics of a setting. To acquire
habitus, one has to coparticipate in situations with those who have
already acquired habitus prior to ourselves. The formation of any
habitus therefore requires *being-in* situations and *being-with* others.
It is this *being-in/with* that is central to apprenticeship and enculturation theories and studies of the cultural reproduction of practices. Relative to teaching, *being-in/with* is the central underpinning
of the 'co' in *co*teaching.

Habitus is not static and closed but an open system of disposi-
tion that is under continuous experience-dependent transformation, embodying its own history and experiential trajectory. These
experiences either reinforce or modify existing structures of *habitus*
such that it will sustain more viable practices. Importantly, *habitus*
is not merely formed by exposure to the social and material world.
Rather, it 'also can be transformed via socio-analysis, that is, via
an awakening of consciousness and a form of 'self-work' that enables the individual to get a handle on his or her dispositions'.[8]
Thus, reflection is an additional, though not principal, mode by
which *habitus* is formed and transformed.

Habitus generates our patterned actions in and with the world,
because it takes (and can take) the world for granted. But in the
notion of *habitus*, strategic choice and conscious deliberation are
not ruled out as modalities of action. First, the sequences of actions generated by *habitus* may always be accompanied by interests, by strategic calculation of costs and benefits, and by other
concerns prevalent in the situation. Second, in times of serious
breakdown, when the normal routine forms of interacting with the
world are brutally disrupted, rational choice indeed takes
over—at least in those agents who are in a position to be rational.

Becoming a teacher therefore means to form the *habitus* that,
according to Bourdieu, can only happen in the experience; if we
coparticipate, rather than individually constructing, we partici-

---

8   Bourdieu & Wacquant, 1992, p. 133.

pate in the patterned activities, practices, which in themselves make sense: we 'are the ways we do things'. We understand ourselves in the way we objectify our experiences of *being-with*. These experiences constitute the ground that reflexively elaborates (objectified) discourse about teaching. As teachers, we never just do things in a stable world, we interact with students who are also agents themselves. Thus, students and teachers construct their Self-Other continuously and emergently as curricula are enacted (i.e., in the situation). 'Teacher' and 'student' arise out of the dynamic of each situation, and personality can only be attributed to individual bodies in a retroactive manner. To be a teacher does not mean to expose a stable Self to the classroom, but to engage in a continuous construction of 'teacher' arising from the interactions in and with the (social, material) classroom.

We develop several central issues relating to teaching and teacher education by presenting cases from our own lived experience of coteaching that we analyze in subsequent metalogues.

A Veteran, Beginning Again

Despite his extensive experience as (science) teacher and teacher-researcher, Ken struggled teaching chemistry in an urban school. His *habitus*, which had developed under different circumstances (students from middle-class situations), generated practices that were not appropriate in *this* situation.

Episode

In my role as a coteacher of high school chemistry I was teaching students in the *Incentive Center* (hereafter referred to as *Incentive*), the same one in which Cam was teaching, of a large urban high school. These students were together because they had failed in one way or another. Many had been incarcerated, some were supporting parents, and most had academic records that were unlikely to qualify them for further studies. Students who have irregular attendance at school, have been expelled from another school for acts of violence, or who are not performing at an appropriately high level are assigned to *Incentive* for a 'last opportunity'.

The roles of teacher and student seemed well established and were typified by a visit to the lab (taught by Mario) in which the students followed a recipe to explore some of the properties of ionic compounds. In one lab session, they investigated some displacement reactions in which precipitates were formed and tested the conductivity of ionic compounds in aqueous solution. I could not see any evidence of students doing or learning science in these activities and resolved to do things differently when I began to teach. I could not see how the curriculum they were experiencing was either engaging, coherent, or of any potentially transformative value. I believed this class of African American students, mainly from circumstances of poverty, would not benefit in meaningful ways from their experiences with chemistry. Even though some would receive high passing grades, these would likely not be negotiable if the students were to seek entry to further studies. Furthermore, many would fail and therefore have to repeat the course in order to gain the necessary credits to graduate from high school. My perceptions were those of an outsider and I could see immediate changes I could enact to improve the quality of the learning environments of these students.

The classroom in which these students were taught science was formerly an art room. It was spacious and had a trough with running water. In other respects the room was not conducive to the teaching and learning of chemistry. Equipment was scarce and supplies nonexistent. I yearned for the lab I inherited in my first year of teaching. As the only science teacher in a junior high school in rural Australia, I taught in a laboratory/classroom that had a demonstration bench at the rear and a storeroom filled with equipment and supplies. As I taught, I could demonstrate and easily get students involved in activities that included experiments and hands on experiences. Thirty-five years later I had virtually no equipment and supplies and the physical space was not conducive to doing chemistry. Appropriate equipment and supplies were hard to locate in the school and getting them downstairs into my classroom was difficult to accomplish. As I searched for activities that would connect to what students knew and could do, I was constrained by the physical resources available to support the curriculum.

What did the students know and how could I mediate their learning of chemistry? Above all I wanted students to show an interest in learning and become autonomous and responsible. The few resources available in the school to support learning hampered my planning. I began to wake up at 3 a.m. to plan until I left for my office several hours later to make the necessary photocopies of daily quizzes, review problems, and at times subject matter I wanted students to learn. My goal was for each student to negotiate a shared language that could be used to engage in the activities of the classroom community. However, I faced numerous dilemmas. Many students did not have paper or pencil and seemed unmotivated to learn. I constantly moved around the classroom, trying to be energetic and positive, and encourage student participation. I was rarely reactive in a negative sense and spoke quietly to students to avoid public confrontations. The textbooks Mario bought were not being used, but I resolved to draw on these books to support learning. As students walked in through the door I asked them to pick up a book and respond to questions I had set them. When some refused to do this, I brought them a book to use. Initially, few students opened the book, made an effort to locate relevant text, or attempted to answer the questions. I noticed that many could not use an index or a table of content to navigate a textbook.

The students had few resources at home to support the learning of chemistry. For example, most of them had no chemistry books, only 2 of 35 had access to computers, and the majority had never used the World Wide Web for recreation or learning. Each day I planned and enacted a curriculum with the intention of meeting their learning needs. However, students would participate, leave, and return the next day without doing any more chemistry. Unlike other teachers in *Incentive* I wanted to assign homework for these students. But first I had to locate suitable resources to support this goal. The chemistry texts in the classroom belonged to Mario and he did not want them to be taken home. Hence, I had to secure texts from the school. 'Impossible!' declared Mario. However, I approached the assistant principal, who was sympathetic and took me to a storeroom that was filled with musty books. I searched for a chemistry book and found *Modern Chemistry*, a text I had used as a reference for my chemistry classes in the late 1960s. Within minutes, 35 copies of its 1970 edition were on their way to my classroom.

I began with the periodic table. 'What could be simpler?' I wondered. This is the key to the electronic configuration and hence to the chemical behavior of the elements. Besides, these students had been taught covalent and ionic bonding prior to my taking over the class. However, the students were unable to make sense of electronic configuration or periodicity, and their resistance to participate in meaningful ways confronted me. I did not want to go all the way back to square one. I wanted these students to attain levels of understanding commensurate with those reached by youngsters from other parts of the school, city, and nation. However, the more I focused on the National Standards the more evident it was to me that they were agents of cultural reproduction and would condemn most of the students in this class to failure. Their extant knowledge, interests and levels of motivation were such that failure was likely. Students did not know the basics and did not have the tools to build the networks of understanding that are at the base of the types of scientific understanding that characterize knowing and doing science in high school grade levels. I quickly realized that these students needed to acquire some staple tools before they would be able to reach the level of scientific literacy I deemed necessary. For example, they had to build a work ethic to enable them to participate in learning activities for 75 minutes, to foster their curiosity and appreciate the significance of studying a phenomenon in detail, and to value persistence in obtaining coherent results in relation to a problem or phenomenon.

Ever so slowly I endeavored to wean students from the highly structured and teacher-controlled environments they had experienced in their middle and high school years. I wanted them to build and use a discourse that was chemistry-like. As they manipulated equipment and materials I wanted them to do more than enjoy themselves. If the students were to experience chemistry, they would have to coparticipate in a classroom community in which we did chemistry. But how would this be possible? Most of the students gave the impression of not wanting to learn chemistry and not knowing how to take academic risks and be successful.

Instead they accepted a state of disempowerment and went through the motions, expecting that they would not understand the subject matter. Indeed, a high proportion did not even go through the motions, but refused to engage and often tried to read a magazine or sleep. Even worse, attendance at school was sporadic and students may be absent for 2–3 days a week.

I had to get some chemicals and equipment in my classroom. When I mentioned copper sulfate I wanted to be able to show students copper sulfate, its color, and how it can dissolve in water. I also wanted them to be able to see how it reacts with a host of other solutions. Initially, the difficulties in getting materials to the classroom were almost overwhelming and my inability to get what I needed made it more difficult to teach in the way I believed would support learning. The solution to the problem of equipment and materials was a process rather than being reached immediately (as was the case with the textbooks).

I wanted the students to prepare their own dilute solutions and systematically mix small volumes with one another to see if reactions occurred. Disaster! Insufficient spatulas! No benches to spread out the chemicals. Not enough equipment to mix all of those solutions and place them so that others could have access to them. The students did not plan what they wanted to do and did not have the knowledge of chemistry to allow them to predict when precipitates might occur. My effort to engage the students in an open-ended lab activity was successful at the level of all students being involved and a non-event in terms of chemistry. The students were actively involved but were not doing chemistry. Many aspects were unsettling to me. The solutions should not be going down the sink! The students were making a mess and there were no paper towels to clean up. Some of the chemicals were corrosive and most students would not wear safety glasses. I expected the students to make a plan and a set of associated predictions rather then engage in random mixing. The events did not proceed as I envisioned and I was pleased there were few outsiders who could sit in judgment.

The students needed more structure and I wanted them to be more autonomous and responsible. The next day I mixed dilute solutions of each ionic compound and placed them strategically in beakers in front of the glass bottles in which the compounds were stored. On this occasion the students showed resistance again because they wanted a structured work plan and were unwilling or unable to generate their own structure. However, they soon were rewarded for making a start. There were many interesting reactions that were possible by mixing the solutions I had provided. I was pleased with the progress at the end of the day and wrote to a colleague that they had not only enjoyed themselves also but had begun to access and appropriate a discourse that was embryonic chemistry. I could hardly wait for them to come in the next day to continue their work on finding interesting reactions between the solutions.

The next day was one of those days when things do not work as intended. My plan was for them to walk in through the door and resume from where they had left off. Once again in hindsight this was not a good plan. From their perspective it was 'Boring! We did this yesterday'. I had assumed that the apparently high level of interest from yesterday would propel them forward into a 3-day activity in which they would become increasingly precise in their efforts to understand the chemical reactions. I had unwittingly projected my interest on to the students and throughout the lesson I had to fight to maintain their focus and emphasize the relevance of the activity.

Day after day as I walked back to my university office I was displeased with significant aspects of what was happening. How could I have enacted the curriculum differently? Despite hours of planning I felt unprepared, and I was not enacting a curriculum that was conducive to learning or potentially transformative. Looking back it was all too clear what I might have done. But when I used those insights to plan for the next day I was just as displeased at the conclusion of the activity. Although some days were better than others, the enacted curriculum was not appropriate for most learners due to physical, social, and cultural constraints.

Michael: In this account of your first two months teaching in an urban school, there are some interesting issues emerging for me. For one, the practices, perceptions, and expectations that had worked for you in the past no longer worked. Thus, despite being an experienced and successful teacher on the surface, in *this* situation, your *habitus* failed you. Having been formed under (social and material) circumstances that are quite unlike those in which you find yourself today, your perceptions, expectations, and therefore your teaching practices are inappropriate. In fact, they are probably so inappropriate that you may be facing a serious breakdown so that your normal routine (and elsewhere expert) ways of interacting with the world of a classroom are radically disrupted. Here, then, it is likely that rationality sets in, possibly calling for objectifications where otherwise your practical sense works without thematizing (objectifying) the setting.

Ken: Mario, the regular classroom teacher, is inexperienced himself and has not established routines that get the best out of the students. As we teach he is usually in the background, but even so, when he does step forward from time to time I am able to learn some things about how best to interact with *these* students in *this* situation. In addition to Mario I have two other colleagues with whom I am teaching from time to time. The first of these, Cam, is a new teacher who has been teaching in *Incentive* for a semester. He has a great deal to learn, but also is able to teach me by working at my elbow. Mostly I notice how he is able to connect with certain students and build relations. As a younger man he is able to get closer to some of the students and I find myself sometimes 'acting like Cam'. This is an interesting turn of events, as the methods instructor is learning from the student teacher.

Michael: Which reminds me of the 'silent pedagogy' required for many aspects of a practice such as teaching. From a teacher perspective, this means 'Do as I do'; from a student perspective, it means 'Acting like the Other'.

Ken: Gale also teaches about twice or three times a week with us. She is a doctoral student and former urban teacher and has extensive knowledge of how to teach science and get the best out of students like these.

Michael: The *habitus* she brings to *this* situation generates more appropriate practices than yours does.

Ken: Yes, and having her in the classroom several times a week enables me to step back and observe how she interacts with the students and builds relationships. Interestingly, there are times when she says and does things that just remind me of the way I teach. I assume she is learning some things by coteaching with me, too, in the way you described it in earlier research.

Michael: Another important issue for me is the construction of teacher and students, of Self and Other in this classroom. Historically, we have been thinking of teacher, student, Self and Other as ontologically stable categories that people bring to a classroom. However, in this classroom, I can see that it makes sense to argue that who we are has to be negotiated in each and every moment. You are not a teacher, unless, in the contingency of this classroom (*being-in*), you and the students (*being-with*) are able to construct you as a teacher. At the same time, constructing you as a teacher means that students construct themselves as learners. Some of the tensions you experience are such that there is a resistance to let you emerge as a teacher from the relationship.

Ken: Negotiating my right to teach has been a constant struggle. It is not just a question of having them accept me as a person but having them accept me as a teacher of a particular type. I feel resistance in many ways and it takes some time for them to construct themselves as learners with respect to me. I find myself working with the class as a whole and with selected individuals at the same time. At the class level I am always emphasizing to them what I will do and why I will do that. I want them to know what they can expect from me and to emphasize the stability of what I am offering. At the individual level I take on the most difficult challenge and endeavor to build a relationship that links to the home. This has so far been extremely beneficial because these students have shown very significant transformations in their interactions with me and in their classroom participation. By meeting my goals with these *project* students I am able to teach with less resistance. I must say that it is not just a case of their having to make changes. I expect to change and the purpose of my making connections with the home is to gain greater insights into what I need to do differently to gain their trust and respect.

Michael: I see here that your construction of a teacher Self has been challenged. In your narrative and our conversation, there is a considerable emphasis on your own goals; your own agency is emphasized. But students resist, and therefore question your agency.

Ken: I see myself as a teacher who is there for my students. I am something that is stable in their lives, a person who can be relied on to look for a way to help them and create learning opportunities. I am much more aware of the need for them to see alternative role models and for me to be a source of unwavering support and reliance. I want them to construct *me* as their teacher and themselves as learners with respect to me. I know I cannot expect them to just assign me this status. I have to earn the right to be their teacher and this can only be negotiated on the basis of interactions with each of them.

Michael: We hear in your account a lot what *you* want for the students, not what they want for themselves. On the other hand, without your effort, the emancipation from their current (wretched) situation which you envision requires some coaxing, a process that engages students such that they create options for themselves. But, I may be off if these students do not consider their lifeworlds as something that should be changed.

Ken: In a social constructivist manner of thinking I see my role as providing students spaces for self-expression and fulfillment. I assume they all come to my class with goals for themselves as participants and learners.

Michael: But can we be sure to know what their goals are? And how do the situation and your goals mediate these goals?

Ken: The goals for the course cannot be theirs alone. Nor can they be mine. I expect to negotiate their goals and associated actions but in a context in which I am a listener who is open to alternatives and always watchful for opportunities to adjust the curriculum to better meet their goals and needs as learners. A critical challenge for me is setting up the conditions for such negotiations.

Michael: An interesting issue lies in the differences between the planned (your) and enacted (your-their) curriculum. In the past, the research community was concerned with the differences between the two. Here, we see such differences arise on a daily basis. And yet there are epistemological problems in thinking that plans relate in a deterministic way to the actions they project. Rather, plans should be seen as guides, but what actually happens is an emergent phenomenon. In your case, it is perhaps that your plan is particularly inappropriate for this situation, and your *habitus* generates practices that set you up for failure.

Ken: In a resource-rich school I would have to plan less. The chronic lack of resources makes it essential for me to identify curricular ideas and materials and equipment to use in their enactment. Getting ready for teaching is harder for me here than it was when I began to teach more than 35 years ago in rural Australia. The point I want to emphasize here is that planning is necessarily context dependent and must take account of not only the students to be taught but also the resources available to support learning. As I do my part in enacting the curriculum I am adaptive and the plan is one of many referents that shape practices. I like to think in terms of generating a new *habitus* because I believe that I learn so much by teaching these students that could not be learned in any other way. Sure, it helps to step back from time to time and observe my colleagues and it helps to talk to others about how to teach in settings like these. But the place to learn what it takes to be successful is in *this* classroom. I regard teaching as an epistemology wherein the knowledge that is teaching is only evidenced in the praxis that is teaching.

Michael: I wonder why it might be useful to think that 'chemistry', or any other subjects in their traditional forms, might be useful to these students and therefore the thing to teach. It is this chemistry and the Discourses that this chemistry is embedded in that may actually be experienced as symbolic violence. In this context, I am also reminded of various analyses of discourse at the high school. The successful jocks have appropriated the disconnected and dispassionate grammatically correct middle-class discourse that is characteristic of science; in their social lives, everything turns around their own career and advancement; and their social structure and norms are adaptive to the corporate context.[9] The burnouts, on the other hand, their language differs from nonstandard English; in their relations to others, friendship and family-like grouping prevail; and their sense of solidarity, their cross-grade relationships, and their egalitarian and cooperative cultures challenge the corporate norms of the school system. Thus, on a multitude of levels, school culture is antithetical to the ways of experiencing themselves and their Self in relation to Other. What you seem to be doing, then, is attempting to bring these children

---

9   For example, Eckert, 1989.

into mainstream culture rather than changing the very conditions of culture.

Ken: Coming into this setting I was determined not to teach the students chemistry. I had thought in terms of adapting the curriculum to have relevance in terms of its connections to the communities in which these students live their lives. I coined the phrase 'street science' to describe what I wanted to do and I came prepared to do this. I envisioned the class as a laboratory and the field as the place where most of the activities would occur. However, my goals were the idealistic dreams of a university professor.

Michael: But of one who is willing to test the dreams in a situation.

Ken: To begin with I could not take these students out into the streets and have them engage in meaningful learning. I do not mean that I could never do this, just that I could not do it *then* and I could not do it *now*. Each Thursday and Friday I take the class downstairs to a computer laboratory. I still find it difficult to get all of the students to the room without losing some of them and to prevent them from disrupting other classes on the way. Although I would like to think I trusted the students enough to take them out into the streets, I do not. They have not learned yet how to structure their own environments to support learning. This is presently my highest priority.

Michael: But you also need particular institutional structures as resources so that the enacted curriculum can unfold in such a way as to afford the type of learning you envision. If you attempt to do it on your own, you are likely to internalize a societal problem that should be dealt with at a collective level.

Ken: The school principal is a great supporter of what I am doing with the class. However, prior to my starting she showed some concern that I might not teach chemistry (my plan was not to teach it). She described a scenario of several students who might be able to learn enough knowledge and acquire enough motivation to pursue a degree in science at university. Of course she is right in terms of rhetoric. I want these students to have access to the same opportunities as high school students from the middle class. In our efforts at reform it is necessary for us to look carefully at what is needed to enter the gates that society has constructed to allow some through and keep others out. These students are excluded from too much because of their lack of educational opportunity. I do not want to see a scenario in which they would be successful learners, only to find that what they had succeeded in learning was not negotiable when they came to a gate they wanted to walk through. Of course this is exactly what is happening because what they are learning of chemistry is not equipping them for higher level studies.

Michael: We then have to come back to the issue of the curriculum. We need to ask, 'Do students have to learn *this* chemistry or are there alternative ways of conceptualizing and teaching science that provide students with the option to participate in mainstream society?'

Ken: Having made this point about curriculum relevance I must still say that I am committed to a version of street science that can connect with the students' lifeworlds and with canonical science. What is learned should be potentially transformative and the implication here is that the knowledge should create a new horizon of opportunities for the manner in which these students can live their lives. At this point I have many images of how this might play out. My caution is that we are not short of curricular ideas. The biggest shortcoming that I see in our profession is a lack of narratives of how to enact curricula to ensure the success of learners like the ones with whom I am working.

Michael: It is interesting to see how a teacher who cares, who is constructed as such by the school as he insists on changing the institution, the rules, and the policies when they seem inappropriate can actually instigate some change. In the past, I have often experienced myself in such situations as I insisted on particular changes that I wanted to precipitate, such as, for example, my model of supervision at a high school where I was department head of science and physics teacher. The change did not come about because I mentioned it once, but by my continuous insistence, modeling the kinds of activities that I wanted others to enact. In the end, a four-tiered model of self-evaluation, coparticipation, peer evaluation, and department head evaluation was not only accepted in the science department but also adopted by the school. Perhaps people begin because they think that giving in a little here and there will eventually stop your drive for change.

Ken: Change from within is incredibly hard. I am constantly negotiating for resources to support the learning of my students. Nothing can be taken for granted, it seems. Initially I was denied access to a computer lab with access to the Internet. Having negotiated access I found that my priority was so low that others could bump me from the lab. I have had to renegotiate and even then I am up against issues of other people having the power to decide what software I can access and the conditions under which I can use this resource. People regard tools and facilities such as computer labs as their own and often create barriers to others using them.

Michael: Thus, the very institutional structures undermine what you consider 'good practice'. Your task is difficult in the double sense that you have to negotiate being the teacher you want to be both with the students and with the institution.

Ken: I have faced similar obstacles with policies that prevent students from taking textbooks home, getting equipment and supplies into my classroom and keeping them there, and building a classroom-based resource pool to support learning. Every resource that comes into the school is brought in for a purpose and seems to be in the control of those who ordered it or negotiated for its purchase. Accordingly, most teachers find themselves without the staples to support teaching and learning. Unfortunately the teachers in the *Incentive Center* appear to have less and ask for less. The general perception is perhaps that the students in the *Incentive Center* do not deserve what others regard as the 'meat and potatoes' of learning.

Michael: In a sense, then, 'teaching' can only be understood as it arises from praxis, from the (socially and materially) situated interactions of individuals. To what extent 'coteachers' emerge as coteachers and 'students' emerge as students is not something that we can know a priori. Perhaps, when we think of *being-in/with* in the classroom, we need to think of all individuals as colearners and explode the traditional one-dimensional teacher-student distinction. As colearners, we can still emphasize difference, but the difference will vary depending on what we choose to focus on. The understandings *these* students bring to and enact in class are then as much referents and resources as those traditionally attributed to the teacher.

Street Science for Street Kids: Curriculum Choices

Teachers often make curricular choices based on what they think students are interested in, only to face trouble when it comes to enacting the lessons they have planned. Despite his best intentions, Ken faced such a situation of breakdown when he wanted to teach 'street science'. In street science, that which is literally in the street (garbage, animal feces) is the central starting point for the emergence of critical literacy and discourses of possibility as enacted by teachers as cultural workers and border crossers.[10] In the situation described below, not feeling assisted by the cooperating teacher, Ken fell back to draw on a tried chemistry lesson to bring the period to a close.

Episode

We were still learning the periodic table. Each morning the sheet I gave the students contained questions to review what we had done the day before. Of the 35 students in the class fewer than 5 of them could be relied on to provide an answer that came close to being correct. One morning, in frustration at the blank faces and the inability of the students to interact in a whole-class interactive lesson, I took a gamble. I had been planning a unit of work on street science for a long time and had advocated this as a possible starting place for building a scientific discourse. Angie Barton's research with the homeless in New York encouraged me to think that I could enact a curriculum about which students had a passion.[11] My switch to street science was seamless. But the protests from students were immediate. I was astonished and caught completely off guard when the previously apathetic students refused to accept the shift. They did not want to talk about garbage in the streets and the ways in which it might be disposed of. They did not want to discuss the smells, good or bad, from their neighborhoods. 'What's this got to do with the periodic table?' I was startled that anyone would even try to connect the discussion I had initiated with what we had previously been discussing. All of a

10   On the notion of cultural workers and border crossers, see Giroux, 1992.
11   Barton, 1998a, 1998b, 1998c.

sudden the students were alive as they rejected my efforts to discuss science in its social contexts. But the class was getting out of control and I did not want that to happen. I eyed the clock. I had 35 minutes still to go and the students were unruly and likely to become more so.

I edged my way to the rear of the classroom where Mario was seated. 'What do you think we should do next?' I asked. My mind was feverishly reviewing the options. 'Stick with it for now', he suggested. I could not wait. I needed to get them engaged again and I did not want them leaving class before it was time to do so. Defiantly I returned to the chalkboard and returned to the initial discussion of electronic structure and ionic compounds. As I wrote on the board, order returned to the room. The students returned to their accepted and familiar roles. Most began to copy, some switched off again, and I breathed a sigh of relief. On this occasion I had managed to keep a lid on an energetic outburst that was beyond my ability to control. I had saved face and was on the way to learning an important lesson about these students and their "hood'.

Tyrone was a student who was repeating grade 9 for the third time. He was part of a group of high-school students, some of whom were in the chemistry class, who were participating in a project in which they went daily to teach science to grade-7 students in a nearby middle school. I had invited a panel of six of the high school students to be teacher educators for a class of graduate students who were preparing to be certified middle- and high school teachers (i.e., Cam and his peers). The issue that the panel of students was to address was 'How to best teach urban students like us'. One student had just finished describing his changing attitudes toward study and academic success when the panel members were asked whether or not they would remain in their neighborhoods when they graduated from high school. Tyrone, who is a tough kid with dreadlocks and a manner of dressing and acting that sends a signal to stay away, was first to respond. He was visibly emotional as he described how his 'hood was a very special place to him. He indicated that he would return and did not like to be away because of the relationships he had with the people with whom he had grown up. The next student to speak also was emotional as he described how being away even for a weekend made him feel homesick. I learned at that moment that many of these students are closely attached to the 'hood and would not like to deal with a curriculum that inferred for a moment that the 'hood was undesirable. Perhaps this is one part of their lives that they can claim as their own, a security that the curriculum ought not to violate either directly, with activities such as those I had proposed, or symbolically. However, the comments from the panel of students had opened a door for me. Perhaps a student essay on life in the neighborhood would be revealing.

Michael: What I find interesting here are all the issues that arise when we see an experienced teacher, willing to learn from any situation he faces, realize that his *habitus*, formed under different conditions, is generating inappropriate practices. First, this episode clearly shows that some of the things that we *anticipate* as being interesting to students in fact are not. This has significant implications for curriculum planning. How can we, as practicing teachers, decide whether a particular new activity is appropriate for *these* students? If it is a novel activity, we simply have to test it out. Alternatively, we can engage students in a meta-activity and allow them to coparticipate in curriculum planning. This is what emerged when you allowed the high school students to teach the prospective teachers a lesson on 'How do you teach kids like us?' A related issue is that of what to do when you find out that what you have planned does not seem to work. Should you attempt to continue your 'experiment' to the end, or is it more appropriate to change activity midstream?

Ken: When my attempt to implement street science 'failed', the situation was not chaotic in the sense that it was out of control. I was able to step back and speak to Mario and seek his advice on what to do next. Unlike Loretta in your coteaching vignette (below), he did not act to take us forward. Instead his advice was for me to persevere. 'No way!' was my immediate reaction as I stepped back into the action setting. I knew I had not yet created the *habitus* to support a continuation of this lesson in any way that would lead to productive learning. Chaos was a predictable outcome of continuing without change. Accordingly, when I resumed teaching I started an activity that would ensure compliant participation until the end of the scheduled time. My strategy was optimal in the circumstances even though looking back I can now see what I might have done differently. My reason for raising this is to note that doing something different was not an option in the context of having to act.

Michael: Though an outside observer or evaluator may have marked you low for *not* having done something different.

Ken: *Being-in this* classroom, I did what was appropriate in the context of an interaction between my own *habitus* and those of *these* students.

Michael: Although he did not interact with you in the way Loretta interacts with me, being in the classroom with Mario provided you with an opportunity to ask, 'What next?' Here, as students were not cooperating in constructing teacher and student in traditional ways, therefore leading to a situation in which your *habitus* experienced breakdown, your rational thinking took over to consider alternatives. Whatever your horizon at that moment, you chose to do what you considered to be safe grounds to use the traditional roles of and relationships between teacher and students.

Ken: My practices at the time are now a resource on which I can draw to learn more about teaching and learning. Thinking about what I would have done is not to second-guess myself but to generate possible alternative future courses of action for students and myself. At some later time these alternatives can be enacted and I will have learned something new about teaching.

Michael: We also have a predicament where Mario and you differed in your assessment of the situation and in your projections of where the lesson should go next. Here, you had to make a choice between continuing street science or going back to the periodic table. What is the most appropriate action in the *here-and-now* of *this* situation cannot be evaluated from a removed perspective. In order to know one would have to be there, in *this* situation and without time-out for reflection. This is where I think it would be more appropriate for supervising teachers or teacher evaluators to make their judgments from a position of *being-with* rather than from the sidelines. The range of possible actions, what we call the *Spielraum*, is highly context dependent, situation and perspective specific. Thus, what actions are possible at any one time in any one situation are therefore radically different depending on whether you realize that you cannot take time out to deliberate at some length, or whether you adopt a removed, theoretical, and timeless stance. Praxis, because there is no time-out, requires a different conceptualization. *Praxeology*, an understanding of praxis that has arisen in and from praxis, attempts to account for the temporal aspects of praxis rather than looking at timeless structures and (procedural, declarative) knowledge.

Ken: As we think about the roles of those who assess the quality of teaching from the sidelines it is well to think of what we mean by teaching, how we come to know about teaching, and how we can determine whether or not given actions are appropriate. When I looked recently at a videotape of my own teaching just last week, I did not want to show it publicly because of a fear that people would assess it as overly traditional and inappropriate for what we expect of students these days. I felt they would see it as too structured and expect to see students engaged in more open ways that foster their own autonomy and responsibility. However, unless someone has tried to do this with *my* students I do not think he/she would have any idea how incredibly hard it is to accomplish. I am not saying that it cannot be done, even at this moment, just that it is easier to exhort and assert than it is to roll up the sleeves and do. My strong advice for any system that needs viable measures of teaching performance is to require coteaching to ascertain what can and cannot be done. Advice that is given from the back of the room, or the side of it, without having direct experience of teaching the students concerned, is likely to be fallible in ways that detract from its utility. On the basis of my experience so far in this study I would like to see coteaching experiences as a significant component of the roles of cooperating teachers, new-teacher supervisors, and administrative personnel involved in teacher assessment.

Teaching Alongside a Veteran

The initial vignettes involving Cam and Ken serve to highlight the power of regarding teaching as an epistemology of practice. Throughout the vignettes and the associated conversations there is a theme that brings into the foreground the potential of coteaching as a way to learn to teach in given circumstances. The vignettes also highlight the difficulties of master narratives of best practices. These vignettes raise questions about such issues as methods courses in universities and teacher assessment in the many circumstances in which it is practiced. The final two vignettes serve the purpose of exploring further the potential of coteaching. Unlike the initial four vignettes, the final two are not set in urban environments and the teachers do not encounter the same extremes of social and cultural difference.

When two or more individuals experience *being-in* the classroom and *being-with* another teacher, that is, when they *co*teach, many learning opportunities arise even for teacher veterans. The episode described below comes from one of six studies on coteaching. Nadine, a new teacher completing a 4-month internship, and Michael worked for the entire time at each other's elbows.

Episode

In 1998, I cotaught with Nadine a unit on water: its components included the physical and chemical properties of water and water ecology (which focused on a local watershed).[12] Nadine and I planned many lessons together, or each proposed to take on a demonstration, whole-class discussion, or activity. We always shared the classroom in the sense that one or the other could enter the ongoing conversation, or have a separate conversation with small groups of children. The current episode had its curricular origin during several previous lessons. First, I had elicited student hypotheses as to the nature of the bubbles that are visible when water is boiled; these hypotheses included vapor, oxygen, hydrogen, and air. Second, Nadine had told students the chemical formula of water without any further rationale or context that might help them to connect it to other things they knew or could see. Thus, I decided to set up a context that might allow students to

---

12   Details of learning about teaching and mastery in questioning can be found in Roth & Boyd, 1999; Roth, Bowen, Boyd, & Boutonné, 1998; Roth, Lawless, & Masciotra, 2001; Roth, Lawless, & Masciotra, 2000; Roth, Masciotra, & Boyd, 1999.

eliminate two of these hypotheses (oxygen, hydrogen) and to hinge a class discussion around the water formula and the different quantities of gases delivered by electrolysis.

I set up an electrolysis apparatus (see diagram) that produced oxygen and hydrogen, which show characteristic reactions when a glowing splint and burning splint, respectively, are brought to them. (Oxygen makes the glowing splint burst into flames, hydrogen, when lit, produces a small explosion.) To scaffold the discussion, I had prepared the experiment in such a way that, from the students' perspective, hydrogen would be produced in the left column corresponding to its left-handed position in the chemical formula (H_2O). By the time we came to the whole-class discussion, there was twice as much of the gas in the left column as in the right column.

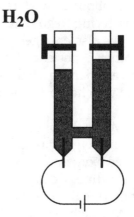

H_2O

Michael:	These [columns] contain different gases. Which one do you think is hydrogen, and which one is oxygen, given that you already know that this [H_2O] is the chemical formula of water?
Tony:	Hydrogen is right, oxygen is left.
Michael:	Why would you say that this [right column] is hydrogen?
Tony:	Because there is less hydrogen and more oxygen in a water molecule.
Michael:	[((points to '2' in H_2O)) [Does everyone agree with that?
Stan:	Yeah.
Jon:	Yeah.
Michael:	Where did you get the information from that there is more oxygen than hydrogen in the water?
Tony:	There is two little ones and one [big one, and one big oxygen.
Michael:	[((points to 'H_2' in H_2O))
Stan:	The little Mickey,
Jon:	With the ears,
Stan:	The little Mickey Mouse.
Tony:	((Walks to blackboard; draws Mickey model.)) These two [small circles] are the hydrogen and this [large circle] is the oxygen.

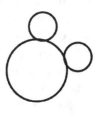

While I was teaching, Nadine stepped slightly backward, yet stayed near where I was. In this way, she perceived the classroom from a position similar to me with respect to the students. When we observed videotaped lessons such as this, and then talked about it, Nadine noted how my taking the lead allowed her to take time out and listen to the way I conducted the interactions:

Nadine: I was listening to your questions and how you've formatted that question at that moment. And that helped me then and there, because it triggered something in my head. I went, 'Oh yeah, I should be thinking about that', or 'I should be asking about that', or 'That was a good question that really got them going on this tangent or brought them back or got them more focused'. Yeah, that was helpful for me to, to listen to your questions and hear your questions then and there, as it happened, and then to think about how it related to the demonstration and where you were trying to go with that question.

We also engaged in conversations about the events. Frequently, another experienced science teacher and graduate student (Mike Bowen) participated in these conversations as an outside observer who watched our teaching from the back of the room.

Michael: So, of the two ideas, oxygen takes more than hydrogen or oxygen takes less than hydrogen, they identified the lesser one as oxygen.

Nadine: Really? But I think that demonstration was great for them to really see that. I do think they got it after.

Michael: See, one thing I wouldn't even hazard a guess about. How many, even if you show the picture on your test, which one is hydrogen, which one is oxygen, how many would get hydrogen and oxygen? I wouldn't be surprised if half said one way.

Mike: Yes. But you know I was really impressed with their observations. What they were doing observation-wise too, like even when they made the observation initially when Michael asked why do you think that the oxygen is the one that is fuller? They did move back and have a rationale of doing it. It wasn't just a guess, it was a statement that was embedded in an understanding they had developed.

Ken: Why would students look at the formula H_2O and realize that twice as much hydrogen would be generated as oxygen? I assume most of them know from the Mickey diagram that each molecule contains twice as many atoms of hydrogen as oxygen, but they also see a huge difference in size. In our macroscopic world, the one in which they live their lives, it is unusual for something to be so much larger and to take up less space. Consider the way it was drawn. The difference in area seems quite large and if you think of that in three dimensions it would seem to be the case that the two hydrogen atoms together, in volume, would be about a half of the volume of the oxygen. So, on the one hand it seems logical to think of there being a greater volume of oxygen being released from the water. What model do these students have for a gas? To what extent have they thought about any of these molecular or atomic level issues? What is the relative mass of hydrogen compared to oxygen?

Michael: I did not set up this whole class conversation around a demonstration for students to get at any right answer. As always, I am interested in allowing a rich conversation to emerge in which students coparticipate. I see my own role as that of starting such conversations and in providing sufficient support (e.g., by asking questions) that allows the conversation to unfold and therefore allows students to enact science talk. As to the way I had planned the activity, I know from my research that what is currently salient in your lifeworld is central to your (discursive and material) actions. So, from a curricular perspective, I was expecting that the material set up in front of the formula might allow students to associate the particular structure of the formula and that of the material configuration, and in this association, generate some hypotheses. Although I had seen Nadine present the Mickey Mouse, the figure was not salient at all in my thinking so that I had not considered it as a possible discursive resource in their hypotheses.

Ken: But why would we expect them to know that there is a greater volume of gaseous hydrogen than oxygen? I am now wondering what to do next. I assume that after testing the two gases they quickly realized that they were mistaken initially and they then could ponder what is happening. This creates a dilemma for both teachers. Where would they want to go with this? Would they regard the kinetic theory of gases as a useful way to proceed? At issue here is the scale up. An equation can show what is happening at the molecular/atomic level and it is clear that twice as many hydrogen atoms are released as oxygen atoms. What is less intuitive to me is that the hydrogen atoms should occupy twice the volume of the oxygen atoms. Could or perhaps should these students try to build a model and see to what extent it conforms to their investigations?

Michael: Throughout the unit, I emphasized the model character of our discourse about atoms. Thus, we used Styrofoam balls to model gases, liquids, and solids in order to make macroscopic properties phenomenally real to the students. This particular case, however, is perhaps difficult because the size relations between oxygen and hydrogen molecules conflict with the notion of equal volumes for each mole of gas. We therefore might have planned another activity in which students attempt to extend their gas model (students in the four corners of the room each holding up one molecule) in such a way as to discuss the differences that they would expect when oxygen was replaced by hydrogen. In this other model we had constructed with the children, the intermolecular distances were very large compared to the intramolecular distances. In this case, they might have come to the conclusion that twice the number of gas molecules take up twice as much volume.

Ken: The whole idea of demonstrations as experience is of interest to me. 'What do students learn from a demonstration of this type and where is the science in the participation?' is the question you raised elsewhere.[13] What is the best way to think about a liquid consisting of molecules and what happens when an electric current passes through the water? Just as students might look at a model for a gas so too they might wonder what a liquid is like and also a solid. How do those Mickey heads arrange themselves in a liquid and what happens when a gas forms?

Michael: This is just what we had done in one activity. We had divided the class into nine groups. Each group built a model for a particular state of matter. We then brought the students into a whole-class discussion where they were not only asked to compare the three models of each state, but also to make suggestions about how the transitions between the states might occur.

---

13   Roth, McRobbie, Lucas, & Boutonné, 1997.

Ken: In this coteaching arrangement the two teachers have some decisions to make as to where to go with an activity like this one. At one level it is neat to see that out of common old water (presumably from a tap) we can see something that rekindles a glowing splint and something else that goes pop. The demonstration can confirm something they might have taken for granted: namely, the formula for water. But as is often the case in science education, the issue soon arises as to what to do next. How do the bubbles produced by passing the electric current through water differ from those formed when the water is boiled? Are there models for the structure of matter that students can construct to account for the data they get from these demonstrations? How do they collect and test the gas from boiling water?

Michael: You raise numerous questions that show there are many issues one can address in such a unit. As a matter of fact, Nadine had sketched out an entire unit plan as part of her methods course and prior to my arrival. However, as we began to enact our curriculum, I began to negotiate an increasing number of activities that made sense from a content and subject matter pedagogical point of view. Our planning sessions became a rich learning experience for Nadine, who did not have a science background. Here, I often introduced new activities and we talked about whether these were appropriate for the particular students we taught. I might then take the lead in guiding the discussion, but in such a way that Nadine could coparticipate in the questioning. Or we planned small-group activities. Here, she often accompanied me to the first group, listened to my questioning, and then drew on what she had heard to enact questioning herself.

Ken: I do wish Cam had similar experiences. Nadine has a wonderful opportunity here to experience teaching alongside of you, a person with a strong grasp of the science, how students think about phenomena such as those embodied in this demonstration and the associated ideas, and where to go to next. It took a high level of skill to get as far as you got in this activity. Many teachers would not have probed to find out why Tony responded as he did. Rather than just say no and call on someone else, you used questions to ask Tony to give a reason for his answer. This is one of the essentials of being scientific. With the explanation came support from Stan and Jon who were able to take the justification even further and show you and Nadine that the idea that there was a greater volume of oxygen was likely to be quite robust. In turn that realization could lead to additional activities such as those described above.

Michael: This form of questioning became central to Nadine's learning. It was after the first lesson that she commented on the differences in the way she asked questions (often requiring one-word answers) and how I enacted them. By coteaching, she learned to enact questioning as a matter of course, by doing as I do, rather than by attempting to follow a long list of rules. What is important to note is that she identified not only the problematic structure of her questioning (e.g., little or no wait time I and II) but also the lack in her subject matter content and content-related pedagogical knowledge. However, in our planning sessions, she constructed herself as being a learner of chemistry and physical science as much as being a beginning practitioner.

Two Veterans Coteach

In our experience, coteaching has been shown to be not simply a viable model for preservice teacher learning. On several occasions, Michael had taught entire units from 2 to 4 months with teachers who have had 20-plus years of experience. This episode shows that even veterans are afforded opportunities for professional growth when they coteach.

Episode

In the spring of 1999, Loretta and I cotaught for a second time a unit on ecology in a grade-seven science class. Loretta was a seasoned teacher with 26 years of experience, an undergraduate science degree, and a master's degree in educational administration. Her own teaching was often directive and, especially in mathematics, centered on textbook-related activities. I motivated this unit, in which children enacted a research project of a local watershed, by drawing on an invitation that was articulated in an article from the local newspaper featuring the activities of an

Elizabeth and Damian's Bug Study

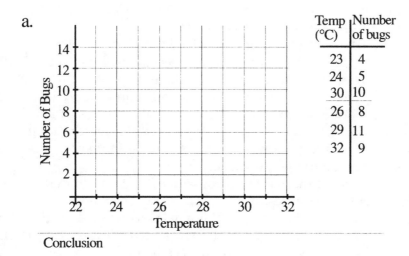

Figure 1.1. Transparency prepared by Michael for an activity intended to allow students to engage in making graphs, drawing inferences, and designing research.

environmental activist group. In this invitation, local residents were asked to contribute to the understanding, preservation, and improvement of the watershed. Loretta and I invited students to frame their own questions. As they began their research, we intended to scaffold their research practices and therefore their learning by designing particular activities that permitted students to make a series of issues problematic.

After the second day in the field, I noted to Loretta that the students appeared to be content to collect a small number of data in support of their claim. Students did not construct a need for collecting more data. In our conversation, Loretta and I decided not to tell students to collect more data, but to design and conduct an activity that could give rise to a discussion about the changes in interpretation when additional information was collected. I offered to prepare an activity.

As I planned the activity, I constructed a scenario that closely resembled the activities in an earlier study involving two grade-eight students, Elizabeth and Damian, who wanted to find out whether small animals have different activity levels at different temperatures. They decided to study relationships between temperature and the number of bugs they found under a rotten tree. I prepared a transparency (Figure 1.1a) and I thought that, covering up the data table partially, I would get students in groups of two to plot the first three data points and write their inferences about a pattern. For this, I would provide students with a copy of the transparency lacking only the data in the table. The process would allow me to control the data to which students would have access. I would then invite students to a whole-class discussion to talk about their (different?) inferences. In the next move, I wanted to question whether they were certain about the pattern they constructed between temperature and the number of bugs, and what they would suggest. Students would then plot the additional information and again draw inferences. In the subsequent whole-class discussion, students would contribute the answers they constructed. I would bring this sequence to a close by asking them to identify the most significant thing they learned from the activity.

On the day I was to teach, the power went off just as I walked into class and did not come on again until we were done. I reconstructed on the chalkboard what I had prepared and began by telling the story of Elizabeth and Damian. I presented the story, the reduced data table, and the graph, and provided each pair of students with their own graph paper (like Figure 1.1a, but without the data). I asked students to plot the data and draw inferences and conclusions. Loretta then asked to step in and take over. She enacted a questioning sequence in which (a) she asked students whether they knew what I meant by 'inference' and 'conclusion' and (b) connected the upcoming graphing activity to the graphing they had done in her mathematics class. After a number of students had indicated that they understood the connection, she suggested, 'Dr. Roth, why don't you continue'.

I invited students to plot the data. As they began their activity, Loretta and I circled in the classroom and asked students questions, correcting their plotting, encouraging them to think of trend (lines), and so forth. I brought the students back to a common forum, plotted the data (black dots in Figure 1.1b), and enacted a whole-class discussion. Many students suggested that the number of bugs increased (linearly) without qualification about what might happen if the temperature rose even more. I asked whether they were certain, how certain they were, and what they would recommend to be done. I used one student's answer to collect more data to suggest that this is what Elizabeth and Damian had done, and completed the data table. Students then plotted the additional data and Loretta and I spent some time with each group, especially encouraging them to write down their new inferences. As we circled, we touched base every now and then to exchange particular observations about student understanding and asked each other to check the understandings of particular students. I then brought students together for the second whole-class session related to this activity and plotted the missing data points (circles in Figure 1.1b). Students ventured a number of different claims but ultimately came to agree that there was a temperature with which the bugs appeared to be most comfortable. To make salient the necessity of the additional data points, I asked students whether they had to change their ideas in the course of the activity. Every now and then, Loretta requested a turn in which she rephrased one of my questions, particularly when she seemed to feel that the pause between question and response was too long.

To conclude, I asked students what they had learned. There were a variety of answers. Many students remarked that bugs liked intermediate temperatures, around 29° Celsius, or that they didn't like the cold. Only after I had elicited a range of responses did several students note the desirability of making more than three measurements to get an accurate answer.

In our debriefing after the lesson, Loretta and I noted that students were engaged with the activity, that they had drawn a variety of inferences, and that even students who were often quiet contributed to the whole-class conversation. As part of the critical and self-reflective analysis of our lesson, Loretta remarked that we should have done the following. We should have asked students to predict how many bugs they would expect for higher temperatures such as 35 or 40° Celsius. I realized that I might have thought of this earlier and agreed that it would have been interesting. In this way, we would have generated further learning opportunities and perhaps further emphasized the point we wanted to make with the activity.

Ken: I want to make a point about you *looking back on your experience* to identify an activity to adapt for use in the class with Loretta. I too have found it very useful to *look back* to identify what was appropriate in the past and to adapt strategies and activities to the contexts of the present. The *looking back* can be intentional and deliberative as in the scenario you discuss here, or it can be automatic when *habitus* projects past experience that has been built about a lifeworld of professional praxis into the future. In this era of Standards-based reform, there is a tendency to identify standards as a source of ideas for the curriculum and perhaps to downplay the importance of the *habitus* and past experiences as sources of current praxis. Coteaching provided Loretta with mediated access to your *habitus* and to the parts of your science teaching expertise that were encapsulated in the activity that was enacted.

Michael: In this, I see an important aspect of practice that existing theories of practice do not contain—time. Teaching is unfolding in time. The practices normally generated by *habitus*, and those generated in times of crisis by deliberate reflection both enfold time as past experience structures future action. At the same time, *habitus*, itself the result of a historical development, is such a powerful concept because it generates situated actions that are appropriate without having to take the time-out required by reflection on action.

Ken: Loretta knew to check on the extent to which her students understood what you wanted them to do. Perhaps her experience with *these* children enabled her to sense that some of them might not fully understand what they were to do after you had set up the context for participation. By stepping in, she was able to deal with her own intuitions about what needed to be done and in so doing you had mediated access to her *habitus* and knowledge of how to teach students like these. The stepping back and stepping forward is the essence of coteaching,[14] and the potential of mediated access to the *habitus* and associated praxis of coparticipating professionals is a rich source on which to build knowledge of science teaching for both of the teacher participants.

Michael: There are really, at least implicitly, two important things in your analysis. On the one hand, we have two differently structured *habitus*. Because of her experience with these students teaching several subjects, her *habitus* had adapted to the contingencies in this classroom; it had adapted to deal with the particulars of each student in this *class*. In my situation, a *habitus* related to science more generally generated my actions. But, because I was unfamiliar with the situation, the (discursive) practices I generated were not always appropriate. However, because Loretta stepped in and took over, I could learn from her how to enact teaching in *this* case. The second important point is that both Loretta and I are experienced practitioners. Thus, as you could see during your visit to our class, our coteaching has structural likeness to a jazz jam session. We can pass the ball back and forth, play solo for a while, and then move with the students into small groups. We are always keeping contact, alerting each other of particular events, constraints experienced by particular students.

Ken: Your experiences with science seem to distinguish you from Loretta in important ways in this vignette. You know how to do science. Your interactions with the students therefore enable them to 'see' some of the conventions of science in action. In particular, your style of questioning has the potential to foster re-

---

14   See the items in our coteaching heuristics (Table 5.1, p. 189).

searching among the students. I sense that Loretta probably learned a great deal from working at your elbow and can see how to work with student answers to go deeper and learn from an activity such as this one. So many teachers just stop when they get the first student response to a question. This is a good example of how Loretta can learn to go deeper.

Michael: Coteaching affords learning for all participants. Thus, I learn a lot from Loretta as we work at each other's elbows. In particular, I notice that she is much more structured than I am in terms of organizing students. Whereas I have thought in the past that structure is bad, I can see in her ways of interacting with students that some structure affords new learning opportunities.

Ken: The stepping back and stepping forward can also bring forward frustrations on the part of either or both teachers. How do you handle styles of teaching that are not coherent in a philosophical sense? What about a situation in which you have a goal of and value for open-ended inquiry and Loretta has a belief (and associated practices) that learning for this class is best when tasks are clearly defined and highly structured? Where are the sites for negotiation of how to approach such issues when coteaching is to occur? I can imagine this can be difficult for new teachers in negotiating with cooperating teachers and supervisors in their field experiences.

Michael: I am not sure how to react to this situation. It may be that in my own coteaching experiences, we always dealt with individuals who somehow worked well together—participating in such an experience in itself may bring individuals together who feel comfortable working in such a situation. In all situations, there was an openness to consider the experience of the Other. Whichever way we go, we do it jointly, supporting each other, and then analyze in long conversations afterward what we might have done better. In all six studies that I conducted on coteaching, these conversations were never sites for blame, but rather sites for learning. In my experience, the resident teachers who have less subject matter knowledge and pedagogical content knowledge often go with my suggestions as to the type of activities; but we rely on their knowledge of *this* classroom in our decisions about how to implement a specific activity.

In the final section, we bring this chapter to a close by working out some of the central issues that teaching as epistemology raises for (preservice) teacher enhancement, supervision, evaluation, and research. Our recommendations for practice are grounded in our own practice, circumventing the traditional route that led from theory to practice.

From Practice to Practice

Grounding our work in (sociological) phenomenology, we develop in this chapter a praxeology of (science) teaching. This praxeology, an objectification of teaching praxis in conversations about teaching, arises from our experience of coteaching. Here, coteaching provides a ground for shared experience, which subsequently becomes the topic of professional conversations. Out of these professional conversations we derive new understandings of teaching, understandings which we term praxeology, which is always situated in praxis, rather than theory, which is always abstracted from praxis. Our framework is rooted in the presupposition that we, from the beginning, experience ourselves as being-in-the-world that we share with others (*being-in/with*). Being-with others, coteaching, teachers develop systems of structured, structuring dispositions (*habitus*) which are generative mechanisms giving rise to the patterned ways in which we perceive and act in the classroom. We found that coteaching provided us with many shared experiences that subsequently led to professional conversations during which we came to better understand teaching in our respective settings. In this section, we therefore propose coteaching as a model for learning to teach and for teacher supervision. We develop our explication of the coteaching/co-generative dialoguing model for research on teaching and teacher assessment more deeply in Chapters 7 and 8, respectively. In each of these cases, the shared experiences provide the ground for more productive conversations that lead to understanding and teacher development.

Learning to Teach

Rational models of learning to teach emphasize the significance of learning about the foundations of education and about teaching methods, and actively practicing in the field where reflection on practice can enhance praxis. In this book we have emphasized teaching as an epistemology whereby the knowledge that counts is what happens when teaching occurs. As is the case in other types of practice, the knowledge that is enacted as teachers' practice is quite different from the knowledge that can be spoken or written about. In this chapter, we have highlighted the complex factors that constrain teaching in particular contexts and the value that comes from learning by doing, especially if others are able to coteach and participate collaboratively. Learning to teach is an ongoing process for any teacher. However, for new teachers, beginning teachers and those seeking professional renewal there may be occasions when the process is formalized. On such occasions we advocate that coteaching be regarded as an essential component of the process planned for learning to teach. We acknowledge the importance of reading research and theory, discussing implications for practice, teaching classes as the 'only' teacher, and reflecting on those practices with a variety of colleagues. In addition we advocate coteaching and associated conversations about practice with the coteacher(s) and students. Because the insider perspective on what is appropriate and possible is so often at odds with the perspectives of outsiders, it is important to include coteaching and conversations with other insiders as essentials in the process of learning to teach.

In this chapter we have shown that even experienced teachers (e.g., Ken) might experience tremendous difficulties when they work in new, especially difficult, educational settings. Although Ken brought tremendous energy and willingness to teach 'Science for All (Americans)', he failed initially because his *habitus* generated actions that did not lead to success in *this* situation (though they might have in other situations). In a very practical sense, therefore, our conversations in this chapter have led to learning and new understanding that allowed Ken (in the year that has followed) to become more successful in teaching students in *Incentive*.

Praxeology: Walking the Walk

In a recent conversation, Peter Grimmett, a long-time advocate of teaching as a craft, told us that teacher educators have to begin to walk the walk.[15] He told about his practice of teaching learning-to-teach courses in the field, where the issues to be talked about arise from the events that happened in the new teachers' classes on the same morning. Rather than teaching students about cognitive development on a particular day because the course outline indicates it, lived experience provides the starting points for professional interrogation and development of understanding through critical and informed analysis.

In the terminology we have developed here, Peter Grimmett talked about praxeology, with its correlate 'method' of hermeneutic phenomenology as the tool for teacher development. That is, he engages students in developing understanding out of their experiences. By introducing relevant existing knowledge in the teaching community, he brings in the resources for a hermeneutic reflection. In this way, new teachers no longer experience a gap when they are asked to move from theory to the praxis of teaching. Rather, praxis is primary, and understanding of praxis, praxeology rather than theory, is developed out of the primary experience.

Some readers may think that we advocate a return to professional schools, immersing student teachers in the field and denying the need for explanatory discourses. However, this is not at all what Grimmett or we have in mind. Rather, the hermeneutic explanation-seeking component in our hermeneutic phenomenology relies on the historically constituted disciplinary knowledge that is used as a resource in the analysis of lived teaching experience. It is only through critical and informed analysis that we can develop understanding; but all critical analysis already presumes and in fact is enveloped by the understanding that arises from lived experience.

In this chapter, we have striven to make the structure of the narrative consistent with the content: Our theoretical analysis of teaching exists in the form of conversations about teaching episodes that we had experienced ourselves. We see our chapter as a

---

15   Personal communication, January 26, 2000.

model for the kinds of conversation that emerge from coteaching. From our perspective, coteaching actually provides a better ground than watching teaching from the outside, because the partners have experienced the lessons from a position that is ruled by the same temporal constraints rather than from a fly-on-the-wall position that is ruled by the objective gaze. We therefore advocate that even teacher supervision, evaluation, and research be conducted from the coteaching situation.

Supervision of Teaching

Teacher preparation programs identify several types of resource persons to teach prospective teachers to teach. These include methods instructors, cooperating teachers from selected schools, and university supervisors who visit the school site and provide an outside perspective on the quality of teaching. The issues that arise from our vignettes suggest that these roles can be productively altered to include coteaching as an opportunity for proactive teachers to learn how to teach by coparticipating with the selected resource persons. We see this as addressing the problems of relevance: The suggestions prospective teachers receive need to be made in relation to what should be tried and what is possible in this situation, at this time, with these students. Tied to the contingently unfolding events in a particular classroom, relevance is reintroduced by linking to the temporality of teacher knowledge. Rather than making suggestions about how to teach given some atemporalized scenario (description of a case) and drawing on deliberative modes of knowing, teachers of teachers move from a telling mode into an enactive mode. Rather than talking *about* appropriate practice, they have to enact appropriate practice without the luxury of praxis-removed reflection-on-action. That is, teacher educators have to, as the popular adage among teachers goes, 'walk the walk' rather than 'talk the talk'. Having to coteach at the elbows of prospective teachers requires all teachers to make their praxis visible in an action setting where all participants can learn from one another. What is appealing to us about this practice is that it avoids the use of master narratives, which imply that certain activities and strategies are appropriate and possible in all settings. Coteaching particularizes practice in specific settings and permits the knowledge that is constructed to be pertinent to the constraints that bring about or diminish what is possible. Thus, coteaching provides an ideal setting in which *habitus* reveals itself as it generates situationally appropriate action. We acknowledge that our suggestions will require most institutions to alter their present practices; however, in so doing, the potential exists to greatly improve the quality of teacher preparation and enhancement programs.

CHAPTER 2

Re-learning to Teach

In this chapter, Ken presents an autobiographic account of his struggle to teach in an inner city school and the learning accruing from the experience. In our professional conversation following the autobiographical account, we critically analyze Ken's experiences and the problems of teaching and learning to teach in inner-city schools.

Initial Urban Experiences

I relocated to an inner city university because of my commitment to make a difference as an urban science educator. I believe the greatest need for educational change is in urban schools where science education invariably falls short of its potential for social transformation. It was time for me to address directly some of the more challenging and enduring problems in science education. I was fed up with studies that claimed to have resolved the equity issues in our major urban centers when it was patently clear to anyone who visited schools in those cities that the problems were manifest and unresolved.

Being in the city was radically different than anything I had experienced. For 6 months I lived in the suburbs and had a short commute to the university. I remember clearly my initial train rides. As we approached my destination the train became crowded with high school students headed for the nearby City

High School (CHS). The students were unlike any I had taught or observed. All were African American and many were from poverty. As I listened to them interact in the crowded conditions of the train I could scarcely understand their dialects. I wondered then whether I'd ever be able to teach students like these. At my station I disembarked, walked along the platform, up a smelly and heavily littered stairwell, and into a dilapidated street just six blocks from my office. The strangeness of the environment was greater than I expected and it was like being in a new country with a distinctive culture. So much was novel. But I was no tourist. I lived and worked here.

My sense making was saturated with deficiencies as I compared this with other places in which I had lived. Even though I had chosen to come to this urban community to practice science education I perceived the environment and its inhabitants through jaundiced eyes and seemed to notice the squalor, disrepair, dirt, trash, neglect, and signs of poverty. To be here was different to such an extent that my life experiences and professional praxis were out of alignment with my expectations and capacity to cope successfully.

Learning to Cope

'You've gotta develop an attitude'. Once more I was on a train, this time in New York City, and a young woman was advising me about riding the trains and walking the streets. I was accomplished in neither of these activities and I was explaining to her that my presence in the streets of Philadelphia was too interactive. I needed to build a way of being that acknowledged others but did not engage them overtly. I knew what she meant about having an attitude but decided that a useful goal was for me to better understand city neighborhoods. I was now living in the city and decided to walk to my office, a four-mile hike that allowed me to traverse a variety of neighborhoods en route to the university. In addition, I began an urban ethnographic study in which I explored local neighborhoods every Saturday and Sunday morning.

I felt heroic in those days and was very conscious of the unusual nature of what I was doing and the associated risks. Being in the streets revealed just how much I had to learn. I could see no alternative than to gain first-hand experience and knowledge of neighborhoods like those of the students I was to teach. Usually I did not feel comfortable and I was alert for possible dangers that might await me. My tendency to feel heroic was potentially problematic, because romanticizing events with me as hero and the urban inhabitants as victims could distance me from those I sought to educate. However, over time I learned to feel at ease in being in the streets, interacting with others, navigating my neighborhood, and walking to different parts of the city. I began to fit in with the environment and no longer felt separate, like a stranger giving meaning to all that happens. The strange was becoming familiar and I could make sense of the smells, sounds, and sights of my urban environment. I regard my learning to become street wise as a necessary component of becoming an urban educator and I am certain I could not effectively teach in this community without first knowing what it means to live here.

Although I was learning a great deal about living in an urban community, I was doing very little to learn about the teaching and learning of science in inner city schools. A growing concern was what to do in my science methods courses. Although I had lots of advice to offer my new teachers I was not all that confident that my knowledge was grounded in good theory, research, or praxis. Most of my new teachers were struggling to enact much of anything I suggested and I began to wonder if it was their relative inexperience, the problems of finding suitable cooperating teachers, unteachable students, or the fallibility of my knowledge of what to suggest.

Just a few weeks into the fall semester of 1998 I realized that most of what I knew about science education was mainly applicable to middle-class values and settings. Even though I had undertaken research in numerous countries my experience in all of them was essentially middle class. Furthermore, my teaching of science methods courses had focused on the teaching of middle-class students in suburban-like schools. What I needed to do was very clear. I had to learn to teach science in urban schools where most students were African American, living in conditions of relative poverty. Otherwise my teaching about science teaching would amount to little more than empty exhortations. I resolved to begin a program of science teaching at CHS, beginning with the most challenging group of students in the school. I declared that I would teach at the school for at least 4 years so that I would not be regarded as a researcher undertaking a short-term study, that is, leaving an unchanged system after attaining my goals.

City High School

My first visit to CHS, where I am presently teaching, also involved deficit seeing. CHS is nothing like the high schools I have experienced in Perth, in Tallahassee, or even in a big city like Miami. It is an urban high school with an enrollment of more than 2,000 students, 98% of whom are African American and living in conditions of poverty. Just like my impressions of the city, my initial impressions of the school were negative. My tendency was to notice the undesirable features of what was there and those missing features that would in my opinion have enhanced the school. As I walked on the pavement alongside CHS I was reminded of a prison by the expansive brick and concrete wall, the few, barred windows, and the heavy metal door at the front of the school. The building was not an architectural masterpiece and from my perspective it was welcoming neither to students nor to faculty.

I am not sure when the switch in my perceptions of the school occurred or what catalyzed the change. Now I look forward to going to the school and as I enter the building I admire the ceramic murals and other decorative contributions of graduating seniors. Learning to regard a school as more than bricks, cement, and metal bars requires a perspective of a school as a social organization, a perspective that evolved as I became part of the CHS community.

The school district adheres to a policy of creating *small learning communities* (SLCs) within each school. The idea is to allow students to experience a small school and to thereby create a feeling of family, belonging, school loyalty, and shared values. At CHS the 10 SLCs each contain approximately 200 students. Students can select an SLC according to their career or academic goals. However, not all students choose the SLC in which they will spend their high school lives. Some fail to meet the entry requirements and others are unable to maintain satisfactory performance levels. In these circumstances they are assigned to an SLC.

My teaching took place in an SLC known as *Incentive*. The school bulletin lists *Incentive* as 'an academic and resource program to assist students who need to acquire additional academic credits because of extended absences or other extenuating circumstances. These credits will enable the students to achieve appropriate grade level or graduation requirements'. However, the description in the bulletin is at odds with the perspectives of most students in *Incentive*. Tyrone, a grade-nine student, told me that '*Incentive* is the bottom of the trash can'. Tyrone also thought that the change to a block schedule, with its longer periods, resulted in a great deal more time being wasted in each of the class periods. He emphasized that 'I don't like it because what they are teaching me is too easy. I'm finished in about 20 minutes and sitting there for about 55 minutes doing nothing'. Tyrone was also riled because he wanted to listen to music on his Walkman when he finished his work. He insisted that others could not hear the music and would not be disrupted.

This Kid Is Trouble

The first time I set my eyes on Tyrone my instinct was to back off. He did not look like the type of person I would want to mix with. His dreadlocks were arranged asymmetrically, his clothes looked like battle fatigues, and his broken front tooth gave him the appearance of a fighter. I was with Mario (the regular classroom teacher with whom I cotaught) in the main office. 'That kid gets in trouble because people are afraid of him. He looks bad so they just get him out as soon as they can'. Mario's words echoed my thoughts. Tyrone was headed toward the main office. Following some distance behind him was an angry male teacher who began to raise his voice as soon as he reached the office door. 'What's the problem Tyrone?' Mario spoke quietly as Tyrone passed by. 'He's suspending me because I went to get my coat', Tyrone replied softly. His response had credibility but events moved too quickly for me to learn more. The raised voice of the teacher became a shout and an assistant principal also began to berate Tyrone for his defiance. Within minutes a stream of colorful language flowed from Tyrone's mouth as he was ushered into the assistant principal's office. 'They just don't know how to handle kids like Tyrone', said Mario with a resigned shrug of his shoulders.

Enforced Absence

Tyrone suggested that teachers and non-teaching assistants (NTAs)[1] stereotyped most male students as thugs and used that as a basis for suspending them from school. He explained to me that his long-running battle with the NTAs resulted in his being absent so often that he was now repeating grade 9 for the third time. I regard Tyrone as an enigma. He is very intelligent, wants to work hard, and wants to succeed. But at the same time he has a spirit that will not be suppressed. He will not allow others in authority to dominate him and he does not condone duplicity when he sees it. Although some might describe him as being smart mouthed, Tyrone regards himself as principled. If an NTA calls him a bastard he will reciprocate with similar or even more profane language. His inability to 'let it go' has cost him dearly with those in authority and he is continually getting suspended. Because of his appearance he is accosted frequently by NTAs and teachers and, because of his enduring spirit, his reactions are such that he routinely earns 5-day suspensions. These absences soon add up to another failed semester.

On the Way to the Forum

I invited Tyrone to participate in a pre-session at Penn's Ethnography Forum. He agreed to participate and I came to the school to walk with him to the session. I located Tyrone in the lunchroom where he was speaking with a friend. He indicated that he would

---

1   Non-teaching assistants (NTAs) are male and female personnel who are hired to maintain order in a school. They keep unauthorized personnel from the school building and enforce rules and orderly conduct.

join me downstairs in the science lab in five minutes. At the designated time Tyrone arrived, but as we were about to leave Cowan (an NTA) burst into the room. 'You and I have business', he shouted motioning Tyrone into the hallway. Although I felt outraged by the event, I waited for Tyrone to return, but to no avail. He was suspended for 5 days for 'dwelling too long on the second floor', and was ushered from the school building. Tyrone later told me what had happened. As he walked down the stairs to meet with me, as we had arranged, Cowan called on him to stop. Without explanation Cowan demanded his identity card, effectively suspending him until the card was returned. In this instance Tyrone was stopped because Cowan assumed that he was breaking a school rule. Tyrone would have none of it and walked away to keep his appointment with me. When Tyrone was taken into the hallway to discuss the 'dwelling' charge and his subsequent walking off his reaction to Cowan's aggression involved his use of profane language and an automatic 5-day suspension. Needless to say Tyrone did not make it to the Forum and it took an intervention from me to have his suspension lifted after 3 days.

Because I have developed a close relationship with Tyrone, it is easy for me to see how Cowan in this and other instances has catalyzed problems based on his preconception that Tyrone is a troublemaker who needs to be controlled proactively. However, I can appreciate another side of this issue because I have been a beneficiary of proactive intervention from an NTA.

Proactive Intervention

My least successful activities are those in which I address the entire class. Invariably someone begins a conversation that is sufficiently loud to be a source of distraction to other students and me. This is a basic classroom management issue. But what is the best way to enforce silence when I am speaking? On this occasion I was speaking to Dante about his annoying habit of speaking loudly to a peer whenever I spoke to the class. I believed that Dante was testing me and I was aggravated by his increasing tendency to be disruptive. However, my making his behavior an issue gave him a public forum in which to impress his peers.

Dante looked at me with disdain and commenced a rebuttal:
'You speaking so loud I have to...'

'Choose you next words carefully'. The softly spoken voice of
an NTA stopped Dante dead in his tracks.

'My bad', Dante said immediately.

The tall young African American NTA smiled reassuringly at
me and left the class without another word. Unnecessary conflict
was resolved before it began. If the NTA had not arrived at the
most opportune of times I would have had a serious problem on
my hands. I would have had to deal with Dante's verbal on-
slaught. I am certain that he would not have complied with any
request I made of him following his anticipated outburst. I had
made a serious error by raising the issue at that time and I was
moments away from possible humiliation.

Refusal to Comply

One thing I learned from Tyrone is never to ask these students to
do something if you cannot deal with the consequences of their
refusing to do what is requested. What could I have done with
Dante? Students like him are not afraid of the law and do not respect authority. Hence, threatening detention is no deterrent as
most refuse to attend. In fact, if a student fails to attend a detention, s/he is suspended for 5 days. These students are not only
unafraid of being suspended; many relish the thought of having a
reason not to come to school and to stay at home or in the streets.
If an optimal learning environment is to be established, it is important to build a community that is self-regulating. In such a community the participants want to learn, and they trust and respect
one another. The students can develop the rules and the custom of
adhering to them, not breaking them.

Why Make This the Line in the Sand?

'Dr. Tobin, this is marvelous. What are we doing here?' The principal entered the room and was focused on three roof-to-floor-
length pendula, two the same length, and one slightly shorter. I

had connected the three close to the roof by looping them over a long dowel rod. Three students were exploring resonance. 'It's not going as well as it might look', I remarked as she entered the room. Fifteen students were present and only five of them were engaged in productive activity. Furthermore, the noise level was unacceptable to me and I was trying to get it down as she entered the classroom.

The principal looked around the class and noticed Clarence wearing his cap reversed. Although Clarence was working, the principal managed to catch his eye and pointed to her head with her forefinger. Clarence continued to work, shaking his head just so perceptibly, but with resolve. 'Young man. Give me the cap. I'll give it back'. The principal moved toward Clarence who once again shook his head ever so slightly. At this stage I felt decidedly aggravated. There was going to be trouble here. So far the principal had broken two of the cardinal rules Tyrone has taught me. She chose to make an issue of something trivial and in so doing interrupted one of the few students who were working. Also, she made a request without thinking through whether she could deal with the consequences of Clarence not doing as she asked. I groaned inwardly. 'Outside, young man!' The principal raised her voice and the stakes. Clarence once again shook his head and continued to work. The principal strode into the hallway and Clarence continued to work.

'You need to go see the principal, man. Don't make this into a bigger problem than it has to be'. Clarence looked at me in stunned silence. Betrayal! He slammed his chair back and walked defiantly from the room, his cap still on his head. The principal began to scold him as soon as he reached the door, but Clarence would have none of it. He continued to walk past the principal and had to be apprehended by an NTA.

Teaching Science at CHS

When I spoke to Mario about coteaching we agreed to focus the curriculum on a form of science that would be relevant to the students and had the potential to transform aspects of their lives. I had in mind investigations focused on the students' neighborhoods, somewhat akin to the science that Angela Calabrese Barton undertook with students from a homeless shelter. I thought of this as street science and envisioned the students mainly learning science outside of the classroom. When I discussed the focus of the curriculum with the principal of CHS she was not enthusiastic and she viewed my suggestions as examples of low expectations and stereotyping. 'Will it prepare these young people for higher studies in chemistry? If your students wanted to study more science, they would be disadvantaged'. The principal was resolved and I did not want this to be the issue that prevented me from teaching in *Incentive*. Accordingly, I agreed to teach a half-unit on chemistry followed by a half-unit on physics.

Getting Started

My initial chemistry activities involved as much hands-on activity as possible. I wanted the students to associate science with doing. However, many students did not enjoy doing science and preferred to sleep, not participate, or talk socially with their peers. Most would not wear safety glasses and if I insisted they would not participate. Also, with few exceptions, the students would not persist with an activity beyond the first day.

The first activity on chromatography involved the students in separating the colors from marker pens. For the remainder of the week I wanted them to use a range of solvents to separate out colors in M&Ms, lipsticks, and other types of ink. The students complained that the activities were boring and that we had done this yesterday! Similarly, the students refused to continue into a second and third day their investigations of chemical reactions between soluble salts (involving temperature changes, color changes, and precipitates). The students wanted fresh activities that were interesting to them and did not develop a curiosity about the chemistry associated with their experiences. It did not appear as if they were able to generate open-ended questions and certainly they did not regard questions as springboards for scientific inquiry and hands-on investigations. In fact, when I asked questions designed to stimulate inquiry the students answered them using as few words as possible.

Relevance of the Enacted Curriculum

Every day I questioned the relevance of the science I was teaching the students in *Incentive*. Sometimes they questioned it too. During an initial discussion of Newton's second law of motion an announcement from the principal interrupted the lesson to provide details about the Stanford-9 testing that was to occur later in the week. One of the students seized the opportunity to declare that he had taken the SAT-9 three times and there never had been a question on Newton's laws. His assertion was received enthusiastically by several peers who joined him to challenge the relevance of studying Newton, force, and motion.

A second example arose the next day when we looked at the physics of delivering a fast ball in baseball. One of the less involved students suddenly showed interest and asked how it was possible to hit a fast pitch for a home run. I decided that the next day students would read a short piece on everyday applications of Newton's second law and respond to questions in writing. The idea was intended to address several problems. First, the students did not appear to learn from oral description of applications or from demonstrations. Second, when students were given questions to respond to in writing they tended to answer in as few words as possible. Third, students had little persistence in answering extended-response questions and were easily distracted.

As the students entered the room I handed them a single page to read. The gist of the science was that Newton's second law could be reorganized to show that force x time is equal to mass x velocity. The implications of losing momentum in a short time-interval were described in terms of punches in boxing, hits in football, collisions involving automobiles, motorcyclists, and cyclists, use of seatbelts and safety, uses of helmets in various sports, and the design of running shoes. Although the list (without a more complete description) does not reflect my concerns about sex equity, I endeavored to include examples that would appeal to both males and females. The reading concluded with five questions that required the equation $\Delta F \cdot \Delta t = m \cdot \Delta v$ to be applied qualitatively to a variety of everyday experiences.

As was customary in the class there were numerous students who refused to engage from the beginning of the lesson. I planned to begin with $F = m \cdot a$, replace a with $\Delta v/\Delta t$, and then use algebra to arrive at the appropriate form of the equation. Then, in a discussion, we would apply the equation to selected examples from the everyday lives of students. I began with baseball since we had explored this the day before when we also debated how auto design could minimize the impact force on passengers during a collision. A very small number of students (2 of 20, both females) showed intense interest, responded to my questions, and nodded their heads at my explanations. However, from the outset, most students were uninterested and only too willing to be distracted at the slightest opportunity. Having fully applied the concepts in several contexts and placed the key points on the chalkboard, I asked the students to read the brief description and respond to the questions.

The initial problem for those who appeared willing to participate was that they did not know what to do. Because the questions were embedded in the text they could not identify them easily or discern how many were to be answered. I responded proactively by calling to the attention of all students the location of each question. Unfortunately, few students were attentive and I had to interact with each individual. As I did this I took care to explain that each question was an opportunity to show how science can be applied. I wanted students to understand that each question could be answered by applying several interconnected ideas and that short answers might not provide a complete response to a question.

With 20 minutes remaining in the lesson I decided to have a discussion of answers to the questions. The first question asked whether laws should require boxers to wear gloves having a greater mass than 8 ounces. I then wrote an extensive answer to the question on the board so that the students had a model of how 10 points could be distributed for the response. Fewer than five students copied my response despite the fact that I had informed them that questions like this would be on their unit tests or SAT-9 tests. As I worked through each question I searched for ways to involve students. However, even though almost an hour was allocated to consider and respond to the questions there were few students who attempted to answer them or were motivated or prepared to contribute.

When the lesson ended I dismissed the students and had an empty feeling in my stomach. Who had benefited from the last 75 minutes? As I looked across to Mario he shrugged his shoulders. 'I am fed up with this group', he said. My sentiments exactly. But I did not share my reservations with him. 'We have got to get to these students', I said with fierce determination. 'We cannot give up!'

I Took Them Outside

I was very apprehensive about taking the students outside. For the most part they were unruly even when I took them down to the computer lab. Taking them into the streets seemed to be an invitation for trouble. Yet, I was a firm believer in doing science out of doors if possible. Accordingly, I decided to enact a series of outdoor activities.

We had been doing sound for some time and the students were not as engaged as I had hoped. The unit on music was not the success I had expected it to be and the students were seemingly bored. We had used a slinky to show longitudinal and transverse waves and also discussed the difference between standing and traveling waves. The students had seen resonance in open and closed pipes and it seemed appropriate to discuss the velocity of sound waves and also to discuss other properties of sound waves such as reflection. We then discussed reverberation, echoes, and ways to measure the velocity of sound.

The students contributed very little to the plan to measure the velocity of sound, although they certainly had the ability to work out a suitable design. Instead, in an interactive way, I led a discussion by explaining what we would do and asking students questions to solicit as much involvement from them as possible. Soon we had the design worked out. I found two large pieces of pine to strike together at one-second intervals to create a loud 'clap'.

The few students in attendance were quite docile. I demonstrated echoes by hitting the wood together some 50–60 feet from a school wall. The echoes were discernible but not distinct because there were so many walls in the vicinity. Then we went to a quiet side street that was flat. I asked for volunteers to move away from Mario, who had agreed to clap the pieces of wood. Only Tyrone volunteered to walk with me down the street until we were far enough away for the sound to take a half-second to reach us. The rest of the students preferred to watch from a distance and crowded under a tree.

When we returned to the classroom I was reminded of the low level of mathematical competence of most of these students. In our experiment the distance traveled by sound in a half-second was 171 meters; none of the students was able to calculate the velocity, or at least have an intuitive idea of what it was. Accordingly, I showed them how to use the data to calculate the velocity. Then, so that they could show what they had learned about the velocity of sound, echoes, and reverberation, I asked them to write a narrative, draw an illustration, or prepare a poster to hang from the ceiling. Although several students commenced the activity, when the folders were submitted at the end of the semester, only a few included their narratives or drawings and none had completed the task.

An interesting irony about the outside field trip is that my fears of losing students could not have been further from what happened. We left the building with 11 students and returned with 13, having picked up two who were late and otherwise unable to enter the building.

Persistent Problems

Sporadic Attendance

I did not satisfactorily contend with the students' sporadic attendance at school. Only a small proportion of the students in my class on any given day was there the day before or the day after. Hence it was difficult to identify issues that were relevant to those in attendance. Since I could not easily predict who would be present on any given day, the enacted curriculum tended to be planned to keep moving forward. The average level of absenteeism in my class was approximately 40%, with a range from close to zero to almost 100% absent. Out of a class of 35 students only 15 might be present on a given day. Of those fewer than 3 would be in the class at the official start time of 8:15 a.m. and even 20 minutes into the class, students would be straggling in. Of those who did come, none would have their materials out ready to begin work and many brought neither paper nor writing tools to class.

I regard it as a high priority to plan for sporadic attendance and late arrival. It is all very well to define this as a symptom of a dysfunctional school, but it is quite another matter to cope with the consequences day after day. One way to address this problem is to have an individualized program that students can access automatically when they arrive in class. If the program includes all assignments and handouts, the students who have missed class can be held responsible for their own progress. The use of computer and Internet technology may provide convenient access to assignments from remote locations such as home, public libraries, and computer laboratories.

Sleeping Students

As many as six to seven students would come into class and put their heads down to go to sleep. What should I do about sleeping students? I could put them outside but then someone else would have to deal with the problem. I would give them a detention, or I could suspend them. None of these possible solutions had more than momentary appeal. Perhaps I could set up my own detentions; however, this has not been an option because I am only at the school for 3 hours a day. There are many reasons why students sleep in class. Punishing them for sleeping or having their heads down does not take into account the reasons for their actions. We need to better understand why students have their heads down and address the problems rather than continually deal with the symptoms. Not only that, I prefer to establish a system whereby students accept responsibility for their own actions, including their need for sleep and their use of class time. I would like to see them as autonomous, accepting responsibility for participating in class, completing assignments, and learning at acceptable levels.

Failure to Do Homework

Getting students to do their homework was a problem for me because I was the only teacher in *Incentive* who set homework and expected it to be done. A minority of the students did their homework, but peer pressure reduced the numbers and also made those who had done it reluctant to go public. Should I go over homework when students had not attempted it? Should I ask students who were here the previous day to complete the homework while I re-taught yesterday's lesson for those who were absent? What about students who were absent for several consecutive days? Should each student have an individualized program? I decided for the future that an individualized approach might be planned and enacted in such a way as to address many of the problems I encountered.

Not having a suitable textbook to take home until midway through the semester limited the types of activity I could set for homework. When we finally got a textbook it was more than 20 years old and unsuitable for many reasons that included content with little relevance to current times and a failure to include minorities and females in substantive ways in texts and pictures. Also, for many students the conceptual difficulty and reading level were too high. This problem was exacerbated by the fact that few books were in their homes and my students were unwilling to access books from public and school libraries.

Signs of Progress

Reggie looked stern as he walked directly toward me. I noticed his bandaged left hand and thought about the stories of him slugging the officer who had pulled him over during a car chase earlier in the week. I didn't flinch as his right fist brushed against my jaw. He broke into a broad smile as he grabbed at my gut. 'You outta shape man!' He gave me a high-five and continued down the hallway. Reggie was back in school and 5 months earlier this incident could never have happened. Students were beginning to acknowledge my existence.

Options to Consider

Teach Those Who Want to Learn

Some of the conventional wisdom of teaching does not appear to work well with these students, at this time. For example, monitoring of the students while they work is sometimes constructed as 'being in their faces'. I had developed the habit of moving around the class, getting to see what each person is doing, looking at his/her work, and as necessary providing scaffolding to facilitate the learning of individuals and groups. Also, if students appeared to be unsettled I often stood close to them to encourage their participation by my proximity. Students have often shown their displeasure with my roaming from group to group and will exclaim: 'Back off man! Get out of my face'. When Tyrone observed my teaching on videotapes he also advised me, 'Back off. Only teach them when they want to be taught'. I have taken this advice seriously and now approach most students only when I am invited.

Tyrone's advice to teach only those who want to be taught is also a potential way out of the relative failure of whole-class lecturing. When a whole-class presentation is seen as desirable, it might be that those who are interested in learning can be invited to a part of the classroom where a focused presentation can be given to them. Students who elect not to participate can be offered an alternative activity such as copying notes or reading and responding to questions. Providing students with alternative ways of participating is an approach that has potential. I will ensure that at any time students have the option of doing what they are good at doing and can pursue their interests. For example, all students seem to know how to read and answer questions from the book. As sad as it may seem, allowing them to read and write science is one way to increase the rate at which students participate and presumably learn. Let them start from what they can do, and over time, when they learn how to participate consistently, then they can learn new ways to participate.

I have now changed the focus of my attention from the whole class to individuals. I endeavor to recruit one student at a time to join a community of learners in which science activities are constructed around the interests and values of the students and what they can do. For example, in a lesson on motion the students were building and racing balloon powered cars. Thirteen students were present, seven were seemingly asleep and, of the six awake, four were participating. When I began 5 months ago my efforts would have been directed toward getting the seven sleeping students awake and involved. Now I realize that my efforts are better spent teaching the four participants. Facilitating those who want to learn has become my goal as I endeavor to build a community of learners. As for those who are not participating? That is their decision. The door is always open if they take the initial step to get started. Of course, I do not abandon them and still make invitational overtures to them to get involved. However, I do not allow that to be my principal goal, as it was when I first started. It is better to focus my energy on those who will participate and want to learn than to antagonize those who are determined to resist and disrupt the learning of others.

Enact Multiple Activities in Each Lesson

For each lesson I now think in terms of multiple 10–15 minute activities in which students participate. Creating variety through the use of short activities separated by well-managed transitions appeals as a possible way to increase student participation and achievement. In my classes I soon realized that students needed to learn to concentrate and sustain their participation. I was unsuccessful in implementing anything close to six activities in a 90-minute lesson, but I regarded the inclusion of short, varied, and interesting activities as a way to address the goal of having students learn to learn.

Encourage Alternative Ways of Participating

Creating a management system to allow me to focus my efforts on students who want to learn makes a lot of sense. In *Incentive* my biggest challenge is to effectively deal with those who are unwilling or unmotivated to learn on a particular day. Rather than placing the onus on me to get students to participate, I would prefer to allow them to choose to participate in alternative ways. If alternative activities are available and the students have the responsibility for all assignments, there is merit in providing them with autonomy and the associated responsibility. In addition, I recommend an opt-out alternative that students can select occasionally, perhaps to a limit of five times per semester (still with the proviso that all assignments are their responsibility). The opt-out activity could involve participation in non-science activities of the students' own choosing as long as the activities do not disrupt others in the class.

Setting up a Portfolio System

The students rarely bring notebooks or pens to class. If they have them, they don't get them out. Dealing with this problem every day suggests that something proactive needs to be done. I envision each class having color-coded folders in which students place their notebooks (paper) and pens for science. Their folders will be stacked on a shelf with the students' names prominently displayed on the spines.

Having such a system will solve numerous problems. All assignments can be placed in the folders and students will have the responsibility of completing them even when they have been absent (in which case, they complete them when they return to school). Completed classwork and homework can also be left in the classroom portfolio. This system will provide me with access to student work and allow me to provide them with regular feedback.

Involve Others to Support Learning

To the fullest extent possible, parents, siblings, guardians, and persons from the community should be involved in supporting learning. Many of the students in my class have jobs and need to earn money to support themselves and their families. Some need to support their own children. However, as Tyrone pointed out to me, 'a lot of people from around my way dropped out of school. Now they see the value of education and make sure I go to school'. He also pointed out how influential his brother is in keeping him at school. His brother is incarcerated but has been educated while in jail and is insistent that Tyrone go to school, attend class regularly, and make an effort to learn. It has been my experience that every time I have contacted a parent/guardian I have made progress in getting a student better focused on learning. It is easy to assume that the parents/guardians are not interested in the education of the students for whom they have responsibility. Such an assumption is another example of the adverse effects of negative stereotypes, which eventually inhibit the learning of students such as those in *Incentive*.

Searching Backward While Looking Forward

Since I began teaching the students from *Incentive* I have done whatever I can to increase the quality of participation and learning. When I took over the class I endeavored to teach chemistry in ways that were engaging. It did not take me long to notice that the students resisted any efforts on my part to enact a curriculum that was inquiry oriented and focused on the attainment of goals like those included in the school district's standards. For more than 5 months, almost every effort of mine was unsuccessful in promoting the meaningful learning of science for most of my students. I now realize that there is little difference between what I was able to accomplish as I enacted the curriculum and what Mario achieved during my observations of his class prior to beginning my teaching. Just as I had a jaundiced view of Mario's teaching, I am certain that any observer of my teaching would conclude that my expectations for participation and achievement are too low and that these are the primary causes of the problems I experienced. However, such judgments would be harsh and would not take account of my goals and the difficulties of attaining them with these students.

Had I not had the experience of teaching these urban high school students, my advice to new teachers encountering problems such as those I have experienced would have been to enact problem-centered learning, emphasize inquiry and hands-on activities and, to as far as feasible, participate in field trips. Certainly I would have advocated small-group work and minimized activities associated with reading and answering questions from a text. I would have encouraged the students to connect their science activities to technology and the lifeworlds of their students and I would have expected all of my suggestions to work. Failure would have been interpreted as the inability of new teachers to teach appropriately. However, for more than 5 months I floundered. Every day I enacted activities that I expected to be successful, but they fell short of my expectations and failed to capture the students' interests. It is imperative that I communicate these findings to new teachers because they should not feel that the research and theory they read necessarily applies in all contexts. It is critical that new teachers understand the significance of elements of social class (especially poverty) and ethnic diversity as factors that will shape enacted curricula, participation of students, and teachers' possible accomplishments.

My decision to begin with more orthodox forms of science was a setback to the enacted curriculum because I never could actually connect with the students' interests and performance capabilities. The initial activity on chromatography captured the students' interests because of its novelty. But students had no interest in follow-up activities, possibly because the topic was imposed on them. It would have been preferable if I had found out about their interests and built a science curriculum around them. Not only that, getting the students involved in selecting what to study would have been good pedagogy and a demonstration of my trust in them.

Science as I knew it, and had experienced it in schools, did not seem to have a place at this time for these students. No matter how I restructured my ideas about what should work or interest them, my few successes were at best short term and were limited to just a few students. It was not as if I didn't ask students about what their interests were, how to improve the class, and what they wanted to get from the course. Questions associated with these issues were asked of students frequently and I tried to learn from their responses. However, I was not able to discern any promising starting points from the students' suggestions and inter-

ests. Instead I enacted a litany of activities that fell short of my
expectations and their interests. It is possible that my lack of experience with these students prevented me from hearing their interests and translating them into science activities.

I wondered about the extent to which the institution of public
schools was a problem when I read a draft of a chapter written by
Deborah Stern in which she described a curriculum oriented toward social justice at a small alternative school for high school
dropouts.[2] Her description of inner city public high schools as
over-crowded and over-regulated institutions where students are
largely invisible is consistent with my experiences at CHS. Despite
the schools-within-a-school policy that led to the development of
heavily tracked small learning communities like *Incentive*, the students at CHS do not participate in curricula that are emancipatory and socially transformative. Stern's students examined issues
of social justice using resources such as newspaper articles about
people like themselves, issues that arose out of gangs, crime, court
decisions, jail, and, life and death in urban communities. Her students could relate to such issues.

What are the comparable topics in science? I have searched for
doorways into the lives of these students, doorways to connect
what they do at school and how they live their lives. What Angie
Barton and Darkside have done in New York City is most impressive, and I have endeavored to learn from their valiant efforts to
break the mold. Their redefinition of science has enormous potential for us to connect social justice, science, and the students' lives.
But they have accomplished their very impressive results outside
the traditional framework of public schools. Whereas Angie Barton can work with volunteers, I teach students who have been assigned to the low track and are required to be at school.[3] It remains to be seen whether or not I can redefine science and elicit
comparable levels of cooperation from students like those in *Incentive*.

Whatever we try in *Incentive* fits within a framework of other
activities that are undertaken in the school. These students have
to learn to learn. Yet there is irony in me making that statement.
The students are streetwise and have survived in very difficult

2   Stern, 2000.
3   Barton, 1998a, 1998b, 1998c.

circumstances. Of course students from *Incentive* know how to learn. It can be argued that what they are not good at doing is joining in small-group conversations and learning from the conversations of others. This too is nonsense! The most formidable challenges I had in *Incentive* involved some of these students when they embarked on tirades to justify a perspective or course of action. The students are extremely articulate and they interact in their dialect at a speed that is overwhelming when the conversation involves a topic that interests them. In terms of science, the most vocal they ever got was when they refused to participate in street science activities on the several occasions I tried to get them involved, and when they protested the relevance of studying Newton's laws. In fact during their protests about learning Newton's laws I stepped back in astonished admiration of how a group of previously sullen noncontributors could spring to life to display an awesome array of discursive resources on which the learning of science could build. No matter how hard I tried, I could not re-create occasions like those they produced with relative ease. I could not find doorways through which they could enter to participate in science. It could be the institution or, more than likely, it is just that I am not yet streetwise within the domain of *Incentive*. I am still on a journey of learning to teach science to students like those I have described in this chapter. Until I become streetwise there is a great deal of potential in those students that will remain invisible to me, even as I continue to see deficits. It is not that I am unwilling to see their potential to learn, it is that I still can't see what is there for others to see and exploit to benefit the students.

For as long as I have been in teacher education I have emphasized the importance of building relationships with students and negotiating the right to teach them. I have been adamant that students do not just bestow the right for people to teach them. All teachers must earn that right and that involves students constructing themselves as learners with respect to would-be teachers. What I did not understand was just how difficult it was to earn the trust and respect of these students. For several months I found many students ignored me when I spoke to them. Most did not respond to my questions or oral remarks, and few initiated any approaches that could be construed as positive. Only now can I say with confidence that I am building rapport with a significant number of students. I regard rapport as a precursor to trust and respect—so there is a considerable distance yet to traverse.

Yesterday as I crossed the street to go to my office, a student from *Incentive* called from the car window: 'Heh old head! How's it goin' man? There's my science teacher'. I was delighted to see Reggie in the passenger's seat with his dad. Both wanted to shake my hand. 'You will be back this year won't you Tobin?' I nodded my head, my affirmation signifying more than just an answer to his question. For me this was a big occasion and I was proud. Reggie acknowledged his teacher in the street. For me there is no higher status than to be acknowledged as Reggie's science teacher. In terms of my becoming an urban science teacher, this is one of many milestones that I still have to pass.

Making Sense

During and following a one-week visit during which Michael co-taught for 4 entire days at City High School, we engaged in a long sense-making process to discuss what we can learn from Ken's experience of becoming an urban science educator. Michael's coteaching experience is crucial, because it allowed him to view Ken's world through the eyes of the teacher.

From: Michael
RE: My week at CHS
Ken, thank you very much for having me and for allowing me this past week to share in the experience of coteaching at CHS. I had read several of your articles about your work at CHS and was therefore very familiar with the situation and your struggles to make a difference. Yet spending a week at the school and coteaching different classes, and talking about teaching with teachers, new teachers, and students changed the way I think about teaching and learning in inner city schools. Not that your articles and presentations were somehow inauthentic—I experienced many of the things you had written about, the prison-like atmosphere, the constant control of students by NTAs and teachers. Similar to your early experiences—and despite being in your presence at all times—I felt uneasy initially with this unfamiliar

world and was afraid that I might not be able to cope and might become a target for violence. This uneasiness subsided as I had many opportunities to interact with students in both formal (teaching) and informal ways. Following you around, and modeling my own behaviors according to your ways of interacting with the students helped me to fit in and learn.

FROM: Ken
RE: My week at CHS

Michael, it was good having you here, because this shared experience at CHS enables us to evolve, through continued (discursive) interactions, our understanding of teaching and coteaching. It is always so easy looking back to see what might have been. When I began to teach at CHS, I did so as a very experienced science educator who realized that I had a lot to learn. I expected to be successful and even in the face of what I considered to be continual failure I looked for solutions and usually came in the next morning with a fresh set of expectations that were success oriented. I knew that there were social and cultural differences that were causing problems for me but without some indication of what these might be I am not sure how to even notice a cultural difference. The most obvious issue was that of respect. I knew before coming that I had to earn the respect of students and in particular to earn the right to be their teacher. I had to build rapport.

Coming to that school, morning after morning, being the first teacher in the hallways, endeavoring to interact with students only to be shunned with silence and looks of complete lack of interest was not only unexpected but somewhat humiliating. I knew the students were being disrespectful and yet I did not immediately realize that my efforts to interact only made me an easier target to disrespect even more. Had someone sat me down and taught me about respect being the currency of the street I might have developed a different strategy for entering the school, the hallways, and the classroom. I felt the disrespect of students and misread many of the signs inside and outside the classroom. For example, one of the older students in my class referred to me as 'old head'. I had never heard of the term before and the way he used it sounded very disrespectful. The very first time he used it I bristled at him in a direct and very confrontational manner. 'What did you call me?'

I challenged. 'Old head!' He pointed to his head and said 'You an old head. Hey old head I need yo help'. I was confused and did my best to help despite a strong feeling that he was still being disrespectful. In retrospect he had no interest in passing the course or learning science and he rarely came to class. However, when he did come he offered me very useful and helpful advice that might have served me well had I constructed myself as a learner with respect to him. For example, he often gave me advice about my teaching. On one occasion when four or five males were being confrontational he pulled at my trouser leg and whispered, 'Back off man. They'll hurt you. They not scared of no one. Leave 'em be or you gonna get hurt'. On that occasion I looked into his eyes and he was sincere. He was not saying this for the benefit of others. I backed off and with the assistance of Mario managed to redirect those in the class that wanted to work.

Knowing the culture of the students—that is, having a sense of their *habitus*—is critical. Through my teaching activities in the past two years I have learned about the culture of schools like CHS and small learning communities like *Incentive*. Knowing what students know, can do, and are interested in is an essential first step. Knowing how to read the students as they approach you, interact, and move on is also important. I now know when to ignore transgressions and when and how to take a stand against a class of students who are not cooperating. I have learned how to focus on those students who want to learn, how to encourage those who appear to be unmotivated, and how to back off from those who are likely to be antagonistic and disruptive to the learning of others if I endeavor to redirect them. At the same time, however, I realize my responsibility to coparticipate with all students. Each one of them is my responsibility and I want them to progress over time from where they are toward some place else that reflects their interests—as they are negotiated between them and me.

When you visited CHS you had a decided advantage in that you had me, transformed through my experiences in the previous year. You did not have to negotiate entry and forge relationships without scaffolding provided by someone who was aware of the major pitfalls. When I began to teach in *Incentive*, Mario expected me to take over. Mario not only retreated into the background, he became an observer from the side and only participated when I encouraged and then insisted. You entered CHS at a time when there was a greater acceptance of coteaching and a better understanding of what that entailed. Accordingly, you were not expected to take a lead role in the class, and when you stepped forward into that role there were other teachers present to reassume responsibility when you decided to step back. In these event-full urban settings, there were always teachers who responded timely to the unfolding events.

FROM: Michael
RE: Contradictions
What struck me most in the situation at CHS is the pervasive presence of contradictions, which, as I understand it, inherently impede teaching and learning to such a degree that these become virtually impossible. On the one hand, these contradictions arise from the difference between the middle-class values and practices inherent in the schooling system and the values and practices of working-class people and the urban poor.[4] On the other hand, these contradictions arise for each student at multiple levels within an activity system that situates him/her as subject with respect to mediated relations involving objects, tools, community, rules, and division of labor in the process of learning. In my view, the contradictions are so pervasive that only systemic approaches at the school level would seem to be able to deal with them. Yrjö and Ritva Engeström[5] provided both analyses and descriptions of actions that allowed administrators, teachers, and students in an inner city school to remove some of the existing contradictions and thereby to contribute to an environment more supportive to learning than had existed before. As it is, well-meaning individuals appear to contribute to the re/production of a system of inequalities despite a passion to make a difference that counts in these students' lives.

FROM: Ken
RE: Contradictions
You raise a significant issue that I did not address: whether a teacher acting alone can make a difference or whether valiant ef-

---

4   Bourdieu & Passeron, 1979.
5   Engeström & Engeström, 2000.

forts simply fuel a cycle of production that leads to re/production. Your application of activity theory highlights the importance of institutional arrangements as mediational agents that sustain the status quo. I fear you are correct in suggesting that without school-level changes (at the very least), hard-working teachers and their heroic actions are unlikely to do more than stem a torrent of low expectations and performance for a short time.

FROM: Michael
RE: Contradictions

At CHS, and probably at other inner city schools as well, many practices seem to mediate what teachers can do to assist students in learning. These practices, then, lead to contradictions and to impediments to creating more favorable learning environments. For example, a major goal of schooling is to allow students to acquire course credits so that they can ultimately enter college or university; many of the students at CHS talked to me about 'going to college' as a stepping-stone to a career. However, suspending students who already have difficulties attending school on a regular basis puts them into the streets and makes it even more difficult for them to graduate. The problem of attendance is simply aggravated when students are prevented from entering when they are late or are suspended for what appear to be minor issues. Here, the institutional arrangements designed to make the school a safe place, by making sure trouble cannot arise, actually militate against learning and teaching. Teachers I talked to are also frustrated by the continuous absence of students—each day they have to contend with students who have missed a week or two. It therefore becomes difficult to make any curriculum a continuous experience—unless everything is individualized and students can complete their courses whenever they are done rather than within the confines of a fixed school year.

In all of our efforts to think through what might be best for these students (or similar students elsewhere in the nation) we seem hardly inclined to rethink the institution itself. In the autobiography, you refer to the work Angie (Barton) does with children in shelters for the homeless. But the difference between her work and others is not just that the activities take place after school, but also that Angie's work embodies a critique of the nature of science in the everyday world. Thus, whereas Angie's students choose most of their own activities, and therefore take ownership and pride, you make most of the decisions for your students. To me, you seem to be caught in the predicament that school science has to look in some ways similar to scientists' science. But you know that I suggested repeatedly elsewhere,[6] there are other ways we can conceive of science. For example, science as enacted by AIDS activists[7] or by a French muscular dystrophy organization[8] has all the attributes of other human activities, the way it is bound up with other aspects of our lives including values, strategies, politics, economics, and aesthetics. This connection to other parts of everyday life makes Angie's science different, and therefore her work also constitutes an ontological critique. However, in this school, as in many others, 'science' means scientists' science. Despite all the efforts of teachers such as you and Mario, little critique addresses the very foundation of an unjust system.

Another contradiction in the students' activity systems lies in the relevance of what students are asked to learn. While I was coteaching a lesson on the chemistry of a single exchange reaction, I overheard several students, among whom there was an expectant mother, talk with great interest about the relationship between food and the growth of babies. Drawing on their experience with the children of their friends and peers, these students seem to know a lot about the relationship between growth and the type and amount of food newborns are fed. I am therefore struggling with the relevance of what we are trying to do in teaching science.

One of the central contradictions, however, is the organization of school life itself. It appears as if the school is less interested in learning and the construction of success than in the re/production of existing differences and the status quo. The school is built on and staffed on the model of Foucault's panopticum and control.[9] There appears to be little interest in assisting students to learn, wherever they are and whatever the resources they bring. Rather, there is a mold and those who do not conform and submit are shaken out of the system. When we look at the way these students

6   Roth & McGinn, 1997.
7   Epstein, 1997.
8   Rabeharisoa & Callon, 1999.
9   Foucault, 1979.

interact outside the school or in the hallways, and when we look at the articulate way in which they talk to us about teaching and learning, we see a striking difference. As Penny Eckert showed, working-class students enact different forms of social relations and different practices of interacting with each other, and, because of their family-like cross-age organization, they enculturate their younger siblings and mates from the same social class.[10]

FROM: Stephanie
RE: Teaching in a culturally appropriate manner
Ken, at least one of my activities turned out to be culturally relevant for my students. Witnessing the battle several of my students waged with asthma, I incorporated a series of lessons focusing on the illness and its link to the African American population. In order to hypothesize about their race's predisposition to asthma, the class members examined trends in diet, living conditions, and geography, while simultaneously exploring the disease's physiological effects. When questioned as to how they would create their own culturally relevant biology curriculum, the students identified health labels, heart disease, sex education, and the contribution of Black scientists as crucial components. The lessons were not only significant to the students' lives, but extraordinarily compatible with the Philadelphia benchmarks as well.

FROM: Ken
RE: Nature of science
Michael, you raise the issue of the nature of science and its place in the curriculum. I have struggled with this mightily over 2 years. I am very persuaded by what Angie has done in her work with the homeless, but it is in different circumstances. You know that Gale (Seiler) has worked with male students at CHS in her 'lunch club' activities.[11] She has accomplished some astonishing progress by beginning with her students' interests and building the science from there. I have not stopped trying to reconstruct the curriculum to begin with the students' interests and knowledge. But it is one thing to intend to do it and quite another to actually pull it off in a classroom. So far the impediments to my efforts

---

10   Eckert, 1989.
11   Seiler, in press.

have been numerous. Students have diverse interests. An implication of this diversity is to allow a significant proportion of time for individualized activities. So far my efforts to individualize the curriculum have fallen short because students need so much personal attention and demand it as and when they need it. They appear to have little tolerance for waiting and I cannot be in so many places at the same time. When I do not respond to them immediately, some students lose patience and refuse to engage. Coteaching is a promising practice that seems to address this issue and is also consistent with creating a community of practice in which all participants are learners and all are teachers.

A significant challenge is to get the students participating in a sustained way for more than 10–15 minutes. The use of block scheduling throughout the school provides 90 minutes of instructional time in most SLCs (*Incentive* has less time in each block). Only on rare occasions have I been able to get the students to participate for anywhere close to the allocated time. Even the best of students use the unfolding events of the classroom to interact socially or just to 'goof off'. It is a concern for me because by doing so they are simply reinforcing the social reproduction cycle.

In my view, educational reform must always involve much more than exhortations to improve. Sitting at the side of Mario's classroom it was very evident to me what was wrong and just as clear what needed to be done to correct the wrongs. As a teacher with a relatively long history of successfully teaching science, it never occurred to me that what I had done elsewhere would not be successful with Mario's students. I was wrong on several counts. The approaches that I considered most appropriate involved changing the nature of the curriculum so that students could employ what they can do, know, and are interested in. I believed in the importance of listening to the voices of the students and endeavored to do that. However, reading and thinking about reform are quite different from enacting reform. In this study I attained few of my goals as a teacher and the main reason for my failure was an inability to see capital in the actions of the students. Despite my efforts to avoid deficit thinking and my stubborn resistance to lowering my expectations for student achievement and performance, what occurred as the curriculum was enacted was barely recognizable as science and students were seldom stretched cognitively. Despite my efforts I was unable to engage most students in higher cognitive thinking about science.

FROM: *Michael*
RE: *Re/production*

Throughout my stay at CHS, I had a strong sense that the school was simply re/producing inequalities rather than seeking to transform an unjust system. The practices enacted in this school and the values that underpin them were those of the middle-class culture that I was familiar with, but did not appear to reflect the understandings and values that the students displayed. For example, I was struck by the discrepancy between teachers' practice of 'threatening' students with low grades, taking points off for late assignments—and the negligible effect these 'threats' seem to have on students. Only a minority of students in *Incentive* or *SET* seemed to be concerned when teachers made such pronouncements. This strategy may work well in the schools frequented by the middle-class kids that you and I taught and researched in the past. But all the evidence shows that it does not seem to work at all in the CHS classes. Here, teachers enact practices that have roots in their own experiences of succeeding in a schooling system, which itself is laid out in ways designed to reward those students who are most able to conform. That is, teachers enact (control) practices that are often without effect in *Incentive*. Yet more than two decades ago Pierre Bourdieu and Jean-Claude Passeron noted the distinction between middle and working class with respect to the systems of punishments and rewards of schools.[12] Thus, the particular sensitivity of middle-class students to the symbolic effects of punishments or rewards underpins their academic docility, which stands in contrast to the 'rebellious' and 'conflict-seeking' behavior of students from other social classes.

Among the values that seem to me typical of Eurocentric middle class societies are 'persistence' with school tasks, 'timeliness', and 'regular attendance'. These values are consistent with a particular way of life, a way that is suited to the needs of the Western economy, work in the factory, and so on. In different cultures, the need to subject citizens to clock time does not seem to exist.

12 Bourdieu & Passeron, 1979.

We may have to interrogate our own teaching and institutional practices to find whether they are the most suited to allow these students to succeed. Are these values characteristic for all students? My and my students' work with and among First Nations people shows that their notions of time (length of pause before speaking, how long before meeting, etc.) are very different than the ones to which we have been enculturated (production cycles of factories, regularities of machines). Yet as educators we rarely seem to ask ourselves about the level of agreement between the primary *habitus* of students and the one of the inculcation efforts of schooling.

Another internal contradiction involves the ways in which teachers such as you attempt to engage the students. Involving students may not work either, because it goes against the *habitus* of the students who have only experienced school and schooling as a teacher's show that one attends to or not with few consequences. Throughout your autobiographical description, we see how much *you* wanted to create opportunities for the students to learn. You attempted to make science relevant and chose topics that you thought might interest them. However, a central problem seems to lie in the fact that the teacher takes all responsibility and decisions, and students are little involved. In the schools where your *habitus* was formed, students may have been more amenable to such innovative approaches to the curriculum.

FROM: Ken
RE: Engaging students
I am not sure I knew how to engage students in the conversation about their interests. They tended to ignore me when I spoke to them or to act with aggression to show their disrespect.

FROM: Michael
RE: Conflicting habitus
I want to come to another instance that you reported in the autobiography. You describe how on one occasion, you were 'speaking to Dante about his annoying habit of speaking loudly to a peer whenever [you] spoke to the class'. This struck me as another situation in which the culture of the students is in conflict with your *habitus*—you wanted to enforce silence and being lis-

tened to, whereas the students in *Incentive* (and *SET*), particularly in whole-class situations, often talk loudly across the classroom. During my week at the school, I noticed other teachers in the school would not interfere with such conversations. As teachers who want to bring about change—both in our own practice and in that of students—we have to think about finding types of activities that do not encourage practices that interfere with the activities of those who are interested in learning. It is then a matter of working more closely with students to have them participate with us in finding activities that minimize disruption and maximize learning. In fact, you and I shared observations of small-group activities, and the recommendations made by those students who talked with us about the lessons converge with our observations. These students suggested to us that their needs are better met in small-group situations, especially when there are several coteachers in the class to attend to the multiple needs arising during the lesson.

FROM: Ken
RE: Conflicting habitus
There were times when observers would come to my class and think they were seeing good science; however, this only reinforces the folly of making judgments from the side of a classroom. Some of my students, like Tyrone, are accomplished at getting activities completed and achieving results such as forming brass on a copper coin. What is more of a challenge for most students is creating a science-like discourse in conjunction with such activities. What that takes, and what was missing from my classroom for the entire semester, is motivation to learn on the part of students. Problems might be anticipated when a teacher's goal is for students to learn science while the students are motivated to accomplish other goals, especially those related to attaining the respect of their peers. The negotiation of goals is an especially important stage in the enactment of a curriculum. In this instance I did not interact effectively with most students. My lack of cultural knowledge about my students was a major obstacle to my becoming an effective teacher. I have much more to learn about how to be a teacher within a community in which respect is so important. I need to learn how to interact as a teacher with these students while not

showing disrespect for them or requiring them to participate in ways that might be seen as earning the disrespect of their peers.

At the same time it is necessary for me to earn respect while being consistent in my actions and beliefs about Self. For example, I believe that successful learning communities are self-regulating and I will not set up a classroom based on punishments and disincentives. Nor do I believe in establishing authority through shouting and physical aggression (involving the use of non-teaching assistants who are in the school to maintain a safe environment and to quell acts of physical aggression). I do not believe in suspending students for 5 days to teach them who is in charge of the school and would prefer to keep students in school rather than act in ways that return them to the streets. However, I do understand that the interests of those who aggressively resist efforts to maintain environments that are conducive to learning may have to be secondary to the interests of those of students who seek to learn. I prefer a community that is self-regulatory. In such a community the students could interact with me about the curricular goals, the activities to be undertaken at a given time, the assessment of what has been learned and accomplished, and the rules for participation. Of course a prerequisite for any of these events is that I must learn how to build and sustain a rapport with students that is constituted in mutual respect.

FROM: Michael
RE: Contradictions, again
Throughout our exchange I have wrestled with the question, 'How do we remove the contradictions that I have noted in my previous letters?' I admit that I do not have an answer to all (or even one) of these contradictions. On the one hand, there are all these arguments about giving students such as these students equal opportunities so that they 'can make it' (in a society that works for and around middle-class values). At the same time I feel that trying to make them fit the middle-class mold is the most inappropriate thing to do, because it is inconsistent with the students' experience of knowing and learning in their everyday life. Those who fit in and are successful in the schools as they are also find their own values and practices from home as the context of their schooling. We know, however, that our success in teaching

students will remain limited as long as we do not deal with the inherent contradictions. Bourdieu and Passeron suggested that the success of any pedagogic work is a function of the distance between the *habitus* it tends to inculcate and the students' existing *habitus*, which was inculcated prior to schooling and in students' homes. As long as this distance is maintained, schools will fail to make a difference in the lives of those students, such as the students attending CHS, who have a primary *habitus* very different from that embodied in the institution.

Teaching and learning to teach in such a situation, then, from my perspective, is one of the characteristic contradictions. Learning to teach means developing a new *habitus*, a *habitus* that breaks with existing ways of re/producing education, society, and culture. As teachers, we need to enact a radical doubt about the nature of education and what it takes for students to break out of their present situation (e.g., of poverty).

Transformation, therefore, needs to be at the heart of our enterprise working in these schools and preparing future teachers. No longer can our goal be the preparation of teachers who maintain the status quo, that is, teachers who re/produce a society in which success is highly correlated with existing social hierarchies. Talk about praxis—including students, new teachers, teachers, supervisors, researchers, and so on—teaches us a lot about what it takes to teach and learn in schools such as CHS. You know that I have been coteaching for years, both while I was still a full-time teacher and through all the years since. I always wanted to walk the walk rather than talk the talk. I feel that there is much that (student) teachers have learned and continue to learn from students themselves about teaching kids like them. If one problem lies with the different *habitus* of students (from situations of poverty and living in housing projects) and their teachers (successful in society as it is), then interacting with each other seems to be a step toward understanding their mutual needs for making the teaching and learning environment work.

FROM: Ken
RE: Contradictions, again
There are no simple answers to the question you raise about the removal of the contradictions. It is advantageous if students

come from elementary and middle schools with the discursive resources on which a scientific discourse can build. They do. But teachers like me are not good at recognizing the capital in what the students know and can do. It is evident that in the neighborhood city schools, the resources that elementary and middle schoolers bring with them from their schooling and home environments do not fit as well with a science-like discourse as is the case with middle schoolers graduating from suburban schools around the country. However, we cannot continue to ignore the needs of high school students from working and unemployed classes and rationalize what is possible in terms of deficits emanating from experiences in urban elementary and middle schools and in the students' homes. Instead, it is time for educators to step up to the plate and spend the time needed to establish a community with its associated mores so that urban students can achieve science learning by coparticipating in safe and pleasurable learning environments.

The students in *Incentive* would be a test for the best of teachers and they are not typical of students from CHS. Students are assigned to *Incentive* because they have not been successful achievers or participants in high school, often due to an inability to settle down and accept their roles as learners. I opted to teach these students because of a sense that the group was abandoned. The rationale was strong. *Incentive* exists so that others can learn. As repugnant as that is to me, I understand the rationale. However, in the past year CHS has expanded from one *Incentive* SLC to two, and just recently to three. This is an alarming trend and it takes little imagination to envision an entire urban school as *Incentive*. The trend must be reversed by teachers and students acting together to create learning communities in which science and other subjects can be taught and learned in a context of safe, caring, and enjoyable circumstances.

Few teachers acting alone with a small set of students can establish and maintain the practices leading to productive learning. Heroic acts of particular teachers, as pleasing and inspirational as they might be, are not sufficient for the reform of urban schools. Nor is an exhortation to collaborative action. The doing of reform extends beyond written or spoken exhortations. From my perspective the initial step is to decide what type of community we intend to be, and that cannot be decided in isolation from the students. Whatever it takes, the first and most critical step is to decide what the community stands for, what is done in this community, and what happens when people interfere with others' efforts to attain the legitimate and negotiated goals of the community. Within that context it is possible to imagine science for all becoming a possibility at CHS and other urban high schools. For my own part, prior to teaching physics in the spring of 2000, I am working with the principal of CHS and teachers within *Incentive* to establish community norms that highlight the significance of inquiry and problem solving.

My building of an appropriate *habitus* for teaching science in urban schools necessitated more than experience of teaching science in urban schools. Prolonged interactions with students such as Tyrone, in one-on-one situations, allowed me to understand how to interact with him in ways that were respectful and how to better understand his perspectives on life. My own culture (White, middle class, and Australian) is so different from that of Tyrone and his classmates. I was unable to build the rapport and respect that was essential for them to construct me as their teacher. No matter what I tried to teach, street science or chromatography, the students were unlikely to cooperate and allow me to be their teacher. On the contrary, working one-on-one with students like Tyrone, interacting with students from *Incentive* in the hallways for several months, and coteaching with numerous new teachers at CHS enabled me to reengineer my *habitus*. Now my interactions with students from *Incentive* are such that I feel more comfortable in predicting success when I teach them on future occasions. Not only did I build knowledge that could be re-presented in speaking and writing, but also I have adapted my *habitus* such that I can now interact differently and my *Spielraum* (room to maneuver) does seem to provide room to maneuver in the classes in which I am coteaching. One implication for teacher education is the significance of learning about culture and building the associated *habitus* and *Spielraum* by engaging in projects with students from diverse social and cultural communities.

What are the contexts for (re-)learning to teach science, this time to relatively poor African American students in urban high schools? Starting out, I assumed that I knew how to teach and I was surprised and embarrassed when my *habitus* for teaching broke down when put to the test. The issue for me was then to identify appropriate resources to support my learning of how to teach these students. Reflection on action was an obvious source for learning and for many hours a day I searched through what I knew and I read widely as I endeavored to create the knowledge that would lead me to success. Then it struck me: no amount of reading and reconceptualizing was going to resolve the classroom problems I was encountering, which were exacerbated by my efforts to succeed. Not only that, being more deliberative in the classroom was creating uncertainty about what I should do and creating a belief that I could not succeed. My attention then turned to the development of *habitus* and *Spielraum* and the resources to support the growth of each as you had written about earlier.[13] Coteaching with Mario was one obvious resource, as we were coteaching with a doctoral student with experience in urban science teaching and coteaching with Cam, a new teacher assigned to teach science in *Incentive*. However, the essential aspects of *habitus* that needed to be developed and the associated *Spielraum* that would enable me to anticipate in action necessitated regular one-on-one interactions with Tyrone so that I could learn how to read and appropriately respond to the signs of urban African American youth. Finally, my *habitus* was reconstructed to incorporate cultural knowledge grounded in an urban ethnography that I undertook. For more than a year I explored the neighborhoods of Philadelphia and built an identity of being in the streets and understandings of the interactions between people with diverse social and cultural backgrounds.

In the past year I have (re-)learned teaching as praxis and at last have the confidence to teach science in ways that are likely to be more successful than my efforts of the spring and summer of 1999. Without wanting to sound too brash I conclude this letter with an exhortation to researchers, teacher educators, and policy-makers. Teaching science appropriately in urban settings extends far beyond selecting what is and is not an appropriate focus for the curriculum. Unless teachers are directed toward the resources for building viable *habitus* and appropriate *Spielraum* for urban

---

13   Roth, Lawless, & Masciotra, 2001.

participants it is unlikely that we will see the improvement in urban science education that our citizenry yearns for and deserves. The issue of whether or not science education can be liberatory and emancipatory extends beyond the prescription of curricular foci and includes as central the issue of building a community constituted in the rapport and mutual respect of all participants.

CHAPTER 3

Becoming a Teacher at City High School

This chapter begins with an autobiographically written account of Mario's experiences during the three years immediately after he completed his teacher education. In his own account, being able to coteach with Ken during his second and third year allowed Mario to learn tremendously and thereby develop as a professional. Thus, our biographical account provides evidence of Mario's *becoming-in-the-classroom*.

The Beginning

I am teaching in the *Incentive Center*. There are six teachers in *Incentive*, four older African American women, one African American male in his early thirties, and myself; a coordinator acts as its director. Together, we have about 60 years of teaching experience.

City High School was not my first assignment. Originally I was to teach at Orange Blossom. Things turned out differently. The principal called me a week before the school year started and said they didn't need me there. They gave me a list of five other schools. I went through the list with them but didn't know any of the schools except CHS. I knew it was a somewhat safe area and chose to come here. I was assigned to the *Performing Arts* SLC for about 20 minutes. The principal came and got me, and we had a walk down into *Incentive*. He told me he was going to place me in an area with rough kids and said, 'If you can teach those kids, you can teach anywhere'.

The principal was right; there is no question about that. I think he placed me in *Incentive* because the mathematics teacher was the only male down there.[1] The other teachers were all older females. Perhaps he thought that another male teacher would be a good role model for the students. So I figured 'OK, I'll do that'. I had a tough first couple of months. The kids weren't doing anything. Exams were horrible; the grades on exams were in the twenties and thirties. I thought it was my fault and started making phone calls telling the parents that their kid got a 20 because he didn't study and so on. Then one day I had a chance to look at credit profiles and realized that it wasn't me. The students were 18 and 19 years old, but had received only 5–10 credits toward graduation. They just didn't want to do the work. And so I tried positive feedback by issuing 'Wall of Fame' certificates. If they got an 'A' or 'B' on the exam, they got a certificate. I signed it, the principal signed it, and the coordinator signed it. First time we did that I guess I had 7 out of the few classes that received certificates then the next exam had about 14–15 so they were starting to see that if they got an 'A' or a 'B' they could at least get a certificate. This made a difference; students received the certificates with pride. One time I bumped into a kid from my first year and he still had the certificate hanging on the refrigerator. So it's like a big mental confidence booster for them.

My First Year

Taking on a Student Teacher

It was around Halloween when the principal asked me to take on a student teacher. He didn't have anybody else who could do it. This was unusual because I was a new teacher. But it was the principal who asked me and I wanted to make a good impression. I thought 'I must be doing something right if he asked me to take

---

1   During the years covered by our research, there had been two principals, one male and one female. Pronouns are chosen correspondingly.

on a student teacher in my first year'. I took his request as a compliment because there are teachers that have been teaching for years and years and they have never been asked to have a student teacher. That is how I looked at it. Here I was the new kid and the principal asks me to take on a student teacher. I didn't ask myself, 'Well how am I going to teach or develop?' I just looked at it this way: 'Well, they asked me to take on a student teacher so I figured I must be doing something right'. So that was when Hakeem came into the picture.

Hakeem and I did not coteach. At that time, it was more like student teachers had to teach two or three classes. It was the same way as when I went through student teaching. You take control of everything. The teacher releases the class to you and just sits in the back and makes sure nothing happens. The student teacher takes control of the class just as I did when I was a student teacher. But there's really no coteaching involved. So Hakeem came in, did his observations for a few months, and then took over two classes. The kids didn't take to him. I don't know why. Perhaps there were personality conflicts.

'He Was Originally from Around This Area....'

Hakeem is African American. He was originally from around this area but he moved to the suburbs. He is intelligent and I think he wanted the kids to be as smart as he was. But they were not, so I think he got frustrated at times. I also think that the kids did not take to him because they might have thought, 'Hey look here's a smart African American from our area and now he's well to do'. They may have been jealous as well. So there was this tension. But he really didn't interact with the kids. He sat in the back doing observation. At least he should have just walked around to help out kids if they needed help. Especially when we did the fly dissection. He sat in the back as the kids were doing the dissection. The SLC coordinator and an NTA were in the room just to have some extra sets of eyes in case something happened. I think the coordinator suggested that Hakeem come on out and interact with the kids. And that's when he finally went to do that.

Hakeem started to take over in January after the Christmas break. He was soft spoken and had a rough time controlling the kids. He often went off on tangents. The kids realized that and they actually told him a few times that he was bullshitting them. They would actually say, 'You're bullshitting us'. These are the types of kids that we have. They are tough, but to the point; and they know if they are being bullshitted or not. So he had all of these discipline problems, classroom management problems. His supervisor at the time sat down to have conferences with him, to give him some good suggestions. I don't think he was following those suggestions or those leads. She came in a few times and we talked in the office about him. She suggested that he take time off and redo the semester. He was just so bad. She was making this judgment from the side. Nice guy, but he wasn't cut out to be a teacher.

My Second Year

Another Student Teacher

The first time I met Cam was when the student teachers were being introduced to the teachers at CHS. Somebody asked me if I wanted another student teacher to take on and I said, 'OK'. Cam came in then—like split personality. He is about my height a little bit smaller than I am, young, and very energetic. The kids took to him right away because he came in and helped out with kids who were having trouble even without my telling him. The kids called him Cammy. At first he got like pissed off about it. So I told him, 'If the kids give you a nickname, that's a compliment'. They also called him 'Our Little Skully' because they call me 'Big Skully'. I said to him, 'Take that as a compliment that the kids like you and are willing to work with you'.

We worked together and co-planned some stuff, but he did not take over any classes until the following January. I did an anatomy/physiology course and that is where we started at coteaching, because I would do a unit then Cam would do a unit then I would do a unit. So it was almost like we're not coteaching but we're doing the same thing. Like here's this course, I'm doing this unit so Cam would do this, give a test, and I'll do the next one and then we'll do the dissection, which he helped with. He taught the biology class because we only had like three classes, I think, and he needed to teach two. So he did that plus he did the biology class and we did a physical science class and then we did an anatomy/physiology class.

Beginning to Coteach

In the spring I went to a school district meeting. That's when Ken and I started to talk about coteaching. I said, 'It's difficult to teach science in the city of Philadelphia, especially chemistry or physical science when the kids don't know six minus eleven is negative five'. So Ken said, 'All right, I'll come to City High School and start coteaching with you'. When he came, we did a physical science unit. I think it was at that time that Ken found out how difficult it really was to actually teach science. It was difficult because the kids do not have the basic math background. They cannot apply the formulas because they do not know how to set them up or how to put in the numbers. For example, they'd reverse the numerator and denominator for the numbers, they would put 40 divided by 2 instead of the opposite. So we had to give them minilessons on how to use calculators. It was almost like we were doing middle school math work again to get them ready for ninth-grade physical science.

As I observed Ken and Cam teaching, I learned from them. For example, Cam started the 'Question of the Day'. He put a 15- or 20-minute question on the board. He told the students that there was no wrong answer as long as they made an attempt. It was really cool. It was based on the lesson for that day or the lesson of the previous day. So I still do that today and the two student teachers that I have now, they also do that in their class. In fact, everybody does it now, almost through the whole building. It has evolved and spread. I never had done the 'Question of the Day' before. I saw Cam do it and thought, 'This is a cool idea. It gets them thinking, gets them opening up a textbook, going through the textbook trying to look for the answers, which none of them

probably ever really did before'. It actually shows the students
that they can successfully answer questions. They feel, 'Hey look, I
can answer these questions'. If they think, 'If you tell me it's no
wrong answer as long as I make an honest attempt', then they're
more willing to do that extra step, writing down the answer, even
though it may not be right. Most kids will not write down an answer if they know that they can't do it. So I learned that from
Cam, my student teacher.

Coteaching with Ken

When I was coteaching with Ken I got some great ideas. I learned
from him how to use different visual aids and about many physical science activities, including that cool paper helicopter investigation. I really liked our sound wave activity, a really great activity where we took the kids out into the street.

We went outside on Elizabeth Street to find out how fast
sound waves travel. We took the whole group over with two by
fours; half of the group stayed on one end of Elizabeth, the other
half went down to the stop sign, which is a good quarter of a mile.
So we actually figured out how long it would take for them to hear
the sound because if you go to a baseball game, you can hear the
bat hitting the ball considerably after seeing the event.

Before we actually went outside, Ken talked to the students
about sound. Initially, the kids were indifferent, sort of, 'Like
whatever....' Then I jumped in and said, 'How many of you ever
went to a baseball game and sat in centerfield?' A couple of kids
raised their hand. I said, 'Well, when you see the ball hitting the
bat do you hear the sound right away?' And they go, 'No'. Then I
asked them, 'What do you hear?' They said, 'About three seconds
later'.

That was when we were saying, 'Well that's because the sound
wave has to travel to you to actually hear it. Unless you're sitting
right on top of the play you won't hear it right away because the
wave has to travel'. So once we made that analogy then they came
to understand. It was at that point, I guess, when they got real excited. When we got outside, all of them wanted to clap the wood
and it actually took about half of a second. We saw the wood

touch, but heard the sound only when the person was already pulling the two pieces away from each other. Then we actually had kids coming off the street to us.

Initially, when I started coteaching with Ken I didn't know how this was going to work. During the first month I just stayed back and jumped in from the back of the class. Then, after a while, I started to participate. We started intermingling, walking around talking. We would take turns teaching: Ken would talk and would explain something; I would explain something; Ken would draw a diagram on the board or something like that. If Ken used words and terminology that the kids did not comprehend, I would jump in and simplify it for them in ways that they could understand.

I thought it was really good, especially when we had four teachers, Ken, Cam, Gale, and myself teaching the chemistry unit. So we had like four, it was almost like four teachers or coteachers because Cam and Gale dealt with the group of kids that was strong in chemistry. So it worked out. It was actually good because you didn't have to worry about 'Okay, if I do this, will the kids actually mess around with the chemicals'. And then we got this sort of working, always going back and forth.

Coteaching: The Next Level

Later we decided to take coteaching to the next level by taking some of our kids, making them into coteachers by having them teach a group at City Elementary School right next door. We took the best of the crop that we thought—even that was hard, just to try and pull them in and these were the best kids in *Incentive*—those that we thought would be successful. It was difficult because we couldn't really plan on working with a stable team, because half the group of 15 would be out one day and then the other half would be out the next day. Eventually we did go to City Elementary, but had a very difficult class. The kids there were so rambunctious and basically our future *Incentive* clientele. It was probably not their fault because they had had substitutes throughout the whole year. So we had a tough time with them, but we also had some good days. The first few weeks I think it went really well.

Our kids were actually interacting with the smaller kids. Some good science was being taught. It was good to see our kids interacting with the smaller kids and the smaller kids' reactions. Like they wanted to participate, but there's a lot of scientific learning that they went through, the hands-on activities that we had planned. We were growing plants from seeds. The elementary kids took the responsibility for watering the plants, and they did this very well. We actually had about two or three really good *Incentive* students who were really fantastic mentors for the kids. They were actually teaching them in the way that we had planned over here at City High. We were planning for two days here and then we would go over to City Elementary School for three days.

So that went well until I guess April or May. There was some friction between some of our students and some of the elementary school kids. It was starting to become ugly so we decided to just drop it before something serious happened.

My Third Year

Coteaching with Pairs of Student Teachers

This year I think a lot of my fellow teachers were surprised that they were getting two student teachers at the same time. I knew this since last May because I had gone to a meeting. It was there that Ken talked about team teaching by those student teachers who specialized in the sciences. So I was not surprised to have two student teachers as some of the other teachers were and I said, 'They are trying to get team teaching'.

My two guys, Mark and Andy, are fantastic. They each have a great personality, very smart, very knowledgeable in their background. So this is how it happened. I started off the school year and then they started to coteach. We all started to coteach in October because they needed letters for evaluations from the cooperating teachers. The only way for me to write them is to see how they teach. So I said, 'Okay, you guys have to teach'. So we started to coteach. We would actually do it every other day. I paired up with Mark one day, with Andy the other day. We each taught for half an hour, half an hour, half an hour, and so on. It was almost like taking your turn, your turn, your turn.... At first, our students had some problems with that because they were used to my style. Then they challenged the new guys because they were new guys. But in the end, I think that went well because they did well on their final exams. In the end, I did less, to let the student teachers get the feel and let them get control. I would go in and maybe do like 5 or 10 minutes of teaching. Sometimes I would just interact with the student teachers and say, 'Well how about if we do it this way?' or I would give an example or draw a diagram if the kids were in trouble.

The Singaporeans

I think it really came together when the Singaporeans came in. Ken sprang this on us at the last minute basically. He said, 'I have a few Singaporeans coming at the end of the week. Do you think you guys can do something?' So this was on Monday or Tuesday, they were coming on a Thursday or a Friday. We decided to use chromatography. We all sat down during lunch, pulled out the chemistry books, and started to develop a chromatography unit. I did the introduction. Mark wrote something up, Andy wrote something up, and I just typed it up in order to make everything coherent and flow. So we have like three versions. I said, 'Here is the rough draft, it looked good last night. Mark and Andy, you read it now and tell me how you really think'. So we have like three sets of eyes that are going through it to get it ready.

Then the Singaporeans came and we started the microteaching experience. Ken and I were running around with our heads cut off making sure that everything went fine, because we had it broken down to this group in this room and the other room. So I was running around while my student teachers were actually teaching, facilitating the smaller groups that were going on and making sure everything was running smoothly. That worked well for 3 or 4 weeks.

Then the semester started again and then Ken wanted the guys to teach their own separate classes so what we did, we took the fourth period class, which was the chemistry class, and broke it down into two classes. Mark and Andy each had a small group of 15 kids. So they taught by themselves and I just went back and forth between the two classrooms, just to make sure that hell'd not broken loose. But they still come and coteach the fifth period of the day; and that is good for them.

Elwyn: A Difficult Student Teacher

A critical issue in coteaching will be the fit in personalities. I'm talking about personalities that can clash. Take Elwyn, for example. He's very smart, very intelligent, and very knowledgeable about a lot of things. If you weren't as smart as he was, he sort of looked down on you, at least, that is the impression I got. When he talked above my level, I would just go 'Hey', and he got real with us again. After seeing that the kids didn't have that high mental capacity, I think he toned it down. We spoke as a group, with the other student teachers, about the fact that his teaching was above grade-nine level physical science classes. What he was doing was really more like AP or freshman year chemistry. But the kids actually let him have it. They said, 'I don't know what's going on'. When I would go on after him, the kids would actually clap that I was going on because I brought the subject matter down to their level. But eventually I could see that he toned it down for our class. I figure he's toned it down or brought it down so the kids can understand where he's coming from.

I remember the day that he was teaching about metallic bonding with us. We interrupted him. That was an example of coteaching. I think he learned from coteaching with Mark, Andy, and myself.

In this instance, I think he was upset at first over the fact that we jumped in. You could see that his train of thought was interrupted. But he was talking about metallic bonding. Ken then talked about the sea of electrons that surround the nuclei at the outer level. Elwyn seemed to get stuck. He actually had a mental block and Ken jumped in. To bring it to the level of the kids, I then drew a lattice of electrons to actually show him how electrons float around. Afterwards I went and looked for some batteries, because we were talking about conduction and electricity. I found the batteries, some wire, and a nail and wrapped it around for a conductor. I had the kids actually feel how hot it gets just to show them, to see electrons; they are floating around and you can feel the energy and the heat. With these materials kids were actually able to understand there is something moving now instead of just being told. I had rigged up that crude apparatus and showed it around the classroom as a little visual aid while Elwyn was continuing with the lecture. I did this just to show the kids that there's something real to it, because they felt how it got hot quickly.

Elwyn has a problem because he tends to show off while teaching. So as he introduced metallic bonding, whereas most people talk about covalent and ionic bonding, he threw in metallic bonding. But he did not show the kids why it was important in any of the cases. From his point of view, he did a review. So what I tried to do was to have him go a bit further to answer the question of so what? And you might remember one kid didn't even know what aluminum was. Then we talked about aluminum foil. Once we started talking and we showed them the chrome on the chairs, then they'd go 'Oh yeah, now I know what it is'. But just the word aluminum, the kids find it tough connecting the word to the actual things they know from their everyday experience.

Advice to Teacher Educators

My major advice to teacher educators would be this: 'The only way to learn to teach is to actually do it. Not through college, just to go up and do it'. Because in university, you never did teaching even though they'd say, 'Here's a small group of your college peers, go teach'. So that might be a microteaching lesson to three of your peers and you get feedback. But there is really nothing to doing that. Field experiences, I thought, would prepare me because I had a diverse group of students whom I taught—I had anatomy class of biology, anatomy, physiology, ESOL classes on the lower level so I advised different activities.

I learned a lot by coteaching with Ken and the new teachers. It worked for me because I generally get along with people. Coteaching works if you have personalities that can feed off each other; it works great for Mark and Andy because those two guys can finish each other's sentence and they plan together during the lunch and I guess on the weekends too. It's almost like a script. They know what to say and they know when to say it and it really works. If you don't have the personalities, I don't think it's going to work, so I think that's one disadvantage of the coteaching. If you don't have the personalities, it's not going to work, or if you have someone who's not into it, it's not going to work. But these guys I think are a good example of coteaching working.

Advice to New Teachers

If I had to give just one piece of advice to new teachers, it would be 'Establish rapport and develop classroom skills'. What I really learned after my teacher training was better classroom skills. Just classroom skills and, especially, developing rapport with the hard-knock kids. If you develop a rapport with the most difficult students, they're the ones that the little ones follow and listen to. If you develop a good rapport with the bad kids and they realize you are a pretty nice person and you want them to be successful, they'll talk to the others. They will say, 'Don't mess around in his class, go mess around in someone else's class but don't mess around in his class because he's really cool. He's gonna help me now, he's willing to help us be successful'. I learned that as one of my most important lessons here at CHS.

The biggest thing I tell the new teachers when we teach is 'Don't bullshit them'. That probably is the most important thing that I learned and that I was told through some people—do not BS the kids, because once you do that you have no respect for them and can't get anything accomplished with them.

I was not told how to get along with the kids. But I treated them with respect. I came into the school knowing that CHS is an all African American school. I saw a lot of the typical stereotyping going on, among my fellow teachers; like a lot of White people are afraid of African Americans, they're intimidated. But I learned not to show any intimidation to them. I got in their faces if they tried to walk out of class. I did not take nonsense from them. So they saw me as a no-nonsense person and that is how I was able to gain control.

As I was teaching, I just picked up little innuendoes. In college I had roommates from North Philly so I picked up the slang and handshakes. My students here at City were surprised that a White person knows their slang and handshakes. Just picking up stuff that goes on in your neighborhood and just being aware of that helped me out, too. You treat them with respect, because they have very difficult home lives, most of them. If you do that then I think you'll be successful. With this as a basis, you keep learning different ways of being successful each year, and eventually you become a good teacher in the inner city.

I try to tell my new teachers that. Treat the kids with respect, do not take any nonsense, and do not BS them. Those three things I think are successful—will make the successful formula for this type of setting in this type of environment.

Now if you go to a different environment, like the suburban all-White area then you would have to change your game plan or just change up just a little bit. That I could not answer because I have never been in that type of situation.

Conversation: Learning to Teach in an Urban School

TO: Michael
RE: Teaching in difficult schools
'Sacrifice a few for the benefit of the majority' appears to be the main philosophy underlying the formation of *Incentive*. Students who are 'disruptive' or 'unsettled' come to one place where they are isolated, self-contained, and conveniently controlled. They are placed in a few rooms on the ground floor with good access for non-teaching assistants (NTAs) who can control disruptive behavior. Of course there is a price to pay for this arrangement. Science is taught in a former art room and so there are no storage rooms and cupboards and no benches for laboratory work. The room is spacious and there is water. But that is it. It is a frustrating place to teach and the two doors through which stu-

dents can come and go create problems because of the nature of the students. The philosophy may have been to contain them but believe me they are difficult to contain! Throughout my first year in *Incentive* the students came and went virtually as they pleased. There was no consistent approach to getting students into class on time and keeping them in there. Not only that, it was not unusual for students from other classes in the *Incentive* SLC to 'sit in'.

Students find themselves in *Incentive* because they are unsuccessful elsewhere in school, which leads to a variety of difficulties. They are unsettled, often unmotivated to participate and learn, and frequently disruptive. For even the most experienced of teachers an assignment to teach in *Incentive* is a challenge. For a beginning teacher the challenge would be daunting to say the least. It really makes me wonder why a principal would decide to place a teacher in *Incentive* in his first year of teaching. Mario is probably right. The principal may have thought that a young male would be most likely to succeed with students of this type, particularly a male with the physical stature of Mario. Mario showed from the outset that he had a sense of the game of teaching *Incentive* students when he enacted a reward scheme to get them focused on achievement and also realized the potential of calling parents and guardians. These are critical elements of building a teaching repertoire that will succeed with these students.

TO: Ken
RE: Difficult schools, habitus, and re/production of inequities

Learning to teach is not easy and, as one of my principals once told me, it takes at least three years to become familiar with a new school. Until then, even old-timers might be seen to have difficulties in their day-to-day work as teacher. It is as if these teachers had to re-learn some of the things they thought they knew. Whereas becoming a teacher is a challenge in the best of circumstances, it is a particular challenge in City High School in general and *Incentive* in particular.

It does not surprise me to see that traditional forms of teaching encounter difficulties in *Incentive*. It has been noted before that the pedagogic work becomes increasingly difficult with the distance that exists between the primary *habitus* of the students and the culturally arbitrary *habitus* to be inculcated at the school.[2] This is because the pedagogic work increases with the distance between the two types of *habitus*. Furthermore, because of the distance between the two types of *habitus*, we can expect much more resistance to the symbolic violence experienced by the students. It is therefore not surprising that *Incentive*, where all those students find themselves who have shown that they do not (or cannot) submit to the practices in the regular classroom, is a place where it is difficult to teach. That is, it is difficult for them when teachers, SLC, and school maintain practices to enact a *habitus* that is characteristic of the middle class. So far, all talk of making schooling more culturally sensitive appears to me a lip service, as long as the *habitus* to be re/produced through the schooling experience remains the same.

I am therefore less than convinced that the principal was right in the sense that Mario would become a better science teacher in *Incentive*. I am convinced, though, that teaching in *Incentive* would allow him to develop a new *habitus* that helps him adapt and survive in this type of situation, that is, teaching where the primary *habitus* and the to-be-inculcated *habitus* are so different. Of course, other cultural practices and constructions of identity complicate the situation. In my case, for example, the First Nations students are often compliant, they are quiet, and they do not rebel. The schools where I work are characterized by the (self-?) exclusion of these children from in-class and schoolyard activities with the children of European and Asian descent. In comparing the two situations, I understand that there must be other practices in the construction of identity that make students from the *Incentive* SLC much more 'rebellious' and 'difficult to teach' than children from other cultures taught by representatives of the White middle-class culture.

Mario is an interesting person in the sense that he does not have his nose high up. In my interactions with him, he appeared a very natural, jovial person who in many ways understands the students. As his autobiographical text shows, he enacts some of their practices—he calls it 'knowing their slang and handshakes'. He moves from his own cultural practices of greeting to those of the students. That is, he narrows the gap between his own *habitus*

---

2   Bourdieu & Passeron, 1979.

and the students'. The latter acknowledge it and in some ways
accept him more than they do other teachers. There are other practices Mario enacts that are closer to the way students perceive
and enact in the world. For example, Mario and the students alike
know when someone 'bullshits' them. That is, Mario has developed a way of perceiving that allows him to recognize situations
in the way the students recognize them. He knew immediately
when Elwyn or Hakeem interacted with the students in ways that
they perceived as 'bullshitting them'.

Whereas Mario developed a new *habitus* that brought him
closer to students, he did not change his *habitus* in other aspects of
teaching. For example, when it comes to grades, he perceives the
world in ways and enacts practices that are imbued with traditional middle-class values. Giving poor marks and threatening
students that they will get low grades and not succeed on exami-
nations are some typical examples. We know at least since Foucault's analysis of the birth of schools that grading is central to the
establishment of inequities.[3] These inequities, at first produced
during the school years, then led to a hierarchical arrangement of
people in their professional lives. Schools became one of the main
mechanisms in which a rising middle class saw an opportunity to
develop and later inculcate practices that would advantage its
own members and disadvantage what was at the time the 'undis-
ciplined country folk'. Since then teachers—themselves members
of the middle class and often from middle-class families—have
continued to contribute to the re/production of inequities. Mario
is one more case of a widespread phenomenon in which a society,
using schools as instruments, re/produces itself and its inequities.

TO: Michael
RE: Learning to teach in difficult schools
Your points about reproduction are well taken. Knowing how
to break that cycle is a matter for significant research. Perhaps the
principal at the time was endeavoring to do just that. Assigning a
student teacher to a first-year teacher was indeed thinking out of
the box. I was somewhat surprised at the principal's suggestion,
but I had been present with Hakeem when his first assigned cooperating teacher quit. A senior biology teacher (also an African

---

3   Foucault, 1979.

American male) did not want a student teacher that year and re-sented the principal just assigning him one anyway. So, it was with some ambivalence that I accepted the principal's suggestion to place Hakeem with Mario. If I had known at the time about *Incentive*, I would certainly not have agreed that this was any place for a student teacher to learn to teach. But there is more to it than assigning a beginning teacher to another beginning teacher in a difficult place to teach.

In hindsight the principal's decision was bold and visionary. This was not the first time he had come up with innovative ideas. Already he had instituted a scheme for his students to act as mentors to student teachers, coaching them on 'How to teach students like me!' In addition, in the second semester of the same year he was to suggest to me that two student teachers coteach without a cooperating teacher at all. Although he never articulated a philosophy of learning to teach by teaching with others in *event-full* classrooms, his practices in placing student teachers are consistent with his knowing (at least at an intuitive level) that the assignment of Hakeem to Mario would be good for both of them. Even though Mario may have seen the assignment of a student teacher as a badge of honor it is more likely that the principal regarded it as a chance for two beginning teachers to support one another in learning to teach by teaching.

TO: Ken
RE: Learning to teach in difficult schools
It is both surprising and not surprising that the principal would act in this way. When I began teaching, in economically de-pressed Newfoundland and Labrador, both of my principals as-signed me to the most difficult classes in these already difficult situations. Rather than assigning teachers according to their competence in some subject, principals often use seniority as a criterion for assigning teachers to more desirable classes. For example, a colleague in Newfoundland taught physics although he had taken only one university course in the subject. The principal assigned me (I had previously earned a master's degree in the subject) to teach physical science in the lowest-streamed grade 9 and science to the 'educationally challenged' students, usually kids from the tough neighborhoods. Therefore, those teachers who have

had many opportunities to develop a *habitus* of teaching in the 'difficult classes' are also those who are often assigned to classes that are more inclined to submit to the cultural arbitrary, to be inculcated, thereby, to the re/production of society.

Learning to teach in this way is difficult, especially when you are left on your own. It is a 'sink or swim mentality'. This is one of the reasons why I think that the principal was right in putting people together, people such as Hakeem and Mario, in putting them into situations of *being-in/with* another, making them resources for each other's learning. Dealing with difficult situations as a collective also has a greater potential for success, especially when, as Mario notes, the personalities of the individual members of the new collective are compatible.

I advocate change in teaching to better accommodate the primary *habitus* of the students. Setting up opportunities for teachers to learn from students how to 'teach students like me' is one way of opening a dialogue. There is the potential that teachers come to recognize and subsequently develop a new *habitus* that is closer to that of the students. Or rather, teachers and students actively produce new ways of acting and interacting, and therefore are involved in the production of new practices of schooling that start from and therefore accommodate the primary *habitus* of both.

We have not brought out sufficiently the episode involving the new teacher, Hakeem, an African American who grew up in the CHS neighborhood. On the surface, one would have expected him to be a prime candidate for working with the students in *Incentive*. Yet Mario tells us that Hakeem had problems, particularly with managing the class. Now, one dimension in a teacher characteristic cannot be the solution to systemic problems. But, from the perspective of Bourdieu, we would think that Hakeem originally developed a similar *habitus* to that of his students, that is, his primary *habitus* was that of an African American growing up in tough inner city neighborhoods.

Of course, many things can happen. I am thinking about the distance between his early primary *habitus* and his newly developed elitist *habitus* that not only conforms to that of the middle class but also is complicated even more through the inclusion of difficult concepts and language from science. It is as if the symbolic violence to which he was subjected in the transformation comes back as anger. Perhaps we see this anger even more strongly in the aggressive behavior of the NTAs and their sometimes violent and conflict-seeking ways of interacting with the students from *Incentive*. But, as Bourdieu and Foucault would argue, African Americans who have made it in an essentially White middle-class system are instances in whom the domination of the lower classes by the middle and upper classes are particularly poignant.

TO: Michael
RE: Learning to teach (by observing versus coteaching)
The idea of *being-in/with* is built on a theory of coparticipation leading to the assumption of new practices. In the case of Mario and Hakeem, they would both participate together. I must confess I groaned when I read Mario's account of Hakeem sitting at the back watching him teach. The traditional model of 'learning by observing' was practiced widely and those roles made sense to both Mario and Hakeem. It made sense for Hakeem to sit until he knew enough about teaching to get started. But there is more to this than is said in Mario's narrative. Hakeem was shocked by the magnitude of the challenge and probably lacked the confidence to even try his hand at teaching. He must have thought that he would eventually see enough good practice to know what to try with the *Incentive* students after watching more experienced teachers teach.

It is interesting that Mario sought help when the class did the fly dissection. Getting the assistance of the coordinator of *Incentive* and the NTA gave him the extra pairs of eyes, and then, the coordinator's insisting that Hakeem coteach provided a level of support whereby the students could receive a variety of assistance and, as necessary, control. This is one early example of coteaching occurring and a tacit acknowledgment that many teachers can facilitate the learning of students. What was not explicit was that having so many teachers teaching science would provide events and resources that would support learning to teach (for all teachers in the room, not just Hakeem).

TO: Ken
RE: Learning to teach (by observing versus coteaching)
It is surprising that the assumption that one can learn by watching someone else (or listening to a lecture) has come to

dominate educational practice. There is no real precedent for this assumption. In traditional societies, people learned through participating and apprenticeship. In both situations, watching others and listening have been part of the process, but learning has not happened unless the individual has also enacted what s/he has seen and heard. Sociologists have reminded us time and again that there is a difference between a material practice and discourse about this practice—what people say they are doing and what they are doing are two different practices.[4] In fact, we have evidence that watching and looking do not work. You and I have daily testimony from teachers and student teachers that there is a gap between what students do and hear in university classes and the practices that they need to enact in the classroom to be able to construct themselves as successful teachers. On the other hand, in the many coteaching experiences I have had over the past decade, we, the participating teachers, have always felt that we learned tremendously and developed in our teaching—more than we did before that and more than we could have learned by taking more courses on teaching.

I do not think that university courses should be abandoned but rather that these courses need to be keyed to the lived classroom experiences of student teachers. Rather then seeing them as 'preservice teachers' or 'student teachers' with little responsibility, I would want to see these individuals involved in the fabric of educational practice. 'Relative newcomer' or 'legitimate peripheral practice'[5] in knowledge and knowledge-building communities appear to me more appropriate ways of looking at the young people whom we introduce to the business of teaching.

TO: Michael
RE: Learning to teach (the traditional way)

It is interesting that the accepted practices of just a couple of years ago can look so out of place nowadays. For example, Mario made me sad when he judged Hakeem's teaching from the side. If things were so bad, why did he let them go on that way? The practice of a cooperating teacher sitting and watching as student teachers make mistakes makes me so pleased that we have

---

4   Garfinkel, 1967; Gilbert & Mulkay, 1984.
5   Lave & Wenger, 1991.

changed our practices relating to learning to teach. Fortunately we have moved away from the heroic image of teaching in which one has to learn alone so as to perform alone. If Hakeem was 'bullshitting', why didn't Mario do something to clarify the topic for students or to ameliorate the bad situation that he could predict would evolve? Tradition! If Hakeem was going to fail, then Mario had to let him fail on his own. The time for advice and encouragement in this model is after the lesson.

Then we go over the notes on the yellow pad and record our judgments. 'One strike against you, Hakeem. It is not only I who think your teaching sucks. See, your supervisor thinks so too!' It is so different now. If the students become unruly, then a cooperating teacher or supervisor has already left it too late to intervene. The time for intervention is when you have the sense that it is time. It should be no big deal for the cooperating teacher and/or the supervisor to coteach with Hakeem and to do what is appropriate at the time as the events unfold. In that way Hakeem can learn by *being-with* Mario (and/or his supervisor) as he acts appropriately *in* the context that is unfolding. Hakeem's supervisor, who was an African American female, could have cotaught and assisted him to enact teaching in ways that were more culturally relevant. I am certain Hakeem would have been relieved to have had the support and associated learning opportunities afforded by coteaching.

TO: Ken
RE: Learning to teach (contradictions and coteaching)
As I reread Mario's comments concerning Hakeem, I am thinking about the situation more and more in terms of the re/production of society which effects itself by re/producing teaching agents that simply maintain the status quo. That is, the pedagogic action to which Hakeem was subjected re/produced in him a *habitus*—a system of schemes of thought, perception, appreciation, and action—that mistakes the culturally arbitrary nature of the contents and form of teaching. Once I frame the issues in this way, I see in Hakeem an individual that his younger siblings (the next generation) could regard as someone 'gone White', acting White despite the color of his skin and his cultural origin.

While I was reading these paragraphs, I also thought about the stories I had heard of African American teachers (in some cases self-reports) who have become much harsher and tougher with young African Americans than any White teacher would have been at that point in time. The pattern is observable among the African American NTAs at City High, who are frequently aggressive in their way of dealing with the male students. It is interesting then that the original pedagogic work that made Hakeem also made him blind to the arbitrariness and the fact that his own practices are even more distant from the students' primary *habitus* than from that of his own teachers.

Mario has come through the old model of teacher preparation, first in his personal experience, then with Hakeem. Later, he began coteaching, beginning with you and Cam and then with Mark and Andy. In his text, there is no strong testimony about the changes, but it appears as if he was sold onto the coteaching idea. He talks in favorable terms about it—though we know that discourse is a tool that enables someone like Mario to enact social actions so that he might talk differently about it in another context.

We find some testimony in Mario's autobiography that he considers coteaching as a context for learning to teach and for growing as a teacher. I also remember him telling me that he wanted to coteach physics with you, because he would learn content and how to teach it (pedagogical content knowledge) from you, in situ, as you were teaching. Rather than talking about taking another physics course, or a physics methods course, Mario expresses his desire to coteach physics. This takes me back to one of the studies on coteaching in a unit on building bridges in a grade four/five class here on the West Coast.[6] The two teachers were convinced after 2 months of coteaching that they had learned more about teaching, the subject matter, the pedagogy, and general pedagogy than they could have learned 'by taking three university courses'. If practicing teachers feel that strongly about the opportunities for learning and growth in coteaching situations, we need to better understand what is going on there, what is the experience of the teachers that brings them such positive experiences.

---

6   Roth, 1998a.

One of the contradictions in this is that Mario still describes Hakeem's problems as in part arising from not following the supervising teacher's recommendations.

Hakeem sitting down with his supervisor is a classic situation of interactions in a field of power that exists because of the participants' institutional relation. The supervisor, having observed the lessons from the outside, admonishes Hakeem for not controlling the class, and later recommends that he ought to stop student teaching and come back for another term. In Mario's account there was no place for Hakeem to negotiate a different solution to the problems. Furthermore, the supervisor simply critiqued Hakeem without having tried to teach or model a class or taught a class with Hakeem so that he could experience, with his body, what a good class might look like. Of course, doing teaching rather than doing talking about teaching frightens many of our colleagues: It is easier to talk about teaching than to actually do it, particularly day in day out with little time to reflect on the events and how and what to learn from them.

I see here a change from the old practice of teacher education to the new practices that you have brought about at CHS. There used to be a 'sink or swim' and 'we have all come through that' mentality. There is a sense of watching a newcomer undergo difficult times in the way newcomers to university have to undergo hazing practices. So Mario did nothing that was particularly different from what he had experienced as a beginning teacher or what others surrounding him also enacted. Mario simply re/produced the cultural practices of teacher training.

You ask, 'Why didn't Mario do something...?' which can easily be read as an implicit criticism of what he did. You know that now, he would not act in the same way after having cotaught for two years and interacted with you and others after school thinking about the practice of teaching in *Incentive*. 'Why didn't Mario...?' Because there was no reason to do anything differently than he did. The robustness of common sense lies in the fact that it generates practices that we do not have to question.[7] So why should Mario have acted in a different way? Here lies one of the challenges for teacher education. Teacher educators often want to bring about changes in current practices without realizing that

---

7   Pollner, 1987.

these very practices are the result of a *habitus* that is re/produced at all levels of society. This re/production begins with schooling, continues in the education of teachers, and pervades the practice of re/producing teacher educators.

Now you are in a different situation. Having experience in and having done research on coteaching, you encourage different practices. If a situation such as that between Mario and Hakeem recurred, you would attempt to get all parties to interact and bring about change. Your questions indicate to me that we have come a long way, but we should not make negative judgments concerning what people have done in the past.

When I initially met Cam and read his comments about Mario, I was horrified. I was thinking something like 'how is it possible to hire someone like Mario to teach science in any school?' Later, when I met and cotaught with Mario, I had a very different impression. Granted, more than a year has passed between the two moments and Mario could have changed. But I do not think that he could have changed as drastically based on my own experience with Mario. He appeared to me a sincere, jovial, welcoming, and easy-to-get-along-with individual who was willing to learn. I do not want to suggest that I agree with how he teaches, or rather, I would not accept from myself many of the pedagogic actions that I see coming from him. But there are many things about teaching that we (you and I) can learn from him, despite the fact that, combined, we have more than 10 times the number of years of teaching experience.

This leads me to thinking about teaching, not along singular and linear scales, but more in terms of heterogeneous and multiply-situated practices. There are many of the dimensions that we might construct for heuristic purposes on which I show more experience and greater competence. But there are many other dimensions, equally constructed for heuristic purposes, on which he would score higher or in a more positive fashion than I would.

It appears to me that the willingness to make a difference in the lives of the students is a central issue in teaching and teacher development. There probably also needs to be a willingness on our (teachers') part to transform ourselves in order to make the necessary changes for the emergence of better ways of teaching. On both accounts, Mario does well and he will continue to do so.

TO: Michael
RE: Learning to teach (the traditional way from a coteaching per-spective)

No wonder Cam was so critical of his cooperating teacher (see Chapter 1). It seems as if he tinkered on the side hoping to see something that would pass as good teaching. Instead of getting in there and trying things out, from Mario's account Cam was helping on occasions and observing mainly. At the same time he was doing his science methods course with me and was highly critical of not being given concrete methods that would work in urban settings. He was critical of the course being too theoretical and unconnected with what he was seeing in his field experience.

Considering what we do now, it is striking that the parts are too disconnected. Today we know that Cam ought to have been teaching while he did his methods course. He should have been trying out what he learned in methods and he should have been bringing challenges and successes from the field to the methods class to provide a context in which he and his peers could learn through discussions of shared experiences. A belief that one can learn to teach by watching and then reflecting on what was seen in a critical way is so obviously a flawed model for learning to teach. Then there are the gaps between teaching experience and the methods course. How can the methods course be successful if there is an expectation that someone is going to deliver a set of appropriate methods to enact, in a manner that is akin to waving a magic wand? Although Cam eventually tried coteaching, he never really accepted the model as superior to someone giving him (validated) recipes to enact.

TO: Ken
RE: Learning to teach (the traditional way, a praxis perspective)

Cam, like Hakeem, is an interesting case, in that we can learn how difficult it will be to bring about change among new teachers. These new teachers bring with them their experiences of how schools look and feel. They bring a *habitus* formed over more than 16 years in school and university environments. During this experience, legitimate knowledge of how the world works and everyday know-how have been devalued, and decontextualized knowledge, which can be obtained from books and in lectures and which gives symbolic mastery, has gained the status of primary legitimacy. Cam and Hakeem therefore expect (part of their *habitus*) that others present them with instances of such symbolic knowledge that they can then apply. But this is where Cam is caught in a vicious circle without realizing it. Working in schools, new teachers experience the difference between enacted and symbolic mastery, but Cam attributes his own failure to enact mastery to his teachers (Mario, you) who, from his perspective, do not assist him in symbolic mastery. If Cam were able to change his epistemological underpinning he could realize that in order to enact masterful teaching he has to enact teaching and recursively work on approaching his understanding (lived experience) and explanation (symbolic mastery).

It is interesting to note that what Cam needs to be successful is a *habitus* of teaching in this situation. I would not say that Cam should have applied in the classroom what he learned in the methods course. Rather, perhaps, there should have been a situation where the students articulated what they might teach in a lesson. With your, the professor's, help, they would reflect on the pedagogical principles underlying teaching a particular subject, that is, for example, the science of sound and what we know about the subject matter pedagogy associated with it. Subsequently, new teachers may try to enact a lesson (not apply it!!!) and make this lesson the subject of an inquiry in which others—the supervising teacher, their peers, students in the class, and other stakeholders—are also involved. I do not subscribe to the 'learn-first–apply-second' model, but see learning occurring as people enact practices.

I am thinking about the role of 'methods courses' rather in the way Peter Grimmett does. These courses should constitute a forum for developing an understanding of primary teaching experiences through critical, explanation-seeking reflection on this (in coteaching shared) experience of being-in the classroom. As long as we continue to make the divide between symbolic mastery (i.e., discourse) and practical (enacted) mastery, the gap between the activities at the university and in the everyday situation of teaching in schools will persist. This type of pedagogic work will give *symbolic* mastery of practices that cannot be reduced to practical mastery; that is, traditional teacher education leads to symbolic mastery of teaching practices rather than enacted mastery.[8]

TO: Michael
RE: Learning to teach (walking the walk)

I have enormous empathy for Hakeem and Cam. It is so difficult to be the heroic lone ranger in a classroom like the one Mario handed over to me. I will never forget when Mario completed his morning messages to the class, turned around and with a gesture of his hand said: 'Dr. Tobin…' I realized then that it was all mine. He walked one way (toward the periphery) and I the other (toward center stage). The initial part of our 'coteaching' experience was just as Mario described it; it was not coteaching at all. I felt like the heroic figure trying to get the job done with several spectators helping out only when I called on them to do so. Perhaps this is not surprising. None of us ever talked about what we meant by coteaching or for that matter what our roles were to be. We made it up as we went along. I think, too, that Mario and I needed time to become friends. There is a large difference in age, experience, and status. I have been teaching since 1964 and I carried with me a status associated with my title and position in the university. Mario was in his second year of teaching and, although he may have had his doubts that I would be as successful as he was, his interactions with me were always respectful and caring. He probably felt that he should defer to me in our arrangements.

As time progressed I found myself learning how to interact with the students by being alongside of Mario. My learning was not conscious as much as it was an evolution in my ways of being-in the classroom. There were times when, like Cam, I strongly disapproved of Mario's actions. And I know there were times when he felt that what I did was stupid and likely dangerous in terms of provoking student anger by showing my disrespect for students' particular actions. Gradually, we learned to teach together and in some respects each of us became like the other. I saw great differences in my own teaching, particularly over a 2-year period.

I am still far too impatient with the students and have a tendency to push too hard to exert my dubious power over them. These tendencies are residual effects of a *habitus* that was molded

---

8   Bourdieu & Passeron, 1979.

in Australian middle-class schools during a decade of teaching in the 1960s and the early part of the '70s. The improvements come from how I approach and interact with students. I know now when and how to push for participation with most students and when to back off. I am also becoming better at getting more from the students. Similarly I can see great improvements in Mario in the way he develops ideas and engages students in a variety of activities. Through his coteaching with me, Gale, and at least six student teachers, Mario has improved his ways of teaching immeasurably. At the same time there are things that he does that show he has much to learn about teaching. As I think about these things they relate to professionalism. A shortcoming of the schools-within-a-school model used at City High School is that there is only one science teacher per school. Except for his coteaching with us, Mario has not had opportunities to work with senior science teachers. Mario makes decisions that senior teachers just would not make, especially when the students have so far to go in terms of learning science. I think Mario would benefit from working alongside a senior colleague who has dedicated her/his life to being a science teacher.

TO: Ken
RE: Learning to teach (walking the walk)
I thought that it might be helpful to better understand both your and Mario's changes as you began to work in the same classroom and with each other. What the two autobiographies and your own past articles provide us with are descriptions of events. What we do not yet have is an articulation, at a new level, of the changes that you have undergone. We have begun to do that in using *'habitus'* to suggest that you now perceive and thereby construct the world in *Incentive* in different ways. It might be helpful for us both to articulate descriptions of the changes your teaching underwent as well as a description of possible mechanisms of these changes. (This will be something like a model of change.)

In some ways, Mario was much more attuned to the students' primary *habitus*. He was also more subtle in interacting with the students based on this primary *habitus* rather than enacting different—as he suggested, dangerous—practices of interacting with students.

People like you and me are often dedicated to causes, and we invest our lives in pursuing them and our dreams. But there are other people, Mario may be one of them, who do not view our cause with the same singularity and almost excessive focus, which leads to the way we characterize them in terms of 'professionalism' or 'publication record', and so forth. I have, in the past, let students 'goof off' but with results that are interpreted much more positively. I allowed a student to read a novel for seven consecutive lessons instead of forcing him to do mathematics, the subject I was teaching him. He not only caught up with his peers but also began to work ahead and excel. He said after the year was over that this was a key moment in his schooling and that his newfound love for mathematics emerged during that particular week when he experienced control over when and how to learn. I had similar experiences with other students and in different places. (I have hardly any memories, perhaps selected memories, of cases where it might not have worked out.) Why would Mario or I enact such practices, which seem arcane and unprofessional to others? It might be a sense of what is right at this moment.

While I am different from Mario and would enact different practices, I am not ready to condemn what he is doing. But I think that we could all learn from each other and develop, you, Mario, your new teachers, and I. Can we enact such developments without setting goals as end-all, and engage in professional development in open-ended ways? Is it possible to enact professional development without framing differences between ideal models and current states, and without viewing development as being achieved when the differences are overcome?

When Mario notes that the students you taught together at City Elementary School will be the future *Incentive* students, I thought that this is not just because of the nature of the children but, essentially, because of the nature of schools. We therefore recognize that *these* students will be in a particular situation in *these* schools. But as happens so often in schooling systems, the blame is entirely placed on the students rather than being redistributed onto the system that re/produces itself, including the social context from which children come and into which their own children are born.

TO: Michael
RE: Teacher transformation in praxis

Because we were introducing an idea that we had not tried extensively, it was imperative that we closely monitor what we did pertaining to coteaching. I did not tell the cooperating teachers how to enact coteaching. I did explain that we regarded student teachers as a resource to support learning throughout the school and the SLC to which they were assigned. Teachers were encouraged to deploy the resources in ways that made sense to them. Part of my research agenda was to ascertain how teaching was organized and to learn from what happened. Through ongoing interactions with the students I felt sure that I could fine-tune the arrangements as the year went along.

Mario refers to two student teachers, Mark and Andy, who did more coteaching, and did it with more success, than Mario did with any of his student teachers. I was particularly interested in how this unfolded because careful study of the evolution of Mark's and Andy's teaching would provide us with evidence about the relative significance of the cooperating teacher in learning to teach science in this instance. From the previous two years it was quite apparent that Mario had had little influence on either Hakeem's or Cam's teaching. Cam had learned to teach by teaching and also by being with other student teachers in the school. Not only that, the school principal who had assigned Mario to *Incentive* had already assigned student teachers in pairs without cooperating teachers from whom they could learn.

As the year progressed, two trends were evident to me in Mario's class. First, he and the four or five new teachers who cotaught in his classes were able to coteach with relative ease—to the benefit of students. Second, as you and I developed a heuristic model for speaking about coteaching (see Chapter 5) I was able to use it to speak to all the student teachers about how to get the best from coteaching. I could also suggest to Mario how to change the way he was coteaching with his student teachers. Having the model enabled Mario and other cooperating teachers to coteach in their own ways but to adapt their practices to emphasize being and teaching with their student teachers.

TO: Ken
RE: Teacher transformation in praxis

Our colleagues would not be happy with such an approach if this was the norm or if this was what we advocated. I think not telling how to enact coteaching is what we had to do at the beginning where we were concerned with finding out what works and what doesn't. As you describe it, Mario knew better what to do and what is expected once we had established the heuristic. I think that this heuristic could become central and we need to make sure that (a) it is a guide for looking at whether an arrangement works and (b) it is flexible in the sense that there may be other criteria that teacher (educators) need to look for. I do not want this heuristic to be yet another instrument in the toolbox of university-based teacher educators to check teacher performance.

What appears to me important in this situation is not that Mario does less, but he does learn from the situation and he does see what works. He learns even if he withdraws, though the highest potential for learning is in those situations in which he actually participates. He makes that very explicit in his desire to coteach physics with you; he knows that he will experience enacted physics lessons rather than having to go by abstract descriptions that he might acquire in a physics methods course.

So he does realize the potential. If he does less coteaching than you might want him to, then there are certainly other mediating reasons why this is so. You remember that in a different note, I wrote about commitment and how we sometimes use it to devalue the contributions of others. We cannot make our own commitment into a yardstick against which we measure the commitment of others. In the lives of teachers, there are many different goals; teaching and earning a living are but two of a whole range. There are likely to be variations in the level of commitment that we enact in each of the different dimensions.

Mario's enthusiasm about coteaching appears to increase with his experience, and he continues to learn by interacting with you and the new teachers. Thus, when I talked to him, he attributed a lot of his own learning during the third year to Mark and Andy. Each, in his own way, contributed to exciting lessons from which Mario learned new ways of teaching himself.

I do not think that we should think of him in terms of 'he is doing it because we/others are around'. Rather, if we think of coteaching and having lots of new teachers in a school as a systemic change in teacher education, then we can capitalize on these schools as places to learn. Your idea of learning communities is one of the key concepts I see. In these communities, some individuals coteach, thereby sharing *being-in/with* that becomes the basis for concrete experiences that they can draw on in their talk about praxis. But the larger community should not be conceptualized according to dichotomies between regular teacher and student teacher, but in terms of legitimate peripheral participation where all of those present at CHS are responsible for what happens and all learn, though they do so in different ways.

At the moment, we still see this difference being re/produced and the tenured teachers are clearly differentiated from the new teachers. This goes so far that during the professional development day when we went to CHS, the new teachers did not participate in the activities of the other teachers; they were not even present in the school. I would like to see some experimentation done where there is more of a common responsibility for and commitment to the education of all new *and* tenured teachers.

As I read the episode involving Elwyn, I am thinking that the kind of situation in which he, as a new teacher enrolling at Penn, will find himself should be really explicit from the outset. In a similar way, the underlying epistemology of the teacher education program needs to be as explicit as it can possibly be made. It might have also helped Cam to see the contradiction that he experienced, and to understand the situations when there is conflict. Practices and artifacts have implicit politics, that is, they embody particular ways of dealing with this world. Sometimes these ways are contradictory to other ways of dealing with the world. This contradiction and the arbitrary nature of the assumptions that underlie teacher education should be more explicit and continuously on the table for discussion.

It was interesting that much of the advice Mario gave me during my coteaching with him and the advice that he had for new teachers was not about how to teach some subject or about the idea that teachers need to know more subject matter. At the core, all of his advice concerned the development of culturally appropriate ways of dealing with the Other (here, the student), how to deal with difference, how to avoid conflict, and so forth. In terms of Shulman's pedagogy, he had a lot of advice on general pedagogy rather than on subject matter and subject matter pedagogy.

TO: Michael
RE: Teaching alone
One issue that always recurs about coteaching is that student teachers must demonstrate that they can handle a class while teaching alone. There is often a skepticism on the part of potential employers about whether a person who has learned to teach by coteaching can actually teach a class without the support of another. Accordingly, we specified that in a whole day of teaching each student teacher should be involved in three 90-minute periods. One of these had to be teaching alone, one had to involve coteaching, and the other could be any approved professional activity in the class, SLC, or school. Often the teaching alone was accomplished by splitting a relatively large class into two heterogeneous halves, each to be taught by a student teacher.

TO: Ken
RE: Teaching alone
This issue of 'handling a class on your own' seems to come out of the same rhetoric that also supports testing people individually, away from the social context in which they work. I see it in a different way. Drivers learn with their instructor sitting next to them—at least in Europe—who can and does also work the pedals. This happens for some time until both feel that the learner is ready to go on his/her own, at which time there is an examination.

For me the critical issue is the easing of a neophyte into the job of teaching. There are so many other jobs where working on your own without contact with your peers is unthinkable and anachronistic. In teaching, we continue to maintain practices that are out of step with getting the most out of the kids that we are teaching.

I understand your concerns for getting the new teachers ready for a marketplace that has certain demands. But after having worked in coteaching situations for a long period of time, with additional time for new teachers to teach on their own in some kind of arrangement to be worked out, I believe that most of the people we are working with are ready. But we can make working on their own a smaller part of the experience of becoming teachers. Why should we disregard the presence of the Other as a resource for learning? Why voluntarily dismiss a better context for learning simply to submit to the rhetoric of the lone ranger?

TO: Michael
RE: Coteaching
It is important that the coteachers like one another to the extent that they can plan and enact the curriculum together. We discuss this issue repeatedly in later parts of the book. Indeed, pairing students such that they are teaching and learning from someone whom they respect and like is a critical ingredient of putting together a successful science teacher education program.

TO: Ken
RE: Coteaching
We can learn from the episode involving Elwyn, which is an example of the synergy between coteachers (even if Elwyn was reluctant at first). Initially you brought in a new and different idea. This became a source of inspiration for Mario to get the materials and actually develop something hands-on, practical, that was more illustrative than your earlier talk and the drawings Mario had put on the board.

The coteaching situation actually allowed you to turn this into a teachable moment, for with several people in the room, you can shift responsibilities and develop the lesson on the spot. We cannot know how anyone would have done the lesson had they been alone. But it is marvelous to see how the lesson unfolds when there are several people in the room. You probably remember the day when I was coteaching with you, Bert, and Stephanie.[9] There, too, we developed the genetics lesson by bringing in interesting personal cases that allowed students to look at the topic in a new and different way.

Of course, the coteaching individuals have to be willing to give each other the space. But it might just be a matter of changing our understandings of what teaching is and what it means to be a

---

9   In Chapters 5–8, we look at this lesson that we cotaught with Stephanie and
     Bert from a variety of different perspectives.

teacher. If we can give up the idea that one teacher is responsible for the learning and accept that we are in there as a group, then it is easy to give up all notions of having to control the unfolding lesson. Rather, capitalizing on learning opportunities is the primary goal. In the instance with Elwyn and the sea of electrons, we see that the three of you (Elwyn perhaps reluctantly) developed the lesson into something that increased the learning opportunities.

TO: *Michael*
RE: *Student teacher 'personalities' and coteaching*
Elwyn was a believer in transmission of knowledge. As Mario noted, he tended to have an elitist perspective on his own knowledge. The way that got enacted was a tendency to show more than the students knew or needed to know. The example of metallic bonding is a good one because he revised covalent and ionic bonding quickly and then threw out metallic bonding without any explanation to the students. He appeared to be flaunting his knowledge and the students looked confused. Our perspective at the time was that, since Elwyn had introduced the topic, he should then go ahead and show the students the relevance of what they were learning to what they already knew. It took Mario and I only a matter of seconds to agree about what needed to be done and what he and I, respectively, would do. I intervened, and as was noted by Mario, Elwyn looked a little aggravated by the interruption and was then at a loss as to how to proceed. That provided the space for Mario and me to enact our plan to provide an explanation, a diagram and also a demonstration.

Elwyn was an enigma in terms of placement with other student teachers and cooperating teachers. Initially we placed him in another SLC but his attitude created significant problems that led to the other student teacher not wanting to continue to teach with him and the SLC coordinator requesting me to reassign him. When he was assigned to Mario he was the third student teacher with whom Mario would be working and coteaching.

TO: *Ken*
RE: *Student teacher 'personalities' and coteaching*
As with many aspects of our work, the workings of many coteaching arrangements cannot be planned ahead of time. If your

new teachers do not know each other, they will not be able to decide whether or not they respect each other or whether they will be able to work with each other. So many of these things will have to be worked out in praxis, seeing what works, providing forums for people to talk and vent issues, and holding conflict resolution sessions. Whether someone will learn from someone else is always open. I cannot accept that a new teacher will say at the outset and without knowing the other (coop) teacher that s/he cannot work with the person.

In his advice to teacher educators, Mario makes a point that is central to the thesis of our book: you learn to teach by teaching. He also critiques the microteaching of peers as an unrealistic exercise that has little to do with the practices you have to enact in the classroom. Furthermore, student teaching does not seem to be the same kind of learning that was afforded to him in the coteaching situation. At the same time, he does not seem to be able to articulate just what it is that you learn by teaching. But underlying his talk seems to be the assumption that you learn teaching by teaching in the same way that you learn to play basketball by playing basketball, not by watching it or by hearing someone else talking about playing basketball.

TO: Michael
RE: Students and primary discourses
Some of the critical issues associated with learning to teach, especially as they relate to the epistemology of teaching, arise because of the social and cultural differences between the teachers and students. The primary discourses of students are so distant from the discourses embodied in the school district standards for science teaching that all teachers are immediately confronted with the challenge of enacting a culturally relevant curriculum.

TO: Ken
RE: Students and primary discourses (deficit mode)
We must make sure that we do not construct the African American students in the deficit mode. When we talk about them developing new discourses that are more science like, or we talk about them making it in the school as it is, we also implicitly talk about their deficits. We need to make sure that we do not use a

deficit model of inquiry, often developed with White college students (e.g., expert-novice) and apply it to African American students. Pathology, 'dysfunction', 'at-risk', and 'special education' are all concepts that characterize traditional deficit discourse about what is needed in education.

TO: *Michael*
RE: *Students teaching students*

The peer teaching with Mario and the *Incentive* students at City Elementary School was a significant experience for us all. As Mario mentions, the *Incentive* students were terrific when they turned up and when they were prepared. It was a wonderful work experience for them too. My great hope is that some of them will decide to be teachers based on those 8–10 weeks that we spent on this ambitious project.

I describe the project as ambitious because we decided that students from *Incentive* would work with the most difficult class at City Elementary. I had several reasons for wanting to do this. First, I felt that the *Incentive* students were being sacrificed in an educational sense for the benefit of others at City High. I wanted to make it possible for them to learn science by getting ready for teaching and then by teaching. Also, I wanted to give them a possible insight into a career, because we desperately need African American teachers. Second, as Mario mentioned, the class at City Elementary needed a break. They had had a series of substitute teachers for more than a year, mainly because of their boisterous behavior. They appeared to run their teachers off!

TO: *Ken*
RE: *Students teaching students: The re/production of society*

Mario was quite positive about the experience where you took the students from *Incentive* and taught a science class in City Elementary School. Trouble might be expected to arise when the younger children see the older ones as tools in the service of the oppressor. Both ideas, involving CHS *Incentive* students in teaching and tools of oppressors, bring me back to Foucault's account of the emergence of elementary schools. He writes that the elementary school became a mechanism of reproduction.[10] Foucault sug-

---

10 Foucault, 1979.

gests that initially, older students simply watched the younger ones, then controlled their work, and finally taught them. In this way, all students at all times were kept busy, some by teaching others by being taught. The older students simply became the tools in the hands of those in power, preparing the younger ones to follow in their footsteps.

It is therefore ironic that Mario talked about the students at City Elementary as being the future *Incentive* students, because, historically, some of them would be right there, teaching other elementary students and bringing them into line. I know that our work is full of contradictions. As an educator, I am part of the machinery that commits the symbolic violence; but I am questioning the nature of this machinery by being critical. It is out of the dialectic of the contradiction that I attempt to become a better teacher.

What does this imply for teacher education? I think that my goal for teacher education would be to help them develop into critical educators rather than into instruments administering the discipline and shaking people out of the system.

TO: *Michael*
RE: *Students teaching students, respect and rapport*
You may have a point about the older students inadvertently being agents of reproduction. Being in the elementary classroom with the high school students and Mario seemed like a good idea and in many ways it was. However, there were so many things we did not anticipate. Although we only went there 3 days a week, frequent absences made it difficult for our high school students to get prepared to teach for about an hour each day. Accordingly, some of them were unprepared in that they did not know what they were to teach. Perhaps even worse, they did not know enough about teaching to know what to do when the younger students misbehaved—which was almost all of the time. Mario and I did our best to coteach with the elementary school teacher and the 7–10 high school students. As Mario noted we had initial successes but over time the situation became more riotous and potentially dangerous in that violence always seemed to be seconds away. I will never forget the final day. It was so tumultuous in the classroom that I decided to get the high school students out of the

room. As calmly as I could, I took them outside to the campus, three floors below the classroom in which we had been teaching. One of the grade-seven students took the opportunity to hurl a flowerpot from the classroom window, striking one of our students in the side of the head. That act finished our project for that year as we all struggled to restrain the high school students from taking justice into their own hands.

The memories of this unfortunate incident are so strong for me that I retrieved an email message from the elementary teacher in which she describes the aftermath of our project. She commented:

> Oh my. I had no idea about the plant. That is horrible. Two of my students ended up getting suspended yesterday and we kept the class for detention until 3:30 p.m. I was at my wits end yesterday. There were maybe 15 fights or something. I absolutely hated them yesterday and I do not feel much better about them today. I am just ready for the year to be over at this point. I have written the rest of this year off, but I look forward to next year still. Okay, well. I think it was a good idea, but not this year or at least not with my class. These kids all know each other. They know Cristobal from out of school. They have seen him do numerous things, bad things. They all have information about one another and I believe that a program like this may work with these HS students working in lower grades, or with kids they do not know. My students do not respect them really. Oh well, it was a learning experience.

Respect. The hallmark of being a teacher in this culture. I was to learn this lesson over and over during my stay in schools like the two in which we have been teaching. This is a theme to which we return throughout the book.

CHAPTER 4

Historical Contexts of Coteaching in an Urban School

In this chapter we describe how coteaching was conceptualized and enacted as a way of learning to teach and learning about teaching. The context for much of the research described in the chapter involves the enactment of coteaching in a teacher education program for new high school science teachers. Initially, we provide brief autobiographical descriptions of our own learning and the experiences that led us to coteaching; then we articulate, from our perspective, the particular challenges that urban schools face. It is to face these challenges that we changed our approach to the education of middle and high school science teachers. The chapter presents the evolution in our thinking about learning to teach and the emergence of a coteaching model. Brief vignettes are provided to introduce coteaching individuals who appear in later chapters.

Getting Started: Ken

When I began to teach science in 1964, I did not employ any explicit theories to frame my experience. I arrived at school and I taught. The biggest concerns for me were mastering the science content I was to teach and motivating my rural students to engage in practices perceived by them to have little direct relevance to their lives. My instincts were to build a community of learners and to lead by example. The building of a community was not difficult in my first school because the town in which it was located was tiny and the students readily formed a coherent group. After two years, when I moved to a large suburban high school, my goals for improvement focused on mastery of the subject matter I was to teach. Once again the students were relatively easy to manage and for the most part could be convinced of the value of learning science. Knowing about theories of teaching and learning was not of importance to me. I talked with colleagues about what worked and what did not. And when any of us learned about promising innovations or resources we readily shared them with others. I became aware of the advantages of applying theory to the practices of teaching and learning only when I became a curriculum developer and needed to persuade others of the appropriateness of alternative activities and approaches to the teaching and learning of science.

As a curriculum designer, my chief role was to support a statewide effort to reform science education. All science teachers in my state (Western Australia) were provided with teacher's guides that recommended ways of teaching subject matter, materials to use, ways to manage instruction, and strategies for assessment. I had many questions to consider. For example, what is teacher knowledge and how does it change? My initial responses were guided by Piaget's clinical studies on the learning of children and adolescents.[1] The obligation to identify the most appropriate ways to teach and learn given subject matter required me to justify, at least to myself, why one approach to teaching was preferable to another. At the time there were numerous curriculum resource guides produced in many countries that encouraged me to use Piaget's developmental theories as a rationale for enacting science curricula.

I entered teacher education after a relatively short career as a middle and high school teacher in Australia and England. Following about 6 years of teaching in Australian schools, I went to England where I taught for a little more than a year. The significance of teaching in England was my exposure to the Nuffield curriculum projects, including Nuffield Combined Science, which was used at the school in which I taught. On my return to Australia I

---

1   Piaget, 1966.

used my knowledge of Nuffield and other projects to prepare curriculum guides for lower secondary science teachers (grades 8–10). The aim of the curriculum projects was to develop major and related concepts from hands-on activities that were carefully arranged to develop a statewide curriculum. After another year of high school teaching, I entered teacher education, as a lecturer in science and mathematics education, in 1974, with the responsibility of preparing teachers for appointments in primary schools (grades 1–7).

Different departments in the teachers college handled the methods courses and the field experiences. However, I carried with me my knowledge of being a cooperating teacher[2] for many new teachers, and strong values and beliefs associated with having taught and prepared curriculum materials for high school grades. In terms of my approach to methods, I wanted to be sure to cover significant topics such as questioning, verbal interaction, wait time, short- and long-term planning, grouping strategies, assessment, and evaluation. I was committed to an approach in which each of these topics was introduced and then exemplified in a sequence of hands-on activities that was potentially usable in primary grades. The new teachers would engage in authentic ways but could readily adapt the activities and materials (such as ice cubes, batteries and bulbs, and colored solutions) to their primary classes when they began teaching. Over a 15-week course it was expected that students would learn about the nature of primary science and address some of the more critical issues associated with planning and enacting a curriculum. Elsewhere in the teachers' college the students learned to teach in a generic sense and in other subject areas. Infrequent discussions were held with the aim of ensuring that the contradictions between different lecturers were not too confusing for students. I visited some new teachers during their field experiences but could not reach all of those I taught in my methods courses. Field experience was considered to be an opportunity for new teachers to put their knowledge into practice. That is, the knowledge they had constructed from

2 New teachers are assigned to cooperating teachers, who assist the former to learn to teach by allowing them to teach in their classes and enabling them to experience all aspects of professional life in schools. Components of the role of a cooperating teacher include specific assistance with planning, with formal observation and evaluation of teaching, and with reflective discussions.

coursework (lectures, discussions, readings, etc.) was to be applied to the field under the wise eyes of a carefully selected practitioner, referred to here as a cooperating teacher, and less frequent visits from a university supervisor.

Over a 2- to 3-year period, the field experiences were arranged so that new teachers learned initially by watching and discussing until they were assigned to their major field experience, which was one semester of full-time teaching. Although different universities arrange field experiences in different ways, the greatest influence while in the field inevitably comes from the school and its associated culture and the practicing teachers/educators at the school site. The most compelling form of evidence about whether or not a person can teach is gained from watching how new teachers perform in the classroom and how they enact their professional roles within the school.

Although there was a recognition that some cooperating teachers were better than others and that some schools were easier sites in which to learn to teach, the general approach was to select carefully the best possible cooperating teachers and to avoid the really 'rough' schools. The best sites for learning to teach were believed to be those in which exemplary teaching and learning practices were to be found.

Strategy Analysis

When I arrived at the University of Georgia in 1978, I was struck by the strong influence of Robert Gagné and derivative behaviorist ways of thinking about teaching and learning. Although I was somewhat opposed to reductionist ways of thinking about knowing and learning, behaviorist models were pervasive within the science education group at the University of Georgia. For a time I was swept up in the compelling logic of developing hierarchical models for complex modes of scientific reasoning. During my time at Georgia we refined models for data processing and created a conceptual scheme for investigation processing.[3] Once developed, these conceptual models served as tools for curriculum develop-

---

3   Tobin, 1982.

ment and analysis of teaching.[4] It was only a matter of time before they became the basis for my approach to educating teachers to teach science. The ideas were closely aligned with the models of teaching proposed by Bruce Joyce, Marsha Weil, and Beverly Showers. New teachers should build an understanding of a conceptual model, apply that model to planning a sequence of activities, and then apply the model as they enacted the curricular sequence. The model could also be used as a basis for analyzing teaching and providing feedback. Adherence to the model then became a criterion for examining the appropriateness of instruction. Over a period of time we were able to develop a number of models of teaching that were consistent with what we valued about science teaching and learning. The approach to teacher education then became one of focusing on understanding and applying models. At this time we instituted a concerted focus on peer teaching and peer- and self-analysis, using the extent of adherence to the model as a basis for analysis and evaluation.

During the 5-year period in which I used strategy analysis as the basis for science teacher education, it became clear to me that students and teachers developed considerable competence in using models to guide their teaching. Complex sets of cognitive actions, sometimes consisting of about 10 components, were enacted as routines. New teachers were learning to teach through the use of a variety of methods. These included (a) interactions about written and oral texts, (b) analysis of teaching in actual classrooms, in microsettings, and from videotapes using written conceptual models, and (c) application of those models in the planning and teaching of science in one-on-one teaching, microsettings and whole classes. On occasions the teaching was to peers and on other occasions to primary students.[5] Although the results were persuasive, I was searching for better ways to make sense of teacher knowledge. This search led me to constructivism and the work of Ernst von Glasersfeld.[6]

---

4   Tobin & Capie, 1980.
5   Tobin, 1985.
6   von Glasersfeld, 1995.

Constructivism

Ontological issues were of importance to me because I wanted to decide for my own research whether to regard knowledge as a social construction mediated by participants from a particular community or as an estimate of truth that iterated gradually toward one correct way of knowing. Did it make any sense to argue that there were correct ways to know and do? Or was correctness inherently a matter of social choice? Because I knew and respected von Glasersfeld, my initial tendency was to read, learn, and think about radical constructivism and ascertain the extent to which it was a suitable referent for my praxis. An initial concern was to figure out, from a radical constructivist perspective, how teachers could mediate their students' learning of science. I also wanted to understand how, from this perspective, teachers could re-present and change teaching. As I began to adopt the principles of radical constructivism as referents for my roles as a teacher educator, I regarded constructivism as a referent for thinking about three main issues. These are how students can learn in given situations, how others can mediate in the process of learning, and how artifacts from an activity setting afford opportunities to learn and participate in particular ways. As a way of thinking, constructivism can be applied to any activity setting and questions can be asked about how to change the roles of teacher and students to promote greater learning. Inevitably the use of constructivism as a referent not only involves the changing of interaction patterns but also the structure of the activity itself. However, constructivism is not only useful as a way to think about managing learning in small classes but can be referenced to learning in any social setting, even to a large lecture class in college biology with more than 1,000 students. From a constructivist perspective, teachers should take account of what students know and can do, how students can negotiate meaning and build consensus by interacting with one another and with artifacts, and what opportunities there are for students to put their knowledge to the test and receive feedback on its adequacy.

There has been a tendency in teacher education to advocate particular ways of teaching and learning. This is not surprising, because many practicing and new teachers seem to value recipes for teaching (just as I did when I commenced my teaching career). It is as if there is a best way to teach that transcends all contexts, and people want to know what it is. I have a problem with quests for master narratives and I use a fishing metaphor to counter requests for recipes. Instead of giving my students the fish they appear to want so badly, I attempt to teach them to fish. Not surprisingly my failure to give them what they want is frequently met with significant resistance.[7] Often the quest for 'methods that work' is subtle. For example, even though I speak about constructivism as a powerful referent for thinking about teaching, learning, and relating to others,[8] people often interpret what I have said as describing a method of teaching that they reject as inappropriate because of the contexts in which they operate. Their reasons usually include the impossibility of using small groups and highly interactive participation of learners, essential characteristics of what they perceive to be constructivist ways of teaching.

Metaphor

When I described my research on metaphor to Mary Budd Rowe, she listened intently and then quickly responded that a metaphor was like a master switch.[9] Her description was apt in that a metaphor can be regarded as a conceptual organizer that aggregates sets of beliefs and constrains actions in given contexts. What was striking to me was that for more than a decade I had worked with teachers to change discrete variables, like wait time, and had experienced the difficulty teachers had in making and sustaining such changes.[10] Yet, in our first study on metaphor, one of the teachers was switching metaphors and, in so doing, was changing sets of associated actions.[11] Throwing the master switch enabled him to teach in a characteristic but radically different manner than before when his actions were constrained by a different metaphor. When the teacher switched from one metaphor for teaching (i.e., captain of the ship) to another (i.e., entertainer) it appeared as if

---

7   Tobin, Seiler, & Smith, 1999.
8   Tobin, 1993.
9   Tobin, 1990.
10   Tobin, 1987.
11   Tobin, Kahle & Fraser, 1990.

hundreds of variables changed as the new metaphor was enacted. From the perspective of teacher education, I was interested to see if teachers could learn new metaphors for teaching and learning, adopt them in their teaching, and thereby make significant changes in their practices. This is precisely what happened, and the use of metaphor became a significant tool in my teacher educator toolkit.[12] I collaborated with teachers to identify the salient metaphors used to conceptualize their most significant roles and ascertain through reflection the extent to which those metaphors were optimal and consistent with what they believed about teaching and learning. The application of metaphors while teaching occurred at a relatively macroscopic level (i.e., at the level of teacher and student roles), which has the potential for making marked changes to classroom environments. In contrast, reflection on the efficacy of alternative metaphors occurred at more of a microscopic level (i.e., more particularized and at the level of variables) as roles were examined in terms of the constituent variables and their associated beliefs and values. Since many metaphors have textual and image components, they can be accessed conveniently while teaching, so it is relatively easy to use them as referents for initiating and sustaining changes in the classroom.

I have had personal experience in constructing metaphors to frame my teaching. For example, some years ago when asked about my beliefs about teaching college science, I realized that I did not have a metaphor to conceptualize my teaching roles. The process of creating a suitable metaphor was protracted in that I related potential metaphors and their associated images to valued referents pertaining to constructivism and to practices I regarded as essential to my teaching. The verbal label I gave to my new metaphor was 'provocateur'. When it was appropriate I preferred to mentally 'push and cajole' students in an effort to obtain deeper levels of understanding. In response to questions about this metaphor, I could say a considerable amount about the roles of both teacher and students and also about the nature of the learning environment. But, as I discussed what I meant by provocateur, I also accessed an image of the teacher as fencing master. I had in mind a duel in which a fencing master practices with an advanced student. There are times when the master allows the student to

---

12   Tobin & LaMaster, 1995.

attack. At these times, the student practices attacking skills and experiences the defense of the master. Then the master attacks. Attacking moves are selected to allow the student to build a successful defense. And so the duel proceeds with the teacher and the student having the freedom to initiate changes to test each other to the limit. There is mutual respect and nobody gets hurt. The student wants to demonstrate competence and is not about to hurt her teacher. Similarly, the fencing master is cognizant of what the student can and cannot do and acts accordingly. Trust is embedded in the metaphor and when the duel is over, both teacher and student bow to show their mutual respect. As they remove their masks it is evident that the master and the student are exhausted at the end of a solid workout.

Having constructed the metaphor I was able to use it as a referent for thinking about teaching and enacting the curriculum. It was relatively straightforward to plan teacher and student roles to cohere with the metaphor. At a later time, when I returned to teach in an urban high school[13] as a researcher-teacher, I once again had to construct a metaphor to constrain the way I interacted with students.

From the first day I was in the class, Nicole caught my attention. Nicole followed the Muslim tradition of wearing a head cover, and she drew attention to herself with her volatile presence. I went to sit in and observe on the day before I started actually teaching the class. On that day, Nicole initiated a dispute with another female that ended in violence as each swung her fists at the other and tore at her hair and clothing. I did not know too much about teaching in circumstances like these. That incident led to my resolution not to push students to the point of conflict and to adopt the metaphor of a cork on a stormy sea. I wanted to be sure that no action of mine would catalyze physical conflict as had happened during my observation. My field notes just prior to the first lesson read as follows:

> I will be a cork on a stormy ocean on Monday. They will be the waves, the currents, the winds, and the tides. At times I am certain to be pulled adrift and even under the surface. However, I will be resilient and bob on the surface, following their lead as I find my way toward a destina-

---

13   City High School, where much of the research for this book was conducted.

tion that is dynamic and probably never ending. I will have more metaphors by the time I arrive in class, but for now this is a reassuring way
to think about my roles. I will not be a counter puncher. I will have no
weapons. I will be totally responsive. Also I will mediate the learning of
individuals whenever the waters are calm. (Field notes, January 8, 1999)

The use of the metaphor enabled me to monitor my teaching at
times when the automatic nondeliberative approaches did not
work as intended. At such times I was able to 'step back' from
practice and think carefully about the context and the most appropriate method of proceeding. For the initial three months the
metaphor served me well as I navigated my way through the
teaching of chemistry. However, as my comfort level with students
and school grew, I realized that the metaphor had limitations and
needed to be adapted to facilitate a more proactive set of teaching
roles. I had learned enough to be proactive in my reading of the
class and in mediating in their participation.

Reflection in and on Action

Reflection in action[14] always seemed something of an elusive goal
for me. To think about your teaching while teaching implies multi-
tasking and assumes that (new or practicing) teachers can monitor
their knowledge in action. I do not regard this as possible or desirable because my experiences in sports suggest that if you think too
much about your actions, then you are certain to lose a close con-
test! From my perspective, reflection on action is most applicable
to teacher education since it allows teaching acts to be reconstructed and to serve as objects for reflection. This process can be
facilitated by the use of oral and written texts either by teachers
working alone or by teachers interacting with others. Self-analysis,
using audio and videotapes, also facilitates reflection on action.
However, it is quite important to note that reflection on action involves cognitive objects that may not be directly related to the
knowledge enacted while teaching. Thus the objects of reflection
can be adapted without necessarily impacting the knowledge of
teaching.

---

14 Schön, 1987.

Arranging opportunities for reflection on action is a significant part of all the teacher education programs in which I have been involved. I usually facilitate this by requiring self-analyses of teaching to be written and to serve as objects for peer and personal review. In addition, each individual has opportunities to review others' teaching and comments about teaching. Reflection on action can also be facilitated through the use of a portfolio and a video narrative that captures aspects of teaching and changes that are considered by a teacher to be salient.

Radical and Social Constructivism

Unlike many of my colleagues, my principal context for research has always been in intact classrooms. Accordingly, even though my focus on constructivism was initially from the perspective of individual teachers and students negotiating meaning and arriving at consensus, my activities were always radically social. Hence, it was essential for me to include in my ways of thinking about teaching and learning a strong component of social processes. Whereas Glasersfeld and others could focus on individual cognitions and personal sense making, the contexts in which I was doing my research necessitated that I understand not only constructions by individuals but also constructions of Self and Others. Any theory to be applied to my research on teaching and learning had to take into account the presence of Others and the manner in which interactions between participants could promote learning.

I did not regard constructivism as a master narrative that could be used as the underpinning framework for all other narratives. In the contexts of my praxis I used constructivism to think through critical issues about teaching and learning and to conceptualize the meaning and place of issues such as power, autonomy, and management in science classrooms. Over a period of a decade, constructivism assumed a central place in a semantic web that focused on issues concerning teaching, learning, and curriculum. My expectation always was that my referents for research would evolve, and I was actively seeking coherent ways of looking that would fit into the semantic web, and enhance my praxis in science education. As concepts were added to the web other parts of it were reconceptualized so as to maximize coherence among the constituents.

Action

The concept of action is a critical part of teacher knowledge and teaching. Just what did I mean by action when I asked, for example, what actions are occurring and what do these actions mean from the perspectives of the actors? The meaning of action was elusive for a number of years as I undertook research in classrooms and explored the theoretical underpinnings of action from a constructivist perspective.[15] Because I regarded an understanding of action as essential to describing and changing teaching, I wanted to know about action in a deep way, not just to be able to define it in a sentence or a paragraph. From a social constructivist perspective, I concluded that action is a holistic entity that can be described in a variety of ways. I conceptualized actions in the following ways: a set of behaviors; a set of associated beliefs and values that provide a warrant for those behaviors considered viable in the contexts in which action is to occur; the constructed context for the action; and a set of the actor's goals. Thus, in the circumstances perceived to exist, an action is an enactment of knowledge, a complex whole that incorporates what a teacher knows and can do and the teacher's values.

Knowing about action also makes it clear to me that teaching is more than learning and having convictions. How the context is constructed will always be a significant component of action. Accordingly, it is imperative that students are given many assignments that require them to identify the most salient parts of the context in which teaching occurs and to understand how the context shapes the teaching and learning environments of others who teach in similar circumstances. Thus, it is important for new teachers to undertake ethnographies of teaching and learning and to identify the constraints that shape teaching as well as aspects of the *habitus* that usually extend beyond what can be written and spoken. The constructivist perspective led me to think of action in a rationalistic way and to almost totally ignore the significance of

---

15   McRobbie & Tobin, 1995.

knowing as doing. My point in mentioning this here is to emphasize that as theory affords it also obscures. In bringing to the foreground issues of behavior, belief, and value, I soon developed the
idea that action was rational and deliberative. Later theorizing
was to radically change my perspectives on how best to think
about teaching and the changing of teaching.

Getting Started: Michael

I became a teacher and teacher educator by accident.

When I was in grade 5, I answered all queries about my career
ideas by saying I wanted to become a teacher. Interestingly
enough, it turned out that I failed and therefore had to repeat that
year. When I became conscious of this turn of events, I also noticed that I had lost all interest in ever becoming a teacher.

At 25, I completed a master's degree in physics and did some
independent work as a researcher. Getting a job without experience was impossible at the time, so I applied for a teaching position in an isolated village, frozen in for 6 months of the year, accessible only by plane and snowmobile/boat, about 500 miles
from the next mining town. Because few teachers wanted to go to
these places, and because the teacher turnover rate was nearly
40%, the school board hired people like me who did not have
teacher training—but I was required to obtain training during the
summers if I wanted to keep my job.

These early years in teaching were crucial for my development
as a science teacher. Although I came to teaching by a fortunate
accident, I loved it on the spot. I decided that I wanted to teach
science so that my students could experience some of the excite-
ment that I had felt doing research in a laboratory rather than the
(drab) lectures I had experienced during my own years in school. I
set up a small laboratory in the basement without running water,
with a six-foot ceiling, heating ducts, and two fire extinguishers
that later turned out not to work at all. Each day and for each
class, my grade-8 and grade-9 students brought buckets of water.
With a few materials from the Introductory Physical Science kit, I
thought up new experiments and engaged my students in thinking
up their own investigations so that what should have been a one-

year course actually taught two years of science. My grade-7 students, taking biology, spent half of their lessons in the open air investigating different forms of succession (bare rock, fire succession, pond), different sampling techniques, and different ways of representing research.

During these first years of teaching, I did not think about pedagogy in any formal way. I had begun to teach without teacher training and had intended to let students learn in the ways that I had found most interesting and exciting in my own learning: doing lab work (during graduate studies) and learning by making sense. My own failures, such as having to repeat grade 5, were constant reminders that there are moments in our lives when we do not understand in the way others expect us to do. Whenever I saw a student struggling, I also saw myself in grade 5 or 7 struggling with mathematics or German, and in fact, struggling to make the grade. My early pedagogy was grounded in these two experiences, learning in (graduate) lab being fun and learning (by teacher standards) being a struggle.

I had students work in small groups, each student progressing at his/her own rate. Each group negotiated with me its progress for the next week, and then endeavored to complete what it had planned. When students ran into trouble, they first attempted to find answers in their group before coming to me. Because we were required to give tests, having groups work at their own rate meant that I had to make up about five different tests for each class. But in the end, even traditionally 'weak' students (i.e., in their other classes) achieved above mastery level for the grade at the end of the year.

Over the course of a year, I spent a lot of time with each student because I also taught mathematics, art (I had several college-level courses and was later certified in art), and physical education (boys'). Life in the small village also brought us together playing soccer, fishing, cutting wood, buying groceries, or sitting around a hot fireplace on cold winter evenings in some crowded living room. The students and I got to know each other well.

When I came to Newfoundland to teach computer science and physical science at a high school, I moved into apparent desolation. About 45% of students never completed high school; nearly 75% of the people in the 18–25 year bracket were unemployed. In a tracked school system, I was assigned as homeroom teacher to a grade-9 class that none of the other seasoned teachers wanted to take. As I spent a lot of time prior to morning and afternoon classes (in addition to 7 science lessons per week) with these students, I soon found out that they needed more than schooling. What these grade-9 students, many of them between one and five years older than other students at that level, needed was friendly and fatherly attention, someone who listened to them and cared about their welfare. They needed someone who trusted them and whom they could trust in turn. They needed someone who respected and appreciated them for what they were at the time. Without that, no lesson could ever be successful.

In Newfoundland, too, I taught science by means of inquiry. I learned that it took about 3 months of five to seven lessons per week before students were willing and able to design investigations and report them in whole-class sessions. Being actively involved seemed so much harder, so much more work.

When I look back at these early formative years, I am aware of my naïveté with respect to teaching and teacher knowledge. Although I was well liked by students and praised by my superintendents—one of whom strongly encouraged me to pursue doctoral work and facilitated my receiving a long leave of absence—I had not reflected a great deal on what I was doing. I simply did what felt right. One thing that characterized these years became evident to me only later when a high school student, who had come to the physics lab along with about 15 others to work on school activities in the evenings, told me, 'You like to learn yourself, don't you?' Students seemed to have recognized in me an enthusiasm about learning.

A few years later, after getting a Ph.D. in science education, I found myself again in the classroom and head of a science department. This time, it was a private boarding school of the 'Dead Poets Society' type (similar traditionalist atmosphere, brick buildings, grassy fields, and caves in which to hide and smoke) that took pride in getting 99% of its students into some form of college or university. At that time, Ken's work on metaphors and constructivism, the notions of reflection in and on action, and social constructivism[16] began to influence the way I thought about teaching and learning.

Despite the conservatism of the institution, I instituted open inquiry and got most of my fellow science teachers to follow me. Our grade-8 students researched different ecozones according to their own questions; grade-10 students built devices that converted solar power into a usable energy form; and grade-12 physics students designed their own curricula (including activities, assessment format) to learn about electricity.

As a department head, I also was responsible for 'professional development' and 'teacher evaluation'. My school viewed both of these activities in traditional ways. Professional development sometimes looked like this: department heads or invited speakers presented 'dog-and-pony-show' activities that could be repeated by the teachers in their classrooms. Department heads also did the 'teacher evaluation', normally by sitting at the back of the classroom and then providing the school with a written report as a form of summative evaluation.

Having begun to read about communities of practice on the one hand, and about the social construction of evaluation and the political nature of all representation on the other, I became dissatisfied with these existing practices.[17] Together with my teachers, I thought of ways in which we could become better teachers and, at the same time, ways in which we could report our activities as formative and summative evaluation to our school administration. The resulting ideas became the ground for my ideas about coteaching as a forum for formative and summative evaluation as we describe it in Chapter 8.

Because of school policy, I could not avoid having to undertake a 'formal' evaluation of each teacher. However, we added three more levels of activities that, eventually, would be adopted by the school as a whole. First, we teachers reflected on our goals for the year and described how we saw our professional growth. We purchased a video camera for the science department that we would use to videotape ourselves as a tool for reflecting on our

---

16 Newman, Griffin, & Cole, 1989.
17 See Lave & Wenger, 1991, on the notion of communities of practice, Suchman & Jordan, 1990, on the social construction of evaluation, and Star, 1989, on the political nature of representation.

practice and growth. This form of inquiry was our autobiographical account of professional development. Although I took the lead in studying my own teaching using videotapes, almost everybody in the department eventually enacted the same practice to look at teaching and learning in their classrooms.

Second, each teacher visited other classrooms or taught several times per year with at least two other teachers. After these experiences in other teachers' classrooms, we discussed our experiences with one another and subsequently wrote brief reports about the similarities and differences between others' teaching and our own. These activities represented our way of building a community of practice by participating in each other's work, while using our reports as a way to articulate our own teaching practices and those of our colleagues.

Third, we visited each other's classrooms for formal evaluations; that is, rather than participating we stood back and watched the unfolding lessons. We provided each other with feedback. Fourth, we maintained the practice of having the science department head do formal evaluations, although I would also engage in all the other development and evaluation activities. In the end, each teacher had developed something like a portfolio in which s/he documented professional growth.

During these years, I began to look more closely at and articulate an understanding of my teaching. In particular, using videotapes shot earlier in the day, I began to analyze my interactions with small groups of students;[18] I used audiotaped interviews to find out more about how students experienced the curriculum that we enacted on a day-to-day basis.[19] Based on my new understanding, I would make changes in the curriculum and teaching strategies. However, I found out that changes did not come as easily as I had thought. Despite careful preparation, I often continued with the same practices that I had enacted earlier. Change came slowly and only through continued reflection, modification of actions, and so forth. Not surprising, the concept of *habitus* made sense to me because of my own experiences as a teacher and the difficulty of changing despite my intentions of doing so.

---

18   See, for example, Roth, 1993; Roth & Roychoudhury, 1994.
19   See, for example, Roth, 1994.

For example, I had noted that in interactions with students, I used to cut them off in their turns and did not do enough to help them to articulate ideas. I also realized that when I did not cut them off or when I used the explain-elaborate-justify strategy to make them expand on what they had said, tremendous learning seemed to occur. I decided to change my practice and allow students to articulate more. Despite my honest intentions, providing consistent space for students to talk and develop discourse without my rapid interventions was difficult. For weeks and even months after making my initial commitment to change, I would notice on the videotapes that I did not enact what I had described in the way I had intended.

I eventually decided to pursue a university career but remained a science teacher at heart. Each year, I spent between 2 and 6 months coteaching science with resident teachers or interns at local elementary schools (covering K–7 in British Columbia). Whenever I worked with a teacher, I articulated an emerging presupposition: We do not learn to teach by acquiring knowledge about teaching (through construction, transmission, or discovery) and then by applying it. Rather, we learn to teach by doing it, especially when we work alongside another teacher, and, while teaching, we also develop a deeper understanding of subject matter knowledge. I said that I would be willing to work *with* them, to supply or construct curriculum materials that would remain in the school as long as they participated. I wanted to be *in* the classroom *with* them so that we could learn from each other. These coteaching experiences, then, became sites for learning to teach and for learning more about coteaching as a means of professional development and understanding of practice.

Like all the teachers I worked with, I learned a lot by working with others, in the praxis of getting the day's work done. *Being-in* the classroom was *being-with* a (significant) Other; *being-in* and *being-with* seemed to be the very conditions for our transformation as teachers, our *becoming-in* the classroom.[20]

As I looked more and more closely at my teaching experience, I noticed that when I was fully involved in teaching, nothing described by traditional theories of teaching was salient. That is, I did not recognize my own experience in the current theories of

20   Roth & Boyd, 1999; Roth, Masciotra, & Boyd, 1999.

teaching such as 'reflective practice' or the tri-part theory of peda-gogy and content.[21] For example, while I was analyzing with Nadine (the teaching intern featured in Chapter 1) a questioning sequence that I had enacted earlier that day, she said that I had all the good questions at the tip of my tongue. Yet I had no recol-lection of having thought about the subject matter (subject matter knowledge) or the literature on children's everyday discourse on the topic (pedagogical content knowledge). The questions that en-couraged children to reflect just imposed themselves; they became salient as the obvious next step in the conversation. I was curi-ously unreflective. At first I felt deficient because I did not meas-ure up to the concept of 'reflection in action', I found out later that other teachers were unreflective too.[22]

Although my experience was not well described by 'reflection in action' or by the tri-part theory of teacher knowledge, I also be-gan to realize that when I had time to stop and think, I could ra-tionalize what I had been saying. I was able to talk about the sub-ject matter in organized ways, articulate children's intuitive lan-guage about some topic, and produce different options that would probably lead to learning. These different options for action that were latently available I came to articulate as *Spielraum*, room to maneuver.[23] Whereas I did not consciously reflect on these differ-ent options for action, they were available to me in the same way as my different options while in a particular situation on the soc-cer field. It is only at the moment of action, without a conscious decision, that one of these options becomes realized.

As a researcher of learning, I struggled with the relationship between knowing-that and knowing-how. How can we make sense of people saying one thing but doing something else that seems to be inconsistent with the action? I found out that the sociological researchers had already worked on this problem. Accordingly, what we say we do and what we do are two different forms of practice each enacted at a different point in time. Even the tradi-tionally accepted relationship according to which situated actions

---

21   For reflective practice in teaching, see Munby & Russell, 1992; for the tri-part theory of teacher knowledge, see Shulman, 1987.
22   van Manen, 1995.
23   Roth, Lawless, & Masciotra, 2001.

followed plans turned out to be reversed: Plans do not cause actions but are descriptions that can be assessed only a posteriori.[24]

In my initial work on teaching as praxis,[25] I began to realize that a 'theory of practice' was an oxymoron because of the ontological differences between theory and praxis. All theories are based on re-presentations, signs, which are (at least temporarily) fixed tokens for objects and events. That is, the temporal unfolding of praxis, the fleeting nature of 'situations' and perceptions, cannot be captured by 'theory'.[26] Praxis, on the other hand, is enacted in an ongoing manner and without any time-out. This quality had to be captured by our understanding of teaching.

As I was thinking through these problems of representing practice, I was reading pieces by natural scientists who hold that the ultimate test of scientific theories is their suitability to describe lived experience.[27]

In the course of writing a number of articles in which my collaborators and I began to conceptualize teaching from a perspective of praxis and lived experience, *praxeology* (Gr. *praxis*, action, and *logos*, talk) seemed to emerge as a natural concept. I became increasingly convinced that what we need at this point in the historical development of our field are models of teaching that are consistent with our lived experience. If a theory does not describe lived experience, then there is something inappropriate in our theory. I felt that once we had models of teaching in which teachers actually recognized their own experience, then we were much closer to dealing with any gap between theory and praxis.

Educating Individuals to Teach in Urban Schools

In this section, we describe the transformation of the secondary teacher education program at Penn from the traditional field-based model to a coteaching model. The section may be read as an ethnography of the challenges that can be faced when changing

---

24 Suchman, 1987.
25 Roth, 1998a, 1998b.
26 Bourdieu, 1990.
27 Varela, 1996.

established patterns of teacher education, at the university and school levels.

Challenges of Educating Urban Teachers

To what extent is it possible to base classroom actions on knowledge that has been constructed from oral and written texts? We believe that at least some of what is learned by talking, writing, listening, and thinking can constrain an enacted curriculum and thereby influence praxis. Hence, it is important to include, as part of the ongoing program of study for new teachers,[28] courses that are tied to the field experience. Discussions between new teachers and others should be scheduled so that what has happened in their classrooms can be described in narrative and propositional forms, thereby becoming objects for reflection and learning.

Much of what can be learned and applied in classroom contexts can be learned while teaching when knowledge is constructed in ways about which the teacher is not necessarily conscious. It is therefore essential that a teacher education program allow new teachers to teach in a variety of contexts where they can learn to teach by teaching. By 'teaching', we mean full participation and integration in the day-to-day work at school and recognition of this as legitimate participation (rather than as an interruption of normal activity). These activities should include the teaching of full classes as students go about their 'normal' curriculum.

There are different ways in which new teachers can obtain practical experience. One way is to place them in front of classes and let them teach. Of course this will allow new teachers to experience teaching and to learn by interacting with students based on their developing knowledge, values, and beliefs. This traditional approach is characteristic of many teacher education programs. New teachers are placed in normal or 'real' situations and learn to teach by taking over a class from the cooperating teacher, receiving feedback on their performance from a variety of sources, and en-

---

28 We remind our readers that the notion of 'new teacher' is more consistent with legitimate peripheral participation in the daily praxis of teaching children; we therefore use this term in preference to 'student teacher' or 'prospective teacher'.

acting changes to accord with the feedback. New teachers can also gather experience by teaching at the elbows of others, including more experienced teachers or peers. One decided advantage of such an approach is that coparticipation is possible as multiple teachers and learners interact to maximize learning.

There are many aspects of teaching and learning in urban schools that are challenging for teachers, irrespective of the length and breadth of their experience. Teacher educators with the responsibility of preparing (educating) new teachers for urban schools must address these challenges. There are many questions that seek answers. What is best learned from coursework, reading, and discussion? How will coursework relate to field experience? Where should the new teachers be placed in the field and for what length of time? Whether or not they are posed, questions such as these are at the core of significant disagreement within the community of teacher educators. Undergirding extant practices is a *habitus* honed around high levels of commitment and hours of labor-intensive practice in the field. The rationale for what is done is also supported by theories of teaching and learning that are grounded in social constructivist theory and conceptual change. There are compelling reasons to continue existing practices and endeavor merely to improve the quality of current programs through fine-tuning of extant roles and practices.

The approach to teacher education and development that we describe in this book differs in its theoretical underpinnings (see Chapter 1) and seeks to change the roles and practices of the key stakeholders associated with learning to teach (see also Chapters 5–8). In our efforts to enact a new approach to teacher education, we have had to address several obstacles. The first of these is current roles and practices and the theories and *habitus* that support them. Participants have a strong tendency to continue with their present practices and understandably do what makes sense to them and is in what they consider to be the best interests of the new teachers and those they teach. A second obstacle is that there are numerous ways to enact roles and practices to enhance learning to teach. For example, we are not sure of the best ways to place new teachers for field experiences or to enact coteaching. We believe it is imperative that participants are given chances to enact coteaching in ways that make sense to them and for us to undertake careful research and ensure that all stakeholders learn from it. As we learn more about coteaching we can better inform stakeholders about potential roles and practices, thereby fostering a community in which learning to teach is supported by numerous participants and a climate of scholarly inquiry.

Field placement is an initial issue to be resolved. If we place new teachers with 'strong' teachers, known to teach effectively, the new teachers inherit smoothly functioning classrooms that have been shaped by the ways of the cooperating teachers. For the most part students enact their established roles and abide by the mores of the extant classroom culture. The influence of the 'coop' continues and, although students may put the teacher to the test, the event repertoire that is encountered is limited by the established culture of the classroom. It is relatively easy to learn to teach in such circumstances. However, we are not sure that the teaching *habitus* developed in these circumstances is viable if a teacher subsequently moves to an urban school. In Chapters 1 and 2, the vignettes featuring Ken show that he had to re-learn to teach in urban schools. His teaching *habitus* developed while teaching in middle-class situations fell short in the urban schools. In the following vignette we describe how one of the best new teachers from 1988–89, whose field experiences were set in a suburban school and a magnet school for high-performing students, was pushed to the limit when she was first appointed to an urban middle school.

Traditional Approaches Do Not Work Well

Sofia's first semester field assignment as a new teacher was to a suburban elementary school where she taught successfully. However, Sofia also wanted to be certified as a high school biology and general science teacher. After one semester of successful teaching in a suburban elementary school, Sofia requested reassignment to a school in which she could teach at both the elementary and secondary levels. The school that met her needs was a magnet school for the most talented grades 4–12 students in the district. To remain at the school students needed to maintain a high grade point average and perform in a satisfactory way. Sofia perceived her teaching experiences at the school as highly successful and so too did her supervisor and 'coop'. She was able to replace the coop by taking over the class almost immediately, and her teaching *habitus* facilitated the learning of her students, who could perform much as they would have with their regular teacher. At the conclusion of her field experience, Sofia was highly recommended and the school principal unsuccessfully endeavored to hire her. However, Sofia was offered a position in an urban middle school.

When Sofia was offered the position she called Ken to discuss her reservations about the job. She was decidedly anxious about teaching in a school and community that she regarded as different from anything she had experienced and potentially unsafe. Sofia had heard stories about the misbehavior of students and the failure of the school to measure up academically. Ken assured her that she would be successful and promised to provide her with some equipment and supplies that she needed.

The evening following the first day of school, Ken called Sofia to discuss arrangements for delivering the equipment that he had promised. She was in tears and determined to quit, deciding instead to pursue the option of going to medical school. 'This is just not worth it!' she sobbed. Ken was astonished. Sofia was one of the best new teachers just one short summer ago. Now she found that her class was completely out of control and she had no ideas about what to do. Ken listened intently and with considerable emotion. As she spoke, he searched his mind for suggestions. 'Earn their respect. Identify the worst offenders and take them to lunch. Call all parents'. None of his suggestions appealed as a suitable remedy for what appeared to be a totally dysfunctional learning environment. 'Implement martial law', he thought. 'Keep your expectations high. Don't be undignified. Identify curricular ideas in which students are likely to be interested. Find out what they expect to do and if it is appropriate see if you can engage them accordingly. Make changes incrementally'. Ken's suggestions were well intentioned, but he was not too sure how helpful they would be. Sofia agreed to call the parents and spoke with Ken at length about his suggestion of taking the main problem students to lunch. Building a climate of student cooperation was the key to his plan for Sofia to become more successful. He also agreed to coteach with her several times a week in a peer-teaching project, described by Mario in Chapter 3.

Sofia received a variety of forms of assistance and over time gradually learned to teach her grade-7 students. These were very different students from those she had learned to teach during her one-year field experience. Although the teacher education program emphasized equity, poverty, culture, and teaching and learning in urban schools, Sofia was not only relatively unsuccessful but had few ideas of what to do. Furthermore, her initial tendencies were to teach in ways that were consistent with the ways in which other teachers in the school taught. Many of these practices were in direct opposition to what we considered appropriate. Yet Sofia's initial efforts were to keep the students busy with seatwork and bribe them through a rewards and punishments system that included hefty punishments for breaking rules.

After a year of emotional trauma and continual struggle, Sofia learned how to teach her students. She earned their respect and by the end of the year she had their confidence and most had constructed her as their teacher. Ironically, after a stressful year in which she learned to teach in an urban middle school, Sofia accepted a transfer to the magnet high school in which she had done her field experience.

What can we learn from Sofia's experiences? During her field experiences at Penn, Sofia learned to teach at schools like those in which she had been a student. However, she was not prepared to teach in the event-full circumstances that characterize urban public schools. Neither her field experience nor her extensive (and successful) coursework prepared her for her initial teaching assignment. There was an immediate need to rethink some of the key assumptions of our teacher education program.

Changing the Internship Experience

Before Ken arrived at Penn, a colleague called him. He had received a grant, together with the principal of City High School (CHS), to undertake a study that included high school students who taught new teachers 'How to teach students like me'. Ken understood this project to involve the high school students as ethnographers who would provide insights to new teachers on how they were teaching in urban high schools. He agreed to participate in the project and thereby committed the teacher education program to assigning approximately 20 new teachers to CHS. That was a break from a Penn tradition of assigning new teachers to schools across the city and to selected suburban high schools. In the past, new teachers had been provided with the option of experiencing different types of schools (e.g., suburban, private, and city magnet schools).

Assigning a relatively large group of new teachers to one high school was consistent with the commitment at Penn to create partnerships with the communities adjacent to the university. The university was actively involved in creating university-school partnerships and the assignment of the new teachers to neighborhood high schools was regarded as a seed around which numerous initiatives could be built. This was not just a token gesture in support of local high schools but an acknowledgment that a productive partnership could create an environment conducive to new and existing teachers learning to teach and to the learning of high school students. Urban high schools were regarded as highly desirable sites for learning to teach; teacher education was seen as a transformative activity that could catalyze new approaches to professional development, curricular improvement, and higher performance of high school students.

During the spring of 1997–98, two pairs of new teachers taught together because of a shortage of suitable cooperating teachers in the urban high school to which they were assigned. The decision to employ coteaching was not whimsical. The school principal at City High School suggested the idea, and Ken was well aware of Michael's research showing the potential of learning to teach by teaching *with* others. In both cases the field experiences were highly successful and we decided to increase the amount of coteaching in the following year. However, the lead time needed to educate supervisors and cooperating teachers was too great to allow for a significant increase in the incidence of coteaching. Despite the goal that coteaching would be done in the fall and gradually increase throughout the 1998–99 year, it was only enacted on a limited scale.

In one instance two new teachers were assigned to coteach with Bert, the science teacher in one of the small learning communities at City High School. The main reason for assigning two new teachers to Bert was not theoretical or any sense that this would be ideal. The reality we faced was a shortage of suitable cooperating teachers. Bert and his two new teachers collaborated on planning and teaching for the entire year and both new teachers showed evidence of significant learning. Their teaching blossomed over the course of the year and Bert, too, adapted his teaching to include many of the innovations introduced by the two new teachers.

Expanding the Coteaching Model

During the 1999–2000 school year, we moved forward in our attempts to redesign the teacher education program around a nucleus of coteaching and to facilitate the emergence of communities of practice in the schools. High schools in Philadelphia are organized into small learning communities (SLCs), which effectively are schools within a school. An important step was the assignment of new teachers to an SLC rather than to an individual teacher. We wanted to acknowledge that teaching, and learning to teach, involved much more than working closely with a cooperating teacher. In these large high schools, the planning that occurs at the level of the SLC was considered to be critical. It made little sense to expect teachers to plan and teach in an interdisciplinary manner unless opportunities were provided for new teachers to learn to teach in such a manner.

Assignments of New Teachers

Teacher education was to be a transformative activity focused on improving learning. We wanted to avoid the perception that the assignment of new teachers to a school was in any way an encumbrance that was detrimental to this goal. Instead we assigned new teachers to SLCs; the coordinators distributed new teachers and practicing teachers so that coteaching would occur in such a way as to benefit the high school students.

In the planning stages, the notion of community was essential. Yet there were preconceptions that had to be overcome. To begin with, the school principal regarded it as a travesty that previous interns could not get positions in her school. Rather than viewing the university students as a transformative resource that had benefited high school students, she saw them as a tax on CHS that needed to be repaid. This was an initial challenge that we addressed aggressively, pointing out that 30 new teachers a year was a resource that could transform the school in otherwise impossible ways. After one semester, the principal was convinced by our results. Based on her initial beliefs about the interns, she had not permitted us to discuss placements with teachers and SLC coordinators until school had commenced. Not surprisingly, her decision to make the assignments without teachers and coordinators was inconvenient and jeopardized our efforts.

We endeavored to group six to eight new teachers in an SLC (consisting of three to four pairs of new teachers, seeking certification in science, mathematics, social science and English, respectively). Several constraints prevented us from enacting such a plan. For example, some new teachers were seeking certification in two of the curriculum areas, and in some SLCs a teacher from a particular certification area was regarded as unsuitable for supervising new teachers. Also, we had to adapt our plans to accommodate the unequal numbers of individuals seeking certification in each of the main four subject areas. We felt that new teachers would plan in teams, sometimes with their coop teachers and at other times with one another. Assigning the students in this way produced opportunities for planning to occur within the disciplines in which certification was sought and in interdisciplinary teams. Also, by assigning new teachers in teams within SLCs we believed they would have opportunities to learn more about the education of the whole child rather than just science education, for example.

Cooperating and new teachers arrived on the same day; the principal read out the assignments in a meeting. Only one teacher protested: A mathematics teacher announced publicly that she did not intend to accept a new teacher. The individual who had been assigned to that teacher was displeased with this unexpected turn of events, but we were able to assign him with relative ease to *Incentive* (despite our previous decision not to place new teachers in such difficult circumstances). This unexpected turn of events forced us to change the way we had intended to place new teachers. This individual did not have others with whom to plan since no other new teachers were assigned to this SLC. In many respects his assignment was consistent with past practices.

When we made the initial assignments we wanted a critical mass of new teachers within the school and within each small learning community. However, seldom was there a conscious effort to create a school-level community and in many cases professional development meetings for school staff overlooked new teachers or declare their attendance to be optional. Similarly, only two of the SLCs to which new teachers were assigned appeared to reap the benefits of creating a community in which planning occurred across the disciplines. The energy required to create and sustain new roles was considerable and unless we were prepared to negotiate new roles, new teaching tended to proceed in a traditional manner.

In the fall semester new teachers were assigned to teach for a half a day each day at one of two urban high schools; effectively they commenced at 8:30 a.m. and taught until 1:15 p.m. They were expected to coteach in at least two classes, one in which they assumed the principal responsibility for planning and the other in which their roles were more of a backup. During the third 90-minute period they could select what their roles would be in the SLC. In the spring semester the field experience was for the full day during the entire week, extending schedules by one class period. New teachers were to teach for two 90-minute periods, at least one of those involving coteaching. In a third period they were to plan for a school-based experience that would enhance their learning to teach. Some of the new teachers opted to teach in a different SLC, some cotaught with a different teacher or observed others teach, assisted in doing an inventory of equipment and supplies in the school, or participated in SLC-level activities.

Methods Course

During the 1998–99 school year, the teacher education students criticized the methods course. Ken had taught it at City High School and required students to bring issues and artifacts from their classrooms to facilitate a close connection between what we did in the course and what happened in the schools. But it did not work in the way he had planned.[29] The students seemed to be critical of their field placements and wanted something different from the methods course. Ken felt that they wanted recipes, and he was more inclined to teach them to think in new ways about teaching and learning—but within the context of what they were doing.

Ken knew from his work in other universities and from his previous years at Penn just how important it was to go and watch the new teachers teaching. Yet, he was not assigned to do this, and other priorities intervened, preventing him from observing new teachers to an appreciable extent in the first semester. This changed when Ken began to teach at City High School during the second semester; he now spent most of each day in classrooms. He also began to coteach with Cam, one of the new teachers in the program. Now the methods courses came to life—Ken was 'walking the walk', teaching himself and observing the new teachers.

During the 1999–2000 school year, Ken and Gale Seiler, an experienced urban educator and doctoral student at Penn, cotaught the course. They reconceptualized the science methods in order to address weaknesses that had emerged from our ongoing research. Their coteaching provided a first opportunity to view coteaching in action. The class met twice a week at CHS and, at times, included high school students as teacher educators. These high school students were to help the new teachers understand 'How to best teach students like us'. Ken and Gale strove to make the methods course responsive to students' needs, concerns, and difficulties by allowing the curriculum to emerge and by allotting considerable class time to coparticipatory activities.

Ken supervised five new teachers and taught the methods course. Including Gale as a coteacher meant that they would both be able to see each new teacher teach regularly and also bring much more of what they observed in the classroom into the methods course. Not only that, since Gale was an experienced and successful urban science teacher she would bring enormous credibility to the course and her background in biology would complement Ken's background in physics. This approach, which linked teach-

29   Tobin, Seiler, & Smith, 1999.

ing and the methods course, was very much appreciated as exemplified in the following quote:[30]

> What proved most beneficial about the methods course was its emphasis on reflection and its fluid (changing with the students' needs) nature. In taking the class I was not looking for suggestions about how to teach specific subjects. In other words, I did not deem it necessary for Gale and Ken to move step by step through the science curriculum offering pointers about what information to cover and how to cover it. Rather, I desired prompts that would encourage me to look at my teaching in-depth and from various perspectives. (Stephanie, teaching in the *Health* SLC, May 31, 2000)

Although Ken and Gale felt partially successful, they were not comfortable with the way the course was enacted. Students seemed to come in fatigued and it was too easy to discuss what happened in what Ken regarded as a superficial way. It was difficult to connect theory and research to the issues that arose and Ken often had the feeling that many of the students regarded the conversations as 'bull sessions'. Gale and Ken reflected on the methods course regularly. Looking back, the sessions that worked best were those where the students first planned something for their field experience, enacted it during the next few days, and then discussed how well it went during the next methods class. The following excerpt articulates, from the viewpoint of a person taking the course, its positive aspects:

> Gale and Ken designed several activities that required me to ask why I had chosen to implement certain lessons in my classroom. This was a crucial step in the trial and error process that I had previously neglected. If a lesson was not well received I tended to dismiss it as no good and look for a new idea. Reflecting on the relevance of lessons initiated several meaningful conversations between my classmates and me. Sharing how and why certain approaches were successful offered us insight about how we might mesh the ideas of others into our unique teaching styles. Rather than having methods forced upon me, I felt free to design my own lessons but was offered much-needed assistance in incorporating them in my urban classroom. (Stephanie, email, May 31, 2000)

---

30 To provide readers with a deeper understanding of particular experience, we use quotes from one new teacher, Stephanie, who features prominently in Chapters 5–8.

In most of the classes we visited, we could see evidence that the new teachers were involved in a methods course. The new teachers learned about particular trends or strategies and then enacted them in culturally appropriate ways. For example, one of Stephanie's major accomplishments was to establish a literacy wall and thereby to connect science to mainstream literacy education, a high priority for the students at CHS. Stephanie noted:

> Literacy was huge!! I would never have thought to place the much-needed emphasis on scientific literacy. Initially I believed that it would be difficult to incorporate science process skills into lessons that focused on scientific literacy. The methods course offered the resources and suggestions that permitted me to implement strategies that did just that. For example, I created an event-based lesson on the Exxon Valdez oil spill. Typically, I would have solely focused on the 'Operation Oil Spill Cleanup' labs, which required the students to hypothesize which supplies would most successfully contain and clean up the spill and then test them in a simulated spill. Discussions in the methods course prompted me to begin the lesson with an article on the Valdez spill. We focused on the language of the science initially, which I believe instilled confidence in the students and allowed them to feel like real experts. (Stephanie, email, June 7, 2000)

As we approached the end of the year, Ken was sure about what had to happen in the following year. On the basis of our ongoing research we were exploring the building of understanding (*praxeology*) in debriefing sessions involving all stakeholders who participate in a class. (We provide greater detail about the nature of these 'cogenerative dialoguing' sessions in Chapters 5–8, including a heuristic that allows us to monitor the functioning of these sessions [Table 5.2, p. 196].) From a distance it would be possible to say that what we were doing in methods class was very close to what we advocated for the *praxeology* sessions. We involved students as teacher educators in both the methods class and the sessions, and in both activities we endeavored to focus discussions on issues emerging from praxis. One difference was that the experiences discussed in methods were not shared to the extent we would want them to be shared in cogenerative dialoguing.

Careful research and evaluation of what we did during the past year suggests that we need to go even further in blurring the boundaries between methods course and field experience. To us this means make them the same. The heuristic for cogenerative dialoguing presented in Chapter 5 (Table 5.2, p. 196) provides a framework for planning ongoing discussions about what is happening in the field experiences. Co-planning during the methods course, however, may actually interfere with the learning of high school students. The essence of the new approach is to ensure that, as methods teachers, Gale and Ken are regularly teaching in the classes of those who are learning to teach. In addition, we believe that the new teachers need more time for discussions of this type and also time to do research on their own teaching and the learning of their students. Accordingly, in addition to a methods course in the fall, a more generic special-topics course in the spring provides the time for all these activities to occur. The following extract exemplifies the positive effect of the research on Stephanie's teaching assignment. Increasing opportunities to participate in action research will likely improve the environment for learning to teach science.

> Taping myself during three situations, full-class lecture, small group, and individual discussion, was probably the most helpful assignment of the year. In my analysis, I recognized that I allowed for practically no wait time and that I would ask simple questions. I also realized that I coddled the girls (led them right to the answers) while I expected the boys to find the answer for themselves. I was directly able to apply the results of this exercise to the classroom. (Stephanie, email, June 7, 2000)

In a revised approach, cogenerative dialoguing will occur intensively throughout the year and the intellectual efforts of the students can provide foci for discussion and critique. The inclusion of coops, students, SLC coordinators, and other stakeholders from the schools in which the new teachers are teaching will enhance the extent to which learning to teach is possible. The following comment speaks to the value of visiting others and learning from diverse experiences to complement coteaching assignments:

> One suggestion I would offer is to mandate cross observation of all students in the methods class. Although Gale and Ken encouraged us to visit other classrooms it was not required. In retrospect, I wish I had observed and participated with other Penn Interns in their science classrooms at City High and West. I think it would have added a more dynamic aspect to our class discussions if we had worked with each other and under-

stood one another's classroom environment. (Stephanie, email, May 30, 2000)

We agree with Stephanie's suggestion of visiting other teachers and within the framework of a year of field experience we will incorporate visits to other schools in which each new teacher will coteach for periods of 3–5 weeks (for one class period of 90 minutes a day). These cross visits will be scheduled on an individual basis over the year and will take place while an ongoing presence is maintained at CHS where all science students will have their primary assignments. The inclusion of more coop teachers will increase the opportunities to learn by teaching with others and in other places.

Coteaching

New teachers were encouraged to learn to teach by teaching. We wanted them to begin their teaching almost immediately—not to take over the control of an entire class but to teach at the elbow of the regular classroom teacher. We envisioned a peripheral (yet legitimate) participation in teaching and acknowledged from the outset that coteaching could be arranged differently in different places. In their roles as methods instructors, supervisors of new teachers, and researchers, Ken and Gale monitored closely what was happening in the classrooms. (In Chapter 5, we provide a heuristic that allows us to monitor the functioning of coteaching [Table 5.1, p. 189].) If they observed new teachers sitting, merely watching the class, they encouraged the new teachers to get up and assist with the teaching. As Ken and Gale moved from classroom to classroom they made efforts to tailor the participation of new teachers and coops in such a way that all were coteaching, that is, teaching at the others' elbows.

On this occasion coteaching was not defined in specific terms, leaving it instead for the participants within an SLC to work out the details to fit the circumstances and opportunities that emerged. In the conversations with new teachers and coops, Ken and Gale made it clear that coteaching involved teaching with another and that there were probably many ways to do this. Since the new teachers were in schools for the entire year there was the potential for different models of coteaching to emerge over time. Because the roles of participants (especially coop, new teacher, and supervisor) were not defined, there was an initial tendency to participate and enact teaching according to a *habitus* built elsewhere from a participant's experience of teaching, learning, and teacher education. Thus, coops sometimes left the room, leaving the new teacher on her own; or new teachers simply watched the teacher from a seat in the back. Supervisors also were encouraged to coteach rather than to effect evaluations by viewing teaching from the side or back of the classroom. The role of the supervisor was not so much to judge from the side as to facilitate conversations between coparticipants from with/in. We will return to the notion of supervising through coteaching in Chapter 8.

When we as university supervisors visited a class we encouraged new teachers and their coops to teach, to participate as teachers, to become teachers in the class with other teachers and in so doing, to build new *habitus* and associated room to maneuver (*Spielraum*). Given our open approach to role definition it is not surprising that coteaching evolved differently in different sites. In some instances coteaching was interpreted as teaching with another new teacher rather than coparticipating in a community of teachers. On other occasions the coop teacher participated by coteaching with the new teachers. Finally, there were very traditional arrangements in which the coop teacher placed greater value on learning first by observing and then allowing the new teacher to participate as an assistant, gradually allowing the new teacher to assume more control until s/he could teach alone. In such circumstances new teachers often felt disadvantaged with respect to their peers. Indeed, throughout the new teacher group there was a strong preference to be assigned to coop teachers in pairs.

In the process of learning to teach, new teachers regarded the cooperating teacher as a major resource. It was not unusual for new teachers to regard their coops as potential experts who would transfer their knowledge of teaching to the novice teacher.[31] Frequently, new teachers expressed disappointment at the quality of their coops. In our earlier experience of coteaching, we had not articulated a list of criteria that would define good coteaching. We

31 Seiler, in press.

needed to do more to ensure that coops and new teachers understood their roles in coteaching and how it is possible to learn to teach by coparticipating in a community that has the goal of learning to teach. The two heuristics for monitoring coteaching and cogenerative dialoguing, presented in the next chapter, go some way in assisting all participants to understand their roles.

Fine-Tuning the Assignments

Although we view the first teaching experiences in terms of their contribution to high school student learning, they also have the goal of helping new teachers learn to teach. As educators we focused on the quality of the learning environment and if it was not optimal we made changes as necessary to foster learning to teach. In some instances this required assignments to be changed. We made a distinctive and conscious break with tradition, where it had been expected that new teachers would overcome adversity; if they were unable to do so, it was taken as a sign of their unsuitability to be a teacher. We rejected the model of learning to teach that emphasizes the 'heroic individual' or 'lone ranger' in favor of forging new roles in which university supervisors would do what they could to optimize the environments in which learning to teach could occur.

Some problems emerged almost immediately when two new teachers seeking science certification, Donna and Elwyn, realized that they could not work together. (Elwyn was later assigned to Mario, who, in Chapter 3, reflects on the experience of having this beginning teacher in his class.) There was a personality clash and Donna quickly pointed out that she 'has worked with people like this forever and knew that it could not possibly work out'. Ken, to whom the request for reassignment was directed, had already experienced Elwyn as a difficult new teacher and was not surprised. Ken's initial efforts to reassign Donna were met with resistance from the SLC. 'Why reassign Donna if Elwyn is the problem?' The SLC coordinator was convincing, so we made plans to assign Elwyn to a different SLC. Since he was seeking certification in both mathematics and science, he was placed with two new teachers in each of these subject areas. Inadvertently we had pushed the coteaching model beyond the two new teachers per coop to a situation where we had three new teachers and a coop working collaboratively.

Donna remained in the original SLC and quickly found that she had a conflict of opinion with her coop. The problem on this occasion involved teaching style and beliefs about learning. Just as it was becoming apparent that the environment was not conducive to Donna's learning to teach, her coop requested that she be reassigned immediately. Reluctantly we searched the building for another site in which she could learn to teach. Donna joined the *Health* SLC where she taught mathematics in the fall and mathematics and science in the spring.

During the fall semester there were seven new teachers teaching science at City High School. Three were assigned to *Science and Technology (SAT)*, two to *Health,* and two to a third SLC. The next section contains an ethnography of learning to teach, primarily in the *SAT* and *Health* SLCs at City High. We describe new teachers' perceptions of City High School as a site for learning to teach in terms of a discussion of resources, the role of expectations of teachers and students in relation to enacted curricula, the management of diversity, and the roles of participants.

Learning to Teach

The tenets underlying our philosophy of learning to teach have evolved over the past three years. Our principal belief is that one learns to teach by teaching. We regard urban schools as *event-full* in the sense that there always is so much happening in any class that it is virtually impossible to take advantage of all of the learning opportunities or to notice and respond appropriately to misbehavior. The wide range of events makes urban schools ideal places to learn to teach as long as the events are manageable. Accordingly, we believe that new teachers should be assigned in pairs so that they can learn by coteaching with a cooperating teacher. This implies teaching in pairs or even threes. During the present year we even have had circumstances in which more than three teachers taught a class (one coop plus three new teachers).

The following comment is typical of those made about the field experience and highlights the strangeness factor and also the potential of coteaching as a way of learning to teach:

> Not only is it providing a completely different learning structure compared to my high school experience but also I like the idea of learning to teach with another new teacher. I feel like even if I do mess up during class I will have the support and understanding of someone who is going through the same things with me right there in the classroom. (Mark, May 30, 2000)

Roles of Participants

Changing the setup of the internship in terms of coteaching also required us to rethink the roles of the different people involved in teacher education. Change in the roles of teacher educators, coops, high school students, and supervisors cannot occur through prescription, nor does it happen overnight. All people involved have to change their habits and their *habitus*. This takes time. Coteaching is not a panacea that automatically yields solutions to the enduring problems of teacher education. Rather, it is a different way of doing and conceptualizing teacher education. As such, time and reflective discussions among insiders (i.e., *with/in* communities) are essential to align the roles of participants and to effect coparticipation oriented toward learning to teach.

So often in the past coops have perceived having a new teacher as an opportunity to give over their classes to the new teacher while they catch up on tasks that might otherwise not get done at all or would have to be done on their own time. Our emphasis on coteaching was designed to actively involve the coops in facilitating the learning to teach of the new teachers while raising the potential that the coops, too, would learn and improve their teaching. However, we did not communicate this goal sufficiently clearly, and in any event, past practices do not easily change. Accordingly, there were too many instances such as the one described below:

> My coop's objectives and direction for this class were unclear and it was quite obvious that she was not working from any short- or long-term plan. So, I offered to create a few lessons for the class. In preparing

a few lessons during this period, I enabled her to leave the classroom and not have to teach. She quickly took this opportunity to attend to her work as SLC coordinator. (William, October 19, 1999)

In the present year we decided to commence the teaching experience when the teachers arrived at the school. We wanted our new teachers to experience and learn about the start-up of a school year, the initial meetings of principal and faculty, and the arrival of the students. One disadvantage of this was that there was no chance for new teachers to meet their coops before the start of the school year. Since we were dealing with numerous teachers who had not previously been involved as coops, there was an initial period of role ambiguity in which teachers had a new school year with which to contend and the presence of new teachers whom they had not previously met. Although we perceived new teaching as a highly valuable and potentially transformative activity, many of the teachers viewed new teaching through traditional lenses and regarded it as potentially disruptive to the ongoing program and a professional obligation that was to be tolerated only once in a while.

The failure to establish rapport between the new teachers and the coops led to problems that had to be addressed in a significant number of cases, especially when teachers had not recently or ever before been involved as coops. In some instances new teachers and coops could not establish a basis for collaboration, and new assignments within the school were necessary. Ideally, new teachers and potential coops would meet to discuss the deployment of new teachers in their SLCs, the goals to be pursued, the associated roles to be enacted, and the expectations of all participants. This may remain a problem in schools where faculty turnover is high and the field experience is for a full year. The magnitude of the problems should diminish as the participating schools develop a tradition of working with a cadre of new teachers that is about 30% the size of the school faculty.

Because new roles have to be negotiated there may be times when the participants are uncomfortable in making changes. For example, Ken focused his role as a supervisor on the building of community in each of the sites in which new teachers were placed. Instead of adhering to the traditional supervisor role of scheduling visits to observe teaching, he visited most classes of the new teachers each day for periods of 15–20 minutes. During his visits he interacted with the coop and new teachers and, as the lesson was taught, he coparticipated as a teacher. He perceived his principal role as being a mediator of the roles of the coop, new teachers, students and other faculty in the SLC. Through his presence he was able to make suggestions on how to structure the resources so as to maximize the opportunities for teachers to learn from one another and enhance the learning opportunities for the high school students. His position as director of teacher education allowed him to change his roles without the worry of what others might think. However, he felt uncertain at times and constantly examined his participation in terms of his beliefs about teaching as praxis and learning to teach. The pressure to adopt more conventional roles as *an expert on the side* was pervasive and evident in the expectations of coops, new teachers, other practicing teachers, school administrators, and colleagues and administrators within the university. (See also Chapter 8 for coteaching as a way of supervising and evaluating teaching.)

Our widespread adoption of learning to teach based on coteaching has shown that there are different ways of organizing coops and new teachers (at different places along the continua of teacher performance). Despite differences, the coteaching teams facilitate the learning of high school science students and, in so doing, learn from one another. However, to maximize the effectiveness of coteaching it is clear that all participants need to actively raise questions about roles (especially university supervisors, coops, new teachers, and high school students) as resources to support learning to teach. One cannot overemphasize the significance of conversations about roles and the reasons why some roles are more important than others. We find salience in the concepts of being *with* others *in* a community, *habitus*, and *Spielraum*. It is not only important to explain to each person what they might do to facilitate learning to teach but also to explain why particular ways of participating are more likely to be beneficial than others. It is in the explication of why particular roles might be productive that theorizing can be beneficial. Although it is accepted that there are multiple ways of participating appropriately with the goal of learning to teach it is also a truism that there are multiple ways of participating that will not be productive. Accordingly it is desirable that discussions among participants *with/in* a community focus on the rationale for the most salient roles and associated modes of coparticipation. It is out of these discussions that we see evolving a viable discourse, a *praxeology* (praxis + *logos*, talk) in the true sense of the word. Our teams, coops, new teachers, supervisors, and so on develop praxis-relevant understanding rather than theory (which does not account for the particulars of a setting that determine the suitability of each practical move).

Teaching Science in *Health*

Bert has been teaching science at City High School for more than 30 years. He is an experienced coop and although new teachers are very fond of him, there are veiled criticisms about aspects of his competence as a science teacher. He is often perceived as not being an exemplary teacher and therefore not an ideal 'coop'. Critical comments about his teaching included references to a lax approach to discipline, limitations in his background knowledge of some of the disciplines of science (e.g., chemistry), and a tendency to teach off the cuff. However, Bert was willing to accommodate the goals of new teachers and organized his classes to allow them to teach for the entire year. In the two years prior to our adoption of a coteaching policy in the teacher education program, Bert had been the coop for pairs of new teachers with whom he had cotaught (i.e., he pioneered some of our early work on coteaching). Even though these new teachers were occasionally critical of aspects of Bert's science teaching, it was apparent that their teaching blossomed in comparison to that of their peers. The contexts created in Bert's classes seemed ideal for learning to teach. This year was no different. Stephanie and Sonny, two new teachers seeking certification to teach biology, were assigned to *Health* with Bert as 'coop'.

From the very beginning, Bert handed over the responsibility for planning to Stephanie and Sonny. Despite initial disappointments, the new teachers soon began to appreciate the opportunities of learning by working with others:

I must admit when I first began working with Bert and Sonny I was somewhat disappointed. Due to his thirty-year veteran status, I had expected Bert to be brimming with insight. It appeared, however, that all of those years had worn him out. Sonny was extraordinarily shy and reluctant to take the lead. I wondered how this coteaching experience was going to teach me anything when it seemed that I was the only one inspired to work at improving the status quo. Over time, however, I believe that the communal experience was of benefit to each of us. We learned to appreciate each other's talents and craft our individual praxis so that it best met the students' needs. What I learned through coteaching was that permitting others to openly critique and evaluate my pedagogy was the best resource for improving my teaching. After a lesson, Sonny, Bert and I would offer our critique and reflect on ways it could be improved. This open communication seemed to inspire each of us to try methods that previously we may have avoided. Bert, for example, would often remark, "You two are so creative and I'm not. I have to just stick to my old ways." After a few months of collaborating, however, his lessons veered away from continuous lecturing and book work, to activities compatible with cooperative learning. While the classroom initially overwhelmed Sonny, she researched topics thoroughly and offered me technical assistance, a skill I much desired to improve. (Stephanie, June 9, 2000)

Because of her prior experience as a teacher in a private school, Stephanie seized the initiative and, before long, her mark on the class was apparent. She planned thoroughly and was innovative in her efforts to create an environment in which students would be interested in science and challenged. Bert facilitated Stephanie's teaching by being enthusiastic about her ideas and Sonny provided support in enacting them. Stephanie and Sonny were willing to enact teaching in ways that were consistent with the theoretical precepts discussed in their methods courses. Because Bert was always inclined to try something that made sense to him, the classroom environment was transformed during the fall semester. For example, the three teachers broke each 90-minute class period into relatively short 15–20-minute activities and, in an endeavor to maintain student focus and engagement they set aside the initial activity each day for the problem of the day. This allowed students to review what they knew from previous lessons and settle down as they entered the classroom. Also, Stephanie and Sonny responded to a school-wide emphasis on reading and literacy with a daily 15-minute activity that focused on the creation of a vocabulary wall. Here, essential scientific terms were displayed to enable students to focus on how to read and write them and ensure that students could provide definitions and use them appropriately in sentences.

As a team, Stephanie, Sonny, and Bert regularly reviewed their experiences of coteaching and possible ways to organize the curriculum to enhance the learning of their students. Their conversations were reflections on what had happened in the previous lessons and focused on their shared experiences that had arisen from *being-in* this classroom *with* their partners. The conversations included plans on what, when, and how to teach the next classes, the problems that were to be addressed, and the roles each of them would assume. Ken's role as supervisor was to coteach rather than observe passively, which allowed him to experience the events from *being-in/with*, giving him a better position to subsequently facilitate conversations between the team of three that directly focused on their roles and goals. These conversations included discussions of curricular ideas that would connect their activities to district standards, of how to manage particular learners who were experiencing difficulties in learning or who were preventing others from learning, and of how to make the classroom discourse to be more science-like.

As problems arose they were identified and resolved through discussion. For example, there was a concern that Sonny was not pulling her weight as a teacher. Stephanie was doing a disproportionate amount of the teaching and Sonny was inclined to stand back. In his role as supervisor, Ken made this issue explicit in one-on-one discussions with Stephanie and Bert. When Ken sought Sonny's perspective she explained aggressively that she was learning a great deal and, for the time being, was more comfortable in a backup role. However, the discussions between pairs facilitated the raising of the issue by Sonny in a meeting of the three teachers. A plan was then devised to ensure that each of them assumed the primary responsibility for one class and backup responsibility for others.

The roles of new teacher, coop, and supervisor have adapted to incorporate coparticipation *with* others *in* a community. There is increased recognition of the goal of building *habitus* and *Spielraum* and less of an emphasis on learning techniques from an exemplary coop and applying methods suggested by university instructors. All three teachers learned from one another, even though Stephanie consistently demonstrated leadership throughout the semester and Bert and Sonny showed in their teaching that they were learning from her. Similarly, Stephanie was a highly motivated learner, and changes in the way she taught were apparent throughout the semester. The enacted curriculum showed evidence of Stephanie having learned from listening astutely to advice from Bert, Sonny, Ken, and her methods instructor. Also, consistent with Michael's experiences with coteaching, all three participants showed evidence of having learned from one another (especially from Stephanie). Because Stephanie had been teaching at the elbows of Bert and Sonny, and at times Ken, there was evidence, too, that Stephanie's interactions with students changed and Bert's approach was noticeable in Stephanie's approach to managing students.

Teaching Science in *Science and Technology*

Initially we assigned two science teachers to *Science and Technology* (*SAT*); however, because of the reassignment of Elwyn to *SAT*, this SLC had three new teachers soon after the start of the semester. Mark and Andy were seeking certification in general science and chemistry while Elwyn was seeking certification in physics, general science, and mathematics. Mario, the science teacher in *SAT*, was certified in general science and biology. The rationale in teaming up new teachers seeking certification in areas other than biology was that as a group the coop and the three new teachers had expertise in all of the subject areas that would be taught during the year. In addition, Elwyn had considerable expertise in computer science and was able to offer to teach special computer-oriented electives.

Ken was nervous about having four teachers coteaching at the same time. Accordingly, he met with Mario to arrange a roster whereby his second period class, in which all three new teachers were assigned to teach science, would be broken down into two halves. This arrangement enabled each of two coteaching pairs (two new teachers, and Mario plus a new teacher, respectively) to teach a half-class. That arrangement appealed to the SLC coordinator, Mario, and the new teachers. Accordingly, we enacted it. In a third period Andy, Mark, and Mario cotaught for the entire semester.

From the outset Andy and Mark took the task of coteaching very seriously as they planned together in detail and approached the in-class assignments collaboratively. They worked within the SLC like seasoned teachers and participated in a full range of professional activities (e.g., SLC-level meetings, field trips, before and after school tutoring of students, parents' night). A more difficult part of the coteaching experience concerned the role of Mario. The following excerpt from an interview with Mark captures some aspects of the respective roles of the new teachers and Mario when the three of them were scheduled to coteach:

> Mario seems to think that we will take over his classes and that he can sit in the back unless 'a fight breaks out' (his words) and then he'll save the day. To date, he is either ON (full charge of class; we act as TAs) or OFF (he's either physically not present or mentally not participating). When we offer ideas, he tells us to run with them, and wants it to take the whole period, even if it is a simple demonstration. He usually doesn't even want to know exactly what we are doing beforehand, and I need to press him to even look over my plan and worksheets. Unfortunately, when we ask for the coop's input on how we can better control the class, he undermines us by telling the class that they will be punished for not having listened to us. Once he gave a pop-quiz and canceled a lab 'because they didn't listen to us' when in truth he didn't even have the lab ready and the quiz didn't even cover the material we had tried to go over—so those kids who listened weren't rewarded. (Mark, May 30, 2000)

Mark's concerns are similar to those raised by Cam in the previous year and those experienced by Ken when he cotaught with Mario. Mario was willing to allow new teachers to learn by teaching and to remain in the background himself. If he perceived he was needed, it was usually because of misbehavior of students. On such occasions he intervened in his own way, in a style that was grounded in what worked for him as a teacher. Mark and Andy coined the metaphor *bear wrestler* to describe Mario's approach to classroom management. The essence of the metaphor is that Mario used his physical stature to present himself as an authority figure and to assert his power as teacher. (He spread his legs, positioned his feet firmly, and endeavored to maximize his size.) His stance was aggressive and he raised his voice to control student noise and movement about the class. Neither Mark nor Andy believed this to be an appropriate way for them to teach and when they endeavored to discuss with Mario how they might teach differently he was not well equipped to participate in *praxeology*. Most of Mario's knowledge of teaching was grounded in praxis and he did not have a strong background in educational theory or research. When Ken joined Mario, Mark, and Andy to discuss teaching, Mario tended to fade into the background or busy himself with other tasks. Mario was willing and able to discuss students, curricular planning, and enactment to a certain extent, but he was usually at a loss for words when it came to discussing teaching and learning roles and strategies.

Mario continued to either take center stage or sit at the back, at the side, or in the faculty lounge during his coteaching assignments. Mario's roles were a concern for Ken, who continued to coteach in the classroom whenever he found the time. However, it was not until the second semester that Ken directly addressed the issue with Mario. Ken's reluctance to address the issue directly was related to his goal that each coop should have the chance to enact coteaching in ways that made sense to him/her. Mario had taken on three new teachers and each of them was learning a great deal by teaching in the SLC. However, in the second semester a social studies teacher, who also was seeking certification in science, made arrangements to teach in *SAT* for one period a day. He joined what was already the most concentrated site for coteaching.

Unlike each of the other three new science teachers, this new teacher was timid and relatively unsuccessful in his teaching. The students were out of control when he taught and Mario was becoming quite critical of the new teacher's efforts. 'Why don't you teach right there at his elbow?' Ken asked. Mario considered Ken's suggestion and agreed that the best way to proceed was to coteach in an active manner. The strategy worked out by Mario and Ken was for Mario to lead and for the new teacher to assist to the fullest extent possible. However, at that time it became evident that the new teacher retreated as soon as Mario assumed a central role. For example, if Mario spoke to the class, rather than standing right next to him the new teacher retreated to the side of the class and effectively handed over complete control to Mario. Similarly, when Ken taught in the class the new teacher assumed a position that was not that of a teacher. The inability of the new teacher to adopt a role of shared responsibility forced our hand. We felt a great need for our research to catalyze change in what was happening. Developing a heuristic for coteaching and one for *praxeology* was therefore a high priority for us so that we could use it as a means to discuss what was being done by the participants in regards both to these activities and to what might be done to fine-tune practices.

CHAPTER 5

Learning to Teach Science
in an Urban School

Our purpose in this chapter is to articulate the great potential of coteaching/cogenerative dialoguing in preparing new teachers for the challenges in urban schools. We begin by articulating the particular challenges presented by the nature of urban schools and the students who attend them. An ethnography of learning to teach follows, in which we describe how Stephanie, a new teacher at City High School, enacted a curriculum that was culturally relevant for her African American students, acknowledged their minority status in respect of science, and enabled them to pursue the school district standards. We draw on a lesson of monohybrid crosses in genetics and the associated cogenerative-dialoguing session about the praxis of teaching to exemplify several key issues.

At best there have been modest gains in the quality of urban science education despite the concerted efforts of funding agencies, policymakers, teacher educators, teachers, and educational researchers. Without diminishing the efforts of agencies or hardworking professionals, our ongoing ethnographic work shows that a visit to an urban high school is all that it takes to reveal that we still are in the midst of a crisis. The problems of urban schools are pervasive and include inadequate funding, teacher shortage, lack of resources, and high proportions of students from conditions of poverty. Regrettably the problems reflect deep issues concerning race and social and cultural factors that are at the core of life in

the United States.[1] As large cities in the United States and elsewhere struggle to provide high-quality education they are too often
faced by shrinking budgets and shortages of well-qualified teachers, especially in science. According to the 1990 U.S. census about
75% of the U.S. population lives in urban areas. However, a critical issue relates to education in the largest cities in the United
States where the number of children living in poverty is significant.
For example,

> the total population of children in New York, Los Angeles, Chicago,
> Houston, and Philadelphia is in excess of four million. Most of these
> children live in poverty, sometimes extreme poverty. The magnitude of
> this problem is illustrated by the following: four out of every 270 Ameri-
> cans is a poor child living in one of the country's five largest cities; most
> of these children come from minority backgrounds, and the overwhelming
> number of them attend or will attend public schools.[2]

These problems can be understood in terms of the concept of
'underclass', a heterogeneous group of people who are socially
isolated in highly concentrated poverty areas in the inner city.[3]
The underclass is populated almost exclusively by the most disadvantaged segments of the Black urban community, having a
marginal economic position and a weak attachment to the labor
force that is uniquely reinforced by the neighborhood or social mi-
lieu in which they live. Our study explores learning to teach in
schools whose students are largely from the underclass and which
are situated in or adjacent to urban communities in which poverty
is highly concentrated.

Paolo Freire showed that a transformative education has the
potential to take people out of poverty, and therefore allow them
to move out of the underclass.[4] Having a pool of well-educated
teachers to teach in urban schools, especially in those large cities
in which poverty levels are significant, must therefore be a priority. What are not acknowledged in addressing this priority are the
characteristics of urban schools that might necessitate a different
approach to teacher education. This is especially likely to be the

---

1   Pinar & Bowers, 1992.
2   Cookson & Shroff, 1997, p. 1.
3   On the notion and sociology of the underclass, see Harris, 1992, and Wilson,
     1987.
4   Freire, 1972.

case when the majority of students are African Americans for whom schooling may be an agency of hegemony.[5] African American students are required to attend school and participate according to others' standards of what is and is not appropriate. There is little acknowledgment of the culture of African American students as incommensurable with mainstream culture.[6] Even though all students are required to adhere to the rules and conventions of schooling, it is difficult for African American underclass students to make adjustments from their primary *habitus* to the *habitus* of schools, even in schools comprising almost 100% African American students.

In this situation, one of the great challenges for teaching and teacher education comes from the fact that those interested in teaching are not from the underclass. Class differences are *the* major contributing factors to the re/production of middle-class values in schools and the re/production of inequities.[7] Teachers generally have little or no knowledge of what to expect from students who have lived part or all of their lives in circumstances of poverty. To become a teacher in an urban setting, one therefore has to learn to put aside prejudices and tendencies toward deficit models of dealing with students from the underclass.

Home and School: Different Cultures and Discourses

There are decided advantages to viewing science teaching and learning as forms of enculturation into a community with its own discursive practices (e.g., talk, writing, cognition, argumentation, and re-presentation). 'Discourse' is a sociocultural and political entity that subsumes ways of saying, writing, doing, being, valuing, and believing.[8] Thus, discourse facilitates communication and establishes social and cultural identity within a community. Attention to the nature of different discourses is important, for they not only communicate ideas, but, importantly, they construct personal Selves and relations to others.[9]

---

5   Apple, 1979.
6   Boykin, 1986.
7   Bourdieu & Passeron, 1979.
8   The New London Group, 1996.
9   Roth & Harama, 2000.

Two broad types of discourse exist: primary discourses
(learned in the home) and secondary discourses (associated with
other communities, such as classes in which students learn science). Primary discourses play a critical role in learning a secondary discourse. Students who are able to use in school the language they speak at home and in the streets are more likely to develop literacy skills that are a foundation for building more canonical, mainstream discourses; these students succeed even if
schools fail to teach anything.[10] Pierre Bourdieu and Jean-Claude
Passeron suggest that this is so because the difference between the
two discourses is small, leading to less symbolic violence experienced by students, and requiring less pedagogical work from the
teacher.[11] Differences between primary and secondary discourses
have also been observed in science education; that is, the primary
discourses of students from homes of working class or unemployed adults do not to interface well with scientific discourse.
Teachers of such students tend to enact curricula that emphasize
the acquisition of scientific facts and de-emphasize conceptual
learning, inquiry, and scientific habits of mind.[12] Since the conventions of an evolving classroom community might not be transpar-
ent to lower-class students, a high priority is for teachers to make
explicit the rules for participation in science activities.

Because students from circumstances of poverty often enter
school science with discursive resources that differ considerably
from those that schools or science legitimate, they may experience
difficulties in seeing the relevance of activities and in making sense
of science. If school science reflects White, middle-class experiences, and has little relevance to the lives of students from the
homes of the working class and unemployed, there is a risk that
participation in the curriculum will re/produce social and cultural
hierarchies and push these students even further toward the mar-
gins. To counter such tendencies, it has been suggested that 'the
experiences of everyone need to become part of the language of
science if the experiences, beliefs, values and essence of all people
are truly to be incorporated into science'.[13] Consequently, in the

---

10   See Becker, 1972, and Giroux, 1992.
11   Bourdieu & Passeron, 1979.
12   Lemke, 1990.
13   Barton, 1997, p. 155.

process of participating in a science curriculum, learning can be enhanced if students are encouraged to use their primary language resources and the *habitus* of their lifeworld.

Cultural Capital

In this context, 'cultural capital' is an important concept, which is used to describe resources that are desirable, beneficial, and regarded as possessing a high measure of integral worth within a community.[14] In addition to the material artifacts that surround us, these resources include social behavior, language, commonly held values, ethics, moral codes and socially ratified goals, aspirations and beliefs, and other factors that combine to constitute a cohesive, recognized group cultural identity. Students from upper-middle- and upper-class families possess a cultural advantage in terms of school-related success that lower-class students do not; schools tend to reward those who demonstrate knowledge and appreciation of upper-middle- and upper-class culture. This contention is supported by research on social class: the upper-middle-class model of success is the primary cultural norm in schools where students who deviate from expected behavioral patterns are devalued. For example, the interactional patterns of working-class youth in urban high schools differed significantly from those of middle-class youth who find their own same-age preferences reinforced in the organization of schooling.[15] In contrast, the multi-age, within- and across-family groupings of working-class and inner city youth actively interfere with schools, leading to a further differentiation of the language particularities between middle- and working-class students.

Cultural capital can be used to explain how cultural funds of knowledge, brought from students' home lives, provide a basis for making sense of what happens at school, and constitute the building blocks on which new knowledge can grow.[16] This cultural capital includes all that students know and can do based on their sociocultural existence within communities that are saturated with

---

14 Bourdieu, 1992a.
15 Eckert, 1989.
16 O. Lee, 1999.

practices and associated beliefs and values. However, any theoretical model for teaching and learning of African Americans has
to take account of the unique niche they occupy in society. They
occupy a unique niche because 'One ever feels his twoness—an
American, a Negro; two souls, two thoughts, two unreconciled
strivings; two warring ideals in one dark body, whose dogged
strength alone keeps it from being torn asunder'.[17] Boykin asserts
that African Americans have to integrate three divergent psychological perspectives, which he calls mainstream, minority, and
Black cultural.[18] Each of these perspectives is discussed in the
context of planning and enacting a high school science curriculum.

Mainstream Perspectives

If science is to be transformative it is essential that African Americans learn it in such a way that it provides them with options
about their lifestyles, careers, and possibilities for further education. Teachers cannot turn their backs on the expectations of the
community for science education. On the contrary, all Americans,
including African Americans, should attain goals that are appropriate for all Americans. In order to avoid racial stereotyping,
Boykin recommends that teachers consider four dichotomies (not
one or the other, both/and) pertaining to the performance of African American students. These dichotomies are what they do and
do not do, what they can and cannot do, what they will or will
not do, and what they should and should not do. Conversations
between teachers typically describe what students do in minimal-
ist terms and identify what they cannot do as deficits. Boykin
notes that a deficiency approach does little more than find fault
with African Americans, fails to take account of the cultural
foundations for their participation in academic tasks, and is supported by the underlying ideology of mainstream America.

---

17   Du Bois, 1903, p. 17.
18   Boykin, 1986.

Minority Perspectives

African Americans are underrepresented in terms of their achievement in science (K–12) and their participation in science, science-related careers, and further education in science. Furthermore, because of the historical role of science in identifying African Americans as inferior to Euro-Americans it is little wonder that many African Americans are marginalized with respect to the community of science.[19] Boykin notes the importance of addressing their marginality by encouraging their participation in science activities in ways that encourages the attainment of goals associated with both mainstream and African American perspectives.

African American Perspectives

According to Boykin, nine characteristics have salience for the psychology of African Americans: spirituality, harmony, movement, verve, affect, communalism, expressive individualism, oral tradition, and social time perspective. In essence Boykin is describing aspects of the *habitus* of African Americans. If teachers are to make science education culturally relevant, then they need to understand how each of these factors can connect to science and the lifeworlds of students. For example, Carol Lee examined signifying as one particular aspect of knowledge available to support the learning of African American students.[20] She shows that signifying, a figurative type of language use characterized by the application of metaphors, tropes, and irony, requires enormous dexterity in the use of language, abstract thinking, and complex modes of interpreting abstract text. These language skills are closely associated with the processing skills needed to be successful in science and are used implicitly by students when they participate in cultural traditions such as the dozens, make sense of rap songs, and participate in the hip hop culture. If African American students are to attain higher levels of success in science, they must come to know science in terms of their own cultural capital. However, once connections are made between science and

19   Stepan & Gilman, 1993.
20   C. Lee, 1992.

the African American culture, it is essential that African American students continue to learn science in ways that reflect the mainstream culture.

Approach to Teacher Education

A relevant urban teacher education needs to address the challenges posed by urban schools in order to prevent teacher burnout and early withdrawal from the profession. In the past, many school-university collaborations have enacted a sink-or-swim approach to student teaching and internships. Given the current problems in urban schools, such an approach cannot be viable. As we described in the previous chapter, we have adapted the teacher education program at Penn over the past three years to better prepare new teachers and to make use of their potential as transformative resources in urban high schools.

Enacting Culturally Relevant Curricula

According to Boykin, if African Americans are to succeed in social institutions such as schools, it is necessary that they integrate the three divergent psychological realities that he referred to as mainstream, minority, and Black cultural. Stephanie, who adopted what might be referred to as a 'both/and' approach to learning, stressed the mainstream interests in a science curriculum to a significant extent. For example, while emphasizing that the science activities should connect with the lives of the students, Stephanie also emphasized the school district's benchmarks. Furthermore, she encouraged full participation of her students in a subject area in which African Americans have been underrepresented, in an institution that was instrumental in propagating racist 'facts' about the alleged inferiority of African Americans and that unscrupulously undertook unethical experiments on African Americans.[21] More than any other school subject, science is a potential source of symbolic violence for African Americans. However, in Stephanie's enacted science curriculum most activities encouraged

---

21   Manning, 1993.

full participation of African Americans and created for them rich images of potential careers and further studies in science. Thus, the students had opportunities to achieve the benchmarks. In addition, as is clear from the examples provided below, the science activities also were relevant to many of the psychological components of African American culture (i.e., catered to aspects of their *habitus*).

I learned a great deal as a result of my teaching at City High School. Even though I had taught in a suburban private school for three years prior to seeking my certification in biology and general science, I found from the outset that my teaching habitus was inappropriate in urban schools.

One of the most influential bits of advice Bert offered me at the start of the school year was to learn to appreciate noise. He said, 'Noise can be a good thing, don't be afraid of it'. After observing neighboring classrooms in which the teacher wasted an inordinate amount of time and energy by demanding absolute silence, I became especially appreciative of Bert's guidance. It seemed that it was not only difficult for African American students to remain quiet but uncomfortable, even unnatural. Recognizing my students' propensity for making noise, I attempted to create science lessons that celebrated rather than squelched their vivacity. One such lesson was implemented in ninth-grade biology and focused on fertilization, pollination, and the parts of a flower. I deemed it necessary to thoroughly cover this material because it constituted a significant proportion of the school district standards and was to be covered on an upcoming citywide science exam. In what had seemed to me the most mundane of topics in my learning experience, I searched for a way to incorporate the students' love of performance into the instruction of standard botany. After having the students practice reproductive terminology by examining live flowers and sketching the events of cross- and self-pollination, they had gained enough background knowledge to take the lead. They were given free domain of a table buried in craft supplies and given only one instruction, to develop a visual lesson that would teach younger students the principles of fertilization and the roles of male and female flower parts. The explosion of learning that resulted was phenomenal. Each student decided to work within a group. They utilized their notebooks and textbooks in order to create an informative and factually correct dialogue. Whether they developed a puppet show, parody of a sitcom or ABC after school special, the students were completely engaged in learning science. One group titled their presentation, 'Plant Fertilization, Now That's Safe Sex', and rapped their information while another group designed hand puppets and sang to their composition, 'The Flight of a Bumble Bee'. When I accompanied this same class on city beautification day, I witnessed several students picking flowers and reciting the exact lyrics that their classmates had belted out nearly three months earlier.

When I began a discussion on weather systems, I was dismayed that none of our 11th-graders could define 'precipitation' although they all agreed that they had heard it several times. One student's response to my apparent disbelief was, 'I watch the weather every night, but I just look for the temp and whether I see a little red umbrella or not'. In an effort to engage the class in the weather unit I asked the students to keep a week-long journal of terms that were used by meteorologists on TV. Many students seemed to enjoy the task, explaining that their parents and siblings would shout out words while they recorded them ferociously. Once the students had collaborated on a master list of weather terminology, I incorporated each word into a lesson. Building functional barometers, for example, covered the topics of barometric pressure and humidity. In fact, by the end of the unit the students had constructed an entire weather station that enabled them to keep a log of changes in atmospheric conditions. At the culmination of the two-week unit, groups of three students were videotaped giving a report on a city whose weather conditions they had been following. As usual, the students' creativity astounded me as they gathered props (mittens, raincoats, and sunglasses), designed weather tables, and sang catchy jingles to introduce their broadcast.

Tacitly Stephanie seemed to be responsive to several of the salient dispositions identified by Boykin. For example, she gave all students opportunities to be emotional, expressive, and responsive by creating models that were intended to be aesthetically pleasing. In terms of verve, Stephanie frequently involved students in high-energy activities in which they were required to re-present what they had learned by building models, preparing posters for the wall, and teaching their understanding of science to others. She also encouraged a sense of community and social connectedness in her students by having them work in groups and negotiate class rubrics for daily participation grades and rules for behavior. Because she believed in the importance of making it possible for students to be successful by re-presenting what they had learned in a variety of ways, individuals were encouraged to personalize their performance in science and to express their individualism.

I knew intuitively that my students were capable speakers and I allowed them to speak freely in class. My lessons were interactive and I actively encouraged students to speak out on what they knew and what they wanted to know. A good example of a lesson sequence in which students capitalized on their oral aptitude involved food, health and nutrition. I commenced the lesson sequence with an investigation of the labels on food. I wanted to bring math into the process of reading food labels, an idea that was suggested by the students. Although I was initially dismayed by the students' math skills, they worked hard to figure out percentages, fractions, and decimals required to complete their graphs. However, the students were interested in comparing the diets of Americans and Chinese. While they were completing their work, they had lengthy discussions about their own eating habits and how they could improve them. Students who finished early copied their graph onto an overhead transparency and I invited them to present their information to the class. This set the scene as if it were a professional conference; the audience (including the principal) fired questions at the presenters and students were permitted to participate in a mode in which most tended to excel.

An activity sequence on the Exxon Valdez oil spill enabled me to be sensitive to numerous aspects of the African American cultural attributes. For example, when I learned that the students did not know much at all about the disaster I allowed them to have three class periods to study the event rather than the one period I had planned for the activity. My event orientation was in contrast to an alternative that might have adhered to the planned time irrespective of the extent to which students had the prior knowledge and strong interests in learning about the issue.

This activity was also ideal because it was a clear example of mankind being out of harmony with nature. The African American preference for harmony with nature and not manipulating and controlling it can come to the fore in an activity like this one. Not surprisingly, the affective side of African Americans also surfaced when searches on the web identified narratives written by Alaskans who were adversely affected by the disaster. Thus, this activity catered to six of the nine psychological dispositions identified by Boykin: harmony, affect, communalism, social time, oral expression, and expressive individualism.

The lesson was successful because it was event based. When my Philadelphia students read the reflections of their Alaskan counterparts, the tragedy seemed to hit closer to home. In their journal writings the majority of the class discussed the importance of preventing another spill and the need for creating more effective measures for containing and cleaning-up oil.

Throughout the year there were many examples of Stephanie making the curriculum relevant to the students and having them learn science that was potentially transformative to them. Perhaps the SLC theme of 'health' facilitated this trend. The students were interested in learning about themselves and issues associated with African American people. When Stephanie questioned her students about how they would create their own culturally relevant Biology curriculum, the students identified the following as crucial components: labeling of food, heart disease, sex education, and the contributions of Black scientists. One activity that was potentially transformative was a sequence of lessons on asthma:

> Witnessing the battle several of my students waged with asthma, I incorporated a series of lessons focusing on the illness and its link to the African American population. In order to hypothesize about their race's disposition to asthma, the class examined trends in diet, living conditions and geography, while simultaneously exploring the disease's physiological effects.

Coteaching of Genetics

In the course of our work we developed a coteaching heuristic by closely examining videotapes of coteaching involving new teachers, coops, supervisors, and researchers. The descriptors in Table 5.1 are not exhaustive, but they provide an idea of some of the practices that occur during effective coteaching. When a video replay is reviewed or a coteaching lesson is planned and enacted, the heuristics can be used to fine-tune what is intended.

The first part of the lesson involved students spreading jelly onto bread and then testing the hypothesis that the bread always falls jelly side down. The students were very active and enjoyed the lesson immensely. Stephanie was the lead teacher and with the exception of co-planning, which did not occur in this lesson, every practice mentioned in the heuristic applied to the coteacher and the enacted lesson. We were all involved actively in facilitating the students' learning from their participation. However, the activity went over time and there was insufficient time for Stephanie to complete the planned follow-up activities. On the spot, Stephanie made the decision to review inheritance, phenotype and genotype expressions, and calculations using the Punnett Square. Even with three other teachers at hand (Bert, Ken, and Michael), all experienced, though in different ways, such a shift can still be success-

Table 5.1. Heuristics for productive coteaching

1. **Coplanning**
2. **Respect**
3. **Rapport**
4. **Creating Space**
    4.1. Willingness to step back
    4.2. Step back
    4.3. Willingness to step forward
    4.4. Step forward
    4.5. Tolerance of others' actions
    4.6. Reciprocity
    4.7. Anticipation of what is appropriate
5. **Seamlessness**
    5.1. Conductor-less orchestration
    5.2. Compensatory actions
    5.3. Touching base
    5.4. Divide and conquer
    5.5. Coordinated action
6. **Reciprocal Coparticipation**
    6.1. Upward trajectory
    6.2. Playing off/tossing/parlaying/passing the baton
    6.3. Overlapping talk
    6.4. Finishing one another's sentences
7. **Complementarity of Action**
    7.1. Oral
    7.2. Spatial
    7.3. Gestural

ful. After a lengthy transition in which Stephanie prepared some overhead transparencies for a review lesson, she commenced the activity on monohybrid crosses. The three other teachers were at various places in the classroom following the unfolding lesson, ready to contribute when the moment appeared appropriate.

After a brief introduction in which the class reviewed the meaning of 'homozygous dominant', the following interaction occurred:

Stephanie: Homozygous recessive means that there are two recessive genes. Keesha, come around.

Bert:	A good way of remembering this... someone just said phenotype, genotype, and you gave the correct answer. An easy way of remembering this is.... Just think of the first letter. A 'p' for physical expression, for physical appearance. A 'g' for the genes. So if you ever get confused, genes, genotype, physical expression, phenotype.
Stephanie:	All right, Keesha is going to put this on the overhead for us.
Keesha:	[*Completes the Punnett Square for the problem posed.*]

While Keesha walked to the front in order to complete the Punnett Square, Bert saw an opportunity to contribute something that would assist students in remembering how to relate the scientific terms, 'phenotypes' and 'genotypes', to more familiar language. Here, the coteacher used a moment of transition as a 'teachable moment'. Bert provided the students, who previously had been hesitant in answering Stephanie's question about the different forms of expression (phenotype, genotype), with a mnemonic that would allow them to relate scientific terminology to words from their everyday language that are therefore more familiar and easier to use. Bert, in effect, built a bridge between two forms of language, that one that students bring to class and the other that is appropriate in the context of formal science. Such moments not only benefit students but also (new) teachers, who can learn how to better teach students.

The following longer sequence shows the interactions that can arise when teachers are working together, at one another's elbows so to speak.

Stephanie:	Now you did a wonderful job there with your Punnett Square. Now, what percent have blue eyes and what percent are gonna have brown eyes?
Keesha:	Fifty and fifty.
Stephanie:	Good, now write that down.
Keesha:	[*Writes.*]
Bert:	You know what another name for that is? When you really get into genetics? When you think of homozygous recessive? [*Pause.*] And in fact, what we are going to do is a test cross.
Ken:	What is it called?
Stephanie:	Test cross.
Bert:	Test cross. They are starting to determine genotypes.
Ken:	[*Pointing to Michael*] Someone had a question.

In this excerpt, we see an interplay between Stephanie and Bert, both contributing to the lesson. Even Ken's question is a contribution, for there may well have been other participants who did not hear or know what Bert was referring to. Ken also contributed to facilitating another teacher's entrance into the conversation. As neither Bert nor Stephanie noticed that Michael had raised his hand to enter the conversation, Ken made it salient. Michael asked a question central to genetics but in a form that could easily be brought into the classroom as a detective story.

Michael:	I wonder if anyone can figure out a little bit about my family?
Stephanie:	OK?
Michael:	So, I have blue eyes and my wife has blue eyes. I was wondering whether you can figure out what color my son's eyes are?
Natasia:	Blue eyes.
Michael:	Why would they be blue?
Natasia:	You have blue eyes, she has blue eyes....
Stephanie:	This is a good question.
Natasia:	She has blue eyes and you have blue eyes, you all must have recessive genes.
Stephanie:	OK, let's think about that [*begins to write*] let's list the possible...
Natasia:	Make them have all the different combinations....
Stephanie:	Excellent, excellent. [*To Michael.*] A good point. I am glad you brought that up. Natasia has a good point. Let's list all the possible genotypes. OK. He has blue eyes. Question. So phenotype is blue. So what are the possible genotypes he may have? All right. What condition may he have?
Natasia:	He would have to be recessive, because if, if, if all people ... [*in the direction of Michael*] You all have blue eyes?
Michael:	My wife and I both have blue eyes.
Stephanie:	This is the question.
Natasia:	It has to be both recessive genes, because dark color is dominant, like brown eyes would dominate over blue eyes.
Stephanie:	OK, so he would have to have...?
Natasia:	Recessive genes.
Stephanie:	All right [*makes notes on overhead*].
Natasia:	So that would make all their genes recessive genes.

In this episode, Michael, Stephanie, and the student enacted a conversation. Michael did not allow Natasia to provide a simple answer, but encouraged her to provide an explanation. This is in contrast to most of Stephanie's verbal interactions with students in this and previous lessons. Later, Natasia showed evidence of her deep thinking when she asked Michael a question in an attempt to confirm her understanding of a prior contribution.

Although only one student was involved in this exchange, Natasia and Michael modeled the thinking and talking that led to a solution to the problem that was posed. This scenario is consistent with what we know about novices learning from experts thinking aloud as they move toward a solution to a problem.[22] Furthermore, in this vignette, thinking in a social forum was not just accomplished by Michael for the benefit of Natasia. The interactions occurred in a social arena where, in addition to Michael and Ken, there were a teacher, a new teacher, and a student, all of whom showed evidence of active participation. All three contributed to the unfolding conversation in the course of which a solution was produced by social interaction.

The situation constituted a moment of learning for the new teacher. Initially Stephanie closely stuck to calculating Punnett Squares and doing problems involving genes in abstract notation (i.e., 'b' and 'B'). Sensing a need to get the students involved in a different way, Michael contributed a problem that could have been almost a riddle suitable for other social situations. Giving some information about his family, Michael asked students to make inferences about other members of his family.

Michael then requested more space to develop another, more complex problem, but one which was also situated in the context of finding out about his family. (Stephanie would later adopt this story context to relate genetic information [and a case] from her own family.)

Michael:	I have another question.
Stephanie:	He has another question!?
Michael:	I have two brothers and a sister. My brother Ulrich has brown eyes, my brother Axel has brown eyes, my sister Sabine has brown eyes. I have blue eyes. What are the possible eye colors my parents have?

---

22   See, for example, Schoenfeld, 1985.

Lisa:	([*Inaudible.*])
Stephanie:	Say it loud, Lisa.
Lisa:	Your dad might have brown eyes, and your mom has blue.
Michael:	Or?
Several:	Your mom has brown eyes and your dad has blue eyes.
Natasia:	Or they both have brown eyes and are heterozygous.
Stephanie:	Good.
Michael:	OK, so both of my parents have brown eyes.
Stephanie:	How nice…

At this point, and despite the ongoing lesson, Stephanie acknowledges that Michael's question not only contributed but also provided a new light on already established content knowledge in this class. Although she appeared reluctant to do so at first, Stephanie demonstrated a willingness to step back when she realized that Michael's questions were providing students with types of practice that would enhance their learning. She was not only tolerant of Michael's moves but became increasingly encouraging of his participation. Michael continued to expand his scenario:

Michael:	So what kind of brown eyes do they have?
S1:	Light [brown.
S2:	[Light brown.
S3:	[Light brown.
Natasia:	One dark one light.
Michael:	But what condition, what genotype will they be?
Natasia:	Heterozygous…
Michael:	Why?
Natasia:	Or one heterozygous and one homozygous … no, no …
Bert:	Think of genotypes, what letter do they have? What are the genotypes? [(*pause*)] Just give me letters. [(*8 seconds.*)] [*Several students think aloud*]; (*One can hear 'Big B', 'little b'*)
Michael:	Could, could…
Natasia:	Wait, wait!!! You both have at least one big B.
Bert:	One of the parents, both of the parents have both capital B's. What would they be, what would they look like?
Natasia:	They couldn't be.
Michael:	And can one of them be homozygous dominant?
Natasia:	No.
Michael:	If I have blue eyes, I have blue eyes.
Natasia:	No.
Michael:	Because both of my parents have brown?

Natasia: No, because you have both recessive genes.
S4:   Yeah.
Michael: So you could figure out a lot about my family just by
              knowing what eye color they have.
Stephanie: [*To Michael*] Very good. [*To class*] Do you understand
              that?
Ss: Yeah...
Stephanie: All right, very good. What kind of crosses are these that
              we just did?
S: Monohybrid.
Natasia: Punnett Square.
Stephanie: Monohybrid.

The questions Michael raised are actually the reverse of what usually happens in science classes. In this instance, students had to figure out phenotypes and then give possible phenotypes rather than the standard procedure of volunteering phenotypes for given genotypes. For the most part Michael did not allow students to call out a single-word answer but requested an elaboration ('Why?'). For years he had both worked to develop his own questioning and conducted research relating to questioning. In this, then, he had developed a *habitus* of engaging students with questions that lead to elaborate inquiries rather than to simple question-answer sequences. Posing a challenge in the form of a story problem is another example of questioning that goes beyond asking for simple facts and names. By coparticipating in the activity, the students benefited from his praxis as did Stephanie and each of the coteaching partners.

Michael's last utterance was a transitional move to invite Stephanie to resume her teaching of the activity. In effect Michael created space for Stephanie by stepping back in anticipation that so doing was in the interests of the students' learning. Stephanie briefly concluded the activity on monohybrid crosses and made a transition to the final activity on dihybrid crosses. Before she handed over the teaching to Bert, she showed she had learned from Michael's two questions. Stephanie described her own phenotypes for hair and eye color ('I have blond hair but I have brown eyes'.). Subsequently she related these to phenotypes of her parents ('My mom's got red hair, blue eyes, my dad has black hair dark brown eyes') and siblings ('And my sisters both have very dark hair'). Presumably the students were left to wonder about this information as Bert stepped forward to complete the final activity.

Toward Praxeology

Just as we did for the coteaching, we examined video replays of the sessions in which we attempted to construct locally relevant theory (*'praxeology'*) and constructed a heuristic that contains a list of practices that were observed in what we considered to be effective praxeology sessions. The practices are listed in Table 5.2 and can be used as a referent for planning and enacting praxeology sessions. In this section we describe praxeology sessions in which Stephanie participated, and we use the heuristic to facilitate our description and analysis.

Immediately after the lesson that was described above, Stephanie, Bert, Ken, and Michael, together with two student volunteers (Natasia and Shawan), participated in a praxeology session during which they discussed salient aspects of the lesson they had just shared. While the two students were getting some lunch, Ken initiated conversation with a remark that it was an interesting lesson. Stephanie followed up and identified some issues about student participation, issues that she felt required further attention. She expressed a need to develop a strategy to get students actively involved at the beginning of a lesson. Her suggestions were consistent with Boykin's notion that African American students are likely to respond to a task that has verve (i.e., high levels of stimulation, energetic and lively interactions). Based on her experiences with these students she realized that to get the best out of them her lessons needed to incorporate verve (and other dispositions of the *habitus* of her African American students).

The conversation changed course when Bert identified the initial activity as a good one, involving an investigation of whether or not bread with jelly on it falls jelly side down or up. He liked the manner in which the students were involved in identifying and controlling variables. Ken was not so enthused and said so. He was skeptical about the extent to which activities like this one get students involved in identifying, manipulating, and controlling variables. Stephanie immediately sprang to her own defense,

Table 5.2: Heuristics for productive cogenerative dialogue sessions

1. **Respect** (Between participants)
2. **Rapport** (Between participants)
3. **Inclusion of stakeholders** (Student teachers, students, school personnel, high school students, university personnel)
4. **Ways to participate**
   4.1. Coordinating discussion
   4.2. Listening attentively
   4.3. Initiating dialogue/ideas
   4.4. Posing critical questions
   4.5. Providing evidence
   4.6. Expressing an opinion (agree/disagree)
   4.7. Speaking freely
   4.8. Clarifying and elaborating on ideas
   4.9. Suggesting alternatives for actions
   4.10. Evaluating ideas and practices
5. **Opportunities to participate**
   5.1. Contributing to an equitable playing field
   5.2. Listening attentively
   5.3. Making space to participate
   5.4. Showing willingness to participate
   5.5. Making invitations to participate
   5.6. Refusing all forms of oppression
6. **Discussion topics**
   6.1. Learning to teach
   6.2. Teaching and learning
   6.3. Curriculum
   6.4. Teaching kids like us
   6.5. Coteaching
   6.6. Transformative potential of activities/curriculum
   6.7. Links to particulars
   6.8. Quality of the learning environment

explaining that she had just completed the biology praxis examination and needed to know a great deal about identification, control, and manipulation of variables. For this reason she perceived activities like the bread and jelly investigation as being very important to these students.

The conversation continued in a very relaxed manner as each participant successively raised issues that became a focus for discussion. After some general discussion about student participation, Ken raised a question about the participation of one of the students. Stephanie provided an extensive list of issues about the student and indicated that he was a dilemma in that he participated well in terms of producing written work and getting tasks done, but he did not participate in public verbal interaction. Ken raised the issue because during the lesson the class had expressed surprise when the student volunteered a correct answer to a question. In her reflections about the student Stephanie expressed concern about whether she had assigned him a fair grade for daily participation. She then identified a long list of ways in which the student participated and the issue of his peers making fun of him (e.g., does his written work, very bright, writes and reads well, rarely speaks aloud, object of ridicule when he speaks, only male in class). Bert made a comment to the effect that the students liked the class, and he explained why they liked it. In so doing he publicly acknowledged Stephanie's efforts in being well prepared, hard working, and innovative, and the fact that she was well liked by her students.

The initial conversations were relaxing and very much oriented toward issue generating. From the outset when Stephanie raised the issue of sleepy students, the session identified issues that are of considerable importance to urban education. These included classroom management, suspension of disruptive students, oral participation of students, coping with diverse abilities, affective responses to science education, peer pressure, and grading. Perhaps sensing that the conversation was not connecting with some of these issues at a deeper level, Michael made the first move to focus the group on an issue:

Michael: If you were to pick up one issue this morning that you want to talk about in order to learn about teaching … simply to start talking about it professionally in order to make you become more … What would you pick out?

Stephanie: Even in that small of a class, with the levels being so different, I feel like there are always two students who are left behind. And those are the students who need more attention but because the other students are more boisterous and outgoing I'm always drawn to them.

The subsequent discussion quickly focused on the use of peers as teachers and the suggestion that Natasia, who was just about to join the praxeology session, would make an ideal peer tutor.

The conversation was wide ranging and considered advantages and disadvantages of using peer teaching. Bert and Stephanie were equally involved in making suggestions and considering the ups and downs of the possibilities of peer teaching. The conversation was enlightening and no one person took a clear lead in being an expert. All contributions appeared to carry equal weight.

Before the conversation on peer teaching was concluded, the students arrived. Ken focused the conversation on a different topic by directing a question to the students: 'How can we better teach students like you?' The initial responses involved the use of hands-on activities and getting students actively involved. It was clear that this class was popular with students and it had them involved because the teacher did not lecture for too long ('talking is boring') and she engaged them in a 'whole bunch of different activities'. During the conversation the students compared this class to a chemistry class taught by another new teacher. The big difference was that the chemistry class contained far too much talking and not enough hands-on activity.

The conversation that included the students covered much the same ground as had been covered when they were not there. However, on this occasion the conversations were even richer, with many more suggestions and arguments over which alternative was preferable. For example, the discussion about how to deal with sleepy kids was marked with a sharp difference of opinion when Natasia suggested that the same kids sleep through all classes and that Stephanie should just teach those who want to learn. Her recommendation was consistent with one of Boykin's concerns that less time be spent on classroom management. On this occasion Bert took the view that sleepy students should be aroused and encouraged to participate. The discussion, as it had done before, progressed to the issue of how best to deal with diversity. Natasia suggested the formation of heterogeneous groups so that those who could do it could teach those who could not. The conversation then moved on to peer tutoring and to a debate about the relative merits of different ways of arranging peer tutoring and coteaching. At one stage Michael suggested dividing the class into three, with Bert, Stephanie, and Natasia each teaching a third. Bert preferred this arrangement but the students expressed a preference for leaving the class as an intact whole and having three teachers to do the teaching. What was interesting about the conversation was that at one stage Natasia and then Shawan spoke in favor of three teachers with a class of 30 students and Bert began to change his mind.

In the final few minutes of the praxeology session several significant topics were raised. These included the benefits of the vocabulary wall, daily participation grades, pacing and transitions during a lesson, the value of down time, relationship building, and the value of the daily warm-up activity used to commence class. Although these topics were quickly dispensed with, it was apparent that they made a difference to the way Stephanie planned and taught her activities during the next week when, for example, the transitions between the five or six activities in a lesson were very smooth and well managed.

> Initially I did not enjoy coteaching because I preferred to have control of my teaching. When someone came in I regarded it as an interruption. But gradually I warmed up to the idea and now can see many benefits.
>
> The round table discussions (by Ken), in which Bert, two or three students and myself reflected on a lesson, were so inspirational that I plan on continuing them at my new school. Most importantly, the conversations gave students a voice in the manner in which they were taught. Whether it involved a minor detail like their difficulty in discerning my 'r' from my 'n' or a major strategy such as pairing students as study partners, their feedback was a precious resource that aided me in designing lessons that best met their needs. Bert also seemed to heed their advice. When a student informed him that his multiple stories were boring, he smiled and responded, 'I'll try to cut back'. While Bert was affable and turned the criticism into a light-hearted moment, it was a major breakthrough in terms of his pedagogy. It was a practice that I knew needed improvement but was too shy to mention. I am convinced that students always serve as the best consultants.

Lessons Learned

In this section, we reflect together on the lessons that we have learned about becoming an urban teacher, coteaching with others, and engaging in cogenerative dialogue.

Creation of a Teaching *Habitus*

Michael: As I cotaught with you, Stephanie, and Bert, I immediately felt at home. In this class, there was space for a new teacher to participate not only in small-group teaching but also in whole-class discussions. Participating in this class gave me the impression that it is an environment that produces students' learning, accepts different perspectives, and fosters mutual respect among teachers and students.

Ken: One of the most striking parts of this study has been the extent to which Stephanie, Chiew, and Bert learned to teach by coteaching at one another's elbows. Over the course of a year I observed very significant shifts in the manner in which each of them taught. The changes were not necessarily thematized and I am sure that in most cases they are beyond the level of conscious awareness. In addition, there were also issues that needed to be overcome, issues that are endemic to urban schools and that influence everything that goes on within them. Do you have any examples of some of these?

Stephanie: Unfortunately, violence affected my teaching on several occasions. What enabled me to divert these situations and avoid total disruption of the learning process was my coteaching experience with Bert. Having taught within the Philadelphia school district for 30 years, and working as a disciplinarian for a third of that time, Bert was an expert at both defusing situations before they escalated into violence and managing them once they did. While it certainly put me more at ease to have an experienced man in the classroom, I did not look to Bert for help in handling altercations when I had taken the lead. Rather, I approached the situations in the same calm and concerned manner I had observed in his approach. If a disagreement between two girls, regarding perhaps which R&B artist was the superior dancer, was escalating into rage, I might have initially thought to say 'Enough girls, what you're arguing over is silly'. What I learned by teaching with Bert is the importance of validating the opinions of both girls, even if the topic is seemingly insignificant. Listening rather than blaming is crucial. As I spent more time coteaching in the classroom, I gradually became confident in dealing with aggression. When I had the wind knocked out of my sails by a mother, who had unexpectedly arrived in our classroom intending to physically harm the friends of her freshman daughter, the instructors and classmates of my science methods class revived me. The violence was so traumatizing to me that discussing it with others who had experienced similar situations was critical for my survival in that classroom. Although I do not believe it necessary for new teachers in urban settings to undergo a generic 'violence training course', I am adamant that a support network, such as the one provided by my science methods class, be available to permit reflection on the topic.

Ken: The facilities available for teaching science at City High School are consistent with Anyon's description of ghetto schools.[23] Parts of the school are run down and there is a shortage of equipment and supplies.

Michael: These conditions are core data in the argument of critical educators[24] who use the concept of 're/production' in order to account for the fact that so little changes in education for minorities in general and African Americans in particular. So, what you are articulating here are obstacles to teaching—you are articulating them at the level of lived experiences.

Ken: Did you learn to work around these obstacles?

Stephanie: I remember returning from my first day of student teaching and thinking, how am I going to teach science in such barren and gloomy conditions? Our 35 students were crammed into one classroom with no laboratory or even sink access. Brainstorming together, Chiew and I devoted several hours to decorating the room, not only to create a welcoming atmosphere, but to surround the students with science as well. The walls looked festive and were continuous reminders of the students' mastery of science objectives. The themes Chiew and I collaborated on included a science vocabulary wall, science in the news, reaching our science goals, and several others. The lack of laboratory access was astounding to both Chiew and me, especially since several lab rooms were reserved for 'holding' students whose teachers were absent. It seemed that Bert had been so accustomed to this deficiency that it didn't concern him. After several months of listening to us bemoan the situation, Bert took action and informed the administration of our need for lab space. Although it took awhile,

---

23   Anyon, 1997.
24   Pinar & Bowers, 1992.

we were eventually admitted into an ill equipped, yet functioning laboratory space. The methods class was of great help in overcoming the school's poor physical conditions. Providing a network of resources, I felt confident that I could create standard high school lab activities even though City High School did not supply the material. The course allowed the necessary time for new teachers to collaborate on ideas and share supplies. It also inspired me to be resourceful and seek materials from outside sources. I would never have thought to ask stores to call me before discarding leftover stock. I was always impressed by their generosity.

Michael: It is not surprising, for all of us think that teachers like us have to deal with the situation and deal with the 'obstacles' to teaching and learning. A critical psychological[25] perspective would be different. From this perspective, we would argue that the obstacles are simply signs, at an experience level, of problems at the systemic level. That is, as we have learned from sociocultural approaches, the problems at the societal levels have been internalized and are now ascribed to problems at the individual level. Here, the problems are almost impossible to overcome other than in marginally making differences. Of course, we can apply this form of analysis to the students as well. In response to the systemic disregard for their primary discourses and the associated symbolic violence experienced by them, working- and underclass students will enact resistance.[26]

Ken: I can only confirm that with other data. In a study I undertook at City High School,[27] I found it virtually impossible to enact a science curriculum because of repeated student absences from school. It was as if the students were showing resistance to schooling as an overt protest about an institution that was re/producing their disadvantage within the United States.

Stephanie: The high rate of absenteeism at City High School, as with most urban schools, was a significant issue that I had to take into account when planning my science lessons. On average, 20% of my class was truant and those students who did attend arrived at various intervals following the scheduled start time.

---

25 Dreier, 1991; Holzkamp, 1983a.
26 Willis, 1977.
27 Tobin, Seiler, & Walls, 1999.

Michael: I want to reiterate my previous point. What you are doing here by 'taking into account absenteeism' is 'working around' troubles created at a very different level. What happens is that you internalize societal problems and attempt to deal with them at an individual level. So we need to work in a different way, involving as we do students, new teachers, cooperating teachers, SLC coordinators, and so on in a cogenerative dialogue that deals with the systemic problems. That is, we have to articulate the structural problems at a collective level. In the meantime, we have to find ways and means that allow new teachers like Stephanie to deal with these structural problems in a collective forum.

Stephanie: I fully agree that if change is going to take place it must happen at the structural level. I often felt like Chiew, Bert, and I were working tirelessly to meet the students' needs while the majority of City High School teachers were content with maintaining the status quo. Although it often felt like three versus hundreds in a tug-of-war that nobody could ever win, I do believe that our methods had more of an outreaching influence than I had originally estimated. As we engaged the students in discussions about the purpose and reasons behind our methods, they seemed eager to share the outcomes with other members of the faculty. Throughout the year we had several teachers visit from *Health* and other small learning communities, curious to observe the activities that students had been discussing. Although this does not reflect a structural change, it certainly seems like a beginning.

Ken: Your mention of methods makes me wonder about the extent to which the methods course was of value.

Stephanie: Because I was teaching in a block schedule, my methods instructors encouraged the inclusion of a sequence of 10–15-minute activities following the introduction of a topic. I utilized this approach often and organized activities by stations (a different activity at each group of tables). For example, when studying plate tectonics, I designed four stations, including a tectonics puzzle, the construction of a flip book illustrating plate movement, a reading and mini-lab studying earthquakes, and an analysis of an ocean floor model. After we had concluded an opening discussion of the day's topic, the students set out to complete the series of exercises, which were all related and independently incorporated the lesson's objectives, as Bert and I circulated offering instruction and assistance. If a student was tardy, I had the opportunity to catch him/her up without disrupting the pace of the class. The student could then blend smoothly into the action by beginning the station sequence. The stations were designed so that failure to complete all of them was not detrimental to meeting the day's objectives. If a student was absent s/he could work with me to obtain the necessary information and then complete the stations during lunch or after school hours. This approach was also beneficial for students with diverse learning abilities because they were able to move at their own pace without the humiliation of disrupting the progress of the entire class.

Michael: These are very interesting ways of coping with the situation that you have earlier characterized in terms of its shortcomings, lack of resources. But in the long run, we all, including students and their parents, have to endeavor to seek solutions at a structural level.

Coteaching

Ken: One of the big issues for me in setting up coteaching pairs was the extent to which new teachers could learn from one another. Because Stephanie had taught in a private school before entering a teacher education degree program, she was quite experienced compared to Chiew. It was not surprising to see Bert and Stephanie learn from one another to a greater extent than perhaps Chiew learned from either of them. I was perplexed throughout the first semester because it seemed to me that Chiew's role was too passive. She always seemed to be in the background and did not take her turn at stepping forward. When finally I took a stand and spoke to her I was surprised to find that she was very pleased with her roles and her learning. That discussion, plus others with Bert and Stephanie about the same issue, catalyzed action, and a structure emerged in which each of the new teachers would take a turn being a lead teacher.

Stephanie: When we first began working with one another it seemed that we automatically moved into the role that was most comfortable to us. Excited about the opportunity to teach in a new environment, I took the lead role while Chiew preferred to observe. Bert was very supportive of our ideas and served as a coach, offering pep talks after difficult classes. Although our relationship was amiable, this arrangement was not the most conducive in terms of learning to teach from one another. Once Ken encouraged us to communicate our needs, we were able to develop an approach to teaching that we all participated in equally.

Michael: The cogenerative discussions after a shared lesson are, from my perspective, a crucial element in our coteaching design. In these discussions, in which the teachers and student representatives participate, we must attempt not only to understand our shared experience at an immediate level but also to develop this understanding into local theory. On the basis of this new and generalized understanding, we are therefore developing new options for actions, and therefore enlarging our room to maneuver.

Ken: An ongoing challenge for us has also been to connect what occurs in the field experience to the coursework, particularly in the methods course. I think it is imperative for the methods course to be tailored to the unfolding events in the field.

Michael: I can see the 'methods course' function very much as an additional forum or an extension for our praxeology sessions, for the intentions appear to be the same: learning to teach.

Ken: This year we endeavored to create a close link but we still have some distance to go. It is imperative that we get coop teachers and students actively involved as teacher educators in the methods course. Situating the course in the same school as the field experiences is also advantageous.

Stephanie: What proved most beneficial about the methods course was its emphasis on reflection and its fluid (changing with the students' needs) nature. In taking the class I was not looking for suggestions about how to teach specific subjects. In other words, I did not deem it necessary for the instructors to move step by step through the science curriculum offering pointers about what information to cover and how to cover it. Rather, I desired prompts that would encourage me to look at my teaching in depth and from various perspectives.

Ken: As we have changed key parts of the teacher education program it has been necessary to adapt the roles of the stakeholders. One of the most important changes is for new teachers to be researchers of their own and students' practices. This seems to me to be a logical extension of the coteaching and discussions about praxis. If new teachers are to optimize learning from their praxis, it seems that an ongoing program of research can only encourage the growth in teaching.

Michael: It is only if all stakeholders are also researchers that we can aspire to new solutions to pressing problems. It is insufficient to generate new understandings and local theory if they do not lead to a change in the action possibilities. Whether a local theory has some merit has to be tested, right then and there, in praxis. Here, all participants have a role in contributing to theory development and testing, and, therefore, to establishing the relevance of the work to the present situation.

Stephanie: Taping myself during three situations, full-class lecture, small group, and individual discussion, was probably the most helpful assignment of the year. In my analysis, I recognized that I allowed for practically no wait time and that I would ask simple questions. I also realized that I coddled the girls (led them right to the answers) while I expected the boys to find the answer for themselves. I was directly able to apply the results of this exercise to the classroom.

Discussions about Praxis

Michael: A central aspect of coteaching has to be the discussion that follows the shared experience. It is here that all stakeholders can work together to generate solutions to problems articulated in new ways as our understanding evolves. Given that all stakeholders are involved in a collective sense-making and theory-generating effort, we might call this a cogenerative dialogue.

Ken: I found these discussions about praxis an exciting aspect of our study that has great potential for bringing about change. Even though we had worked out the details of how to involve students, the coop, and the university supervisor in discussions about praxis, events unfolded in such a way that we did not seriously enact this part of our teacher education program until toward the end of the year. Even so, it was a significant step forward. I thought the conversations between the new teachers, coops, and students were of particular significance. We had discussions with and without the students and my impression is that they are an order of magnitude better when the students are there. We also had them with and without the coop. I felt it was slightly better in most cases without the coop being present. The students tended to be less restrained in their talk about praxis. However, one key advantage of having the coop present is that the coop can be a major beneficiary, in that issues that arise can be of as much significance to the coop as to any of the stakeholders.

Stephanie: I appreciated having all of the participants present during the praxis discussions. On a few occasions, a subject was introduced that had been troubling me yet that I was too embarrassed to discuss with Bert or Chiew one-on-one. Having the students, supervisor, and coteachers available actually relieved the pressure because the issue could be addressed from various viewpoints, not just mine. The students also enjoyed the dialogue immensely. They would often request to participate in the meetings and were more inclined to approach us with their opinions about lessons after they had shared in a praxis discussion session.

Michael: This is probably a key concern that we have to deal with during transitions between rather different ways of going about education. How do we move from our old *habitus*, which includes the re/production of power relationships alongside other aspects of culture, to a new *habitus* where we take a more democratic approach—as is already happening in various Scandinavian models of work.[28]

Ken: I thought that the power relationships within the discussions on praxis were very even.

Michael: But we have to continue to be watchful with our own perceptions so that we do not succumb to seeing things as more rosy than they are. This is why we need to enact 'radical doubt'[29] and 'suspicion of [our own] ideology'.[30]

Ken: I think that we have good evidence for my claim of flattened hierarchies in the relationships between the various stakeholders. Looking back on the tapes I am struck by the sophistication of the students' perspectives on what is happening in

---

28   Ehn, 1992; Eldon & Levin, 1991; Henderson & Kyng, 1991.
29   Bourdieu, 1992b.
30   Markard, 1984.

the classroom and the extent to which they can identify issues having salience to their learning and to the creation of productive learning environments. Of course we all have to learn new roles within the discussions on praxis. There were times, for example, when I spoke and it might have been just as well if I had remained silent. There also were times when the coop tended to make statements that reified the traditional roles of teacher and student in which the teacher 'instructs' and the student listens and learns. Fortunately we had students who seemed unafraid to speak and be heard.

Stephanie: I never felt that one voice dominated the discussion. It seemed that the students appreciated their roles as consultants and the teachers were very interested in what they had to offer. I think our experience with coteaching allowed this dialogue to be as comfortable as it was. Bert never acted as 'master' nor treated Chiew and me as lowly apprentices. Rather, there was an even exchange of knowledge. Because of this arrangement we were willing not only to learn from one another but to learn from the students as well.

Michael: Shaking the behaviors that came with our traditional roles and our culture-specific *habitus* will be one of the central challenges. I have learned a lot and changed my own ways of interacting with others when I started to teach students from different cultures with very different interactional patterns. Providing space so that all participants can get involved irrespective of their traditional ways of interacting is not easy and we will all have to demonstrate a willingness to be sensitive to others.

Ken: The best way to set up a discussion on praxis depends very much on the circumstances. It seems essential that the teachers at the table should have cotaught. Maybe another way to say that is that all non-students at the table ought to have cotaught—that would include new teachers, coops, supervisors, researchers, and school administrators. I have a preference for two students because they can interact with one another and feed off one another's comments. When we had three students it did not have the same dynamics. I am also concerned that we do not want too many adult coteachers in the group, although it seems fine to suggest that as many coteachers as there are could productively be involved. In this study we had Stephanie, Bert, Michael, two students, and myself. In fact in most of the discussions on praxis in this study we had between six and eight participants.

Stephanie: Even though the participants involved in each praxis discussion were slightly different, I found them all beneficial. I agree that no more than two students should attend. Throughout the year it might be interesting to have one slot reserved for the same student and one slot available for a new face. I don't believe there is a specific recipe for selecting which students participate. During one session, a student who rarely spoke in class volunteered to attend and offered several valuable insights.

Michael: There is probably no single recipe for how to make this 'right' overall. Arrangements for these sessions have to become part of the research conducted locally by involving the stakeholders. In this way, local solutions can be found that are sensitive to the particulars of the setting.

Looking Ahead

Ken: Coteaching in combination with discussions on praxis and adapted roles of new teachers, coops, supervisors, school administrators, and students has the potential to revolutionize practices associated with teacher education. On the basis of what we have learned from our ongoing research it seems as if there is a lot to be gained from assigning small groups of new teachers to a coop in order to prepare teachers for the challenges of teaching science in urban schools. Just how many teachers are optimal? During the past year we have assigned as many as three new teachers to one coop and all four teachers learned a great deal from the field experience. In addition, when we cotaught in numerous settings there were as many as four coteachers practicing at one another's elbows. Even so there was more to do than we could keep up with. I can see no problem in having as many as six teachers coteaching with 20 to 30 students. Just where these teachers should be in the career ladder is not at all clear to me. In terms of being a resource for learning to teach I see the benefits of having a 30-year veteran like Bert as a coteacher, but I also see the benefits of having someone like Stephanie as a coteacher. Throughout City High School our coteachers ranged in the length of their teaching experience from less than a year to more than 30 years. Each of those we employed as coteachers was of great value this year. Of course there were teachers we would not choose to participate in coteaching because of interpersonal factors that are not related to the length of their teaching experience. Some of these issues will frame our research in the forthcoming year as we proceed in the reconstruction of our teacher education program with the goal of improving the learning environments to support learning to teach.

Stephanie: There is no doubt that the coteaching arrangement provided the necessary support for me to succeed in the urban setting and improve my teaching in general. It was obvious from the beginning that my opinion mattered as Bert, Chiew, and the students treated me as a valuable commodity. Starting from that foundation I felt confident in trying new approaches and asking for honest critique, something that might have been intimidating if my role was solely as an observer and part-time participant.

Michael: Having more than one teacher in a classroom may appear to be a utopia to many readers. However, I can see professional development moneys spent on hiring qualified subject matter teachers to coteach with regular teachers rather than on summer workshops and other activities that do not take place in the classroom, that is, where praxis is enacted and experienced. Furthermore, we have not even talked about the potential resource for learning that would be created by tying teacher education more closely to professional praxis. If new teachers were to legitimately (though perhaps peripherally at first) participate in teaching from the beginning of their professional training in the academy, we could easily have a larger number of teachers in each class without additional costs to the school and school system. Therefore, if teachers and principals regarded new teachers not as a burden but as a tremendous resource, we would make crucial inroads toward bringing about improvements in learning. These changes as I am envisioning them here, too, are structural changes that need to occur for lasting transformation of education in praxis.

For me, the central issue for change will have to be solutions for what I perceive to be structural problems. We cannot continue to ask teachers to internalize problems, which therefore become personal problems leading to them blaming themselves or their students, experiencing stress, and in many cases, withdrawing from the system. I am not surprised to hear that there is a considerable number of teachers who change careers within their first 5 years at the job. At a personal level, I have dealt with these problems by enacting resistance. Some of the ways included teaching a different curriculum, but using resources to argue my point and in defense of my actions or allowing students to learn when and where they wanted, provided they were showing achievements that would legitimate this radical departure from school policy. But resistance is not a long-term solution for students or their teachers.

Ken: Some of your own work has resulted in significant changes in the manner in which science was taught. Do you see any of this as having applicability to the problems experienced in urban schools and science classrooms?

Michael: Recognizing one's own problems as the outcome of structural problems, and then seeking solutions at this new level has to become an important goal for the cogenerative dialogue. It may turn out that some of the discussions will be just what Paulo Freire enacted with his peasants. In any case, I envision beginnings as I have enacted them in my own last job as full-time high school teacher, where students and I met as part of the official lesson to talk about how to make it better for students to learn. In this way, one can change institutions from the inside out. For example, I began enacting a more participatory way of conducting the ongoing teacher evaluation that my school required. This actually started my efforts in coteaching, making sense together about what has happened, and collating different teachers' perspectives of what it is like to teach chemistry, biology, or physics to *these* students in *this* school. The solution we had come up with was structural, for the entire school eventually adopted our participatory (and emancipatory) approach to teacher evaluation.

Relating to urban education, our cogenerative dialogue must include students. Given the distance between their primary *habitus* and the *habitus* embodied in the official curriculum and by the largely White teachers, we must search for solutions that are workable for students and teachers alike. This cannot be achieved by answering a teacher-centered question, 'How can I better adapt my teaching to the students?' Rather, the question has to be something like 'What do we have to do in order to enhance learning?' and has to be asked by teachers and students collectively.

CHAPTER 6

Researching as Coteaching and Colearning: Lessons from the Dihybrid Cross

Learning science and how to teach it is the central topic of this chapter. Coteaching and cogenerative dialogue provide the context in which tremendous learning is able to occur. The theme of the case study is the learning of science subject matter and subject matter pedagogy by two individuals who are traditionally regarded as among those who 'should know', such as university researchers, supervisors, and methods instructors. Research and school praxis, research and learning subject matter, and subject matter pedagogy enter a fundamental unity—which is a prerequisite for an adequate understanding of the human experience of learning.[1]

Teachers continue to perceive a gap between what they have learned in the academy and what they experience and know in their daily work. Our research shows that depreciative comments about the use of university-generated knowledge are still rather frequent.[2] This perception is supported by the experience of teachers that much of what they know they appear to have learned by working in the field. The following excerpt is from a cogenerative dialogue among coteachers about the subject matter knowledge that teachers seem to be acquiring from teaching:

---

1   Dreier, 1993.
2   See, for example, Roth, 1998a; Roth, Lawless, & Tobin, 2000.

Michael [20 years' teaching experience]: I often think in terms of a chemistry teacher of mine, a professor, who said, 'Now after 20 years, I feel that I am slowly getting the understanding of the subject matter that I am teaching. And this was a professor. If we think that through in terms of our students, students who tutor other students . . .

Stephanie [new teacher]: Definitely, the best way to learn is to teach.

Bert [30 years' teaching experience]: Absolutely, absolutely. You learn, you overlearn by teaching the material. The more I teach the more I understand something and so forth. I mean, you have to explain, show all types of ways of translating the materials, so that the student picks it up. And in order to do that, you have to really be knowledgeable about what you are doing.

Despite such experiences, (lifelong) learning as teachers and researchers engage in daily praxis is not sufficiently appreciated. The lack of appreciation for learning in praxis is unfortunate, because our own work of teaching in middle and high schools shows that learning science content and learning to teach science appear to be precipitated in and through the coteaching experience. That is, while teachers traditionally have found research of little help, we find that our own coteaching practice leads to direct changes in teaching where and while we work. However, we may want to ask ourselves whether it is necessary to spend 20 or 30 years in the field before knowing a domain sufficiently well to feel that one is ready to teach it. In this chapter, we show how coteaching and cogenerative dialoguing provide for an ideal context and starting point in which teachers can continue their development by learning subject matter and subject matter pedagogy. Teachers and professors do not stop learning once they have received their diploma or tenure. Rather, they continue to learn throughout their life, though mostly in 'informal ways', on the job, and without taking more coursework in formal institutions.

Engaging in a continued cogenerative dialogue that led to the building of praxeology allowed us (Ken and Michael) to further and deepen our understanding of genetics, Punnett Squares, and dihybrid crosses and how to teach these topics. We present a case study of learning by two of the participants in a biology lesson, which included, among others, a problematic sequence on the topic of the dihybrid cross. (The patterns of learning evidenced here are exemplary. Our choice of a sequence is pragmatic in the sense that we have to choose one over many others.) In other contexts, we would have been characterized as 'researcher' or 'methods teacher/supervisor'. We might have engaged in evaluating the subject matter errors committed by the teachers, or evaluating the level of competence in their subject matter pedagogy. However, we find such research limited in the sense that it does not further the learning of teachers or necessarily lead to changes in the classroom where we conduct our research. Having made a commitment to change practice by participating in it, we are, in the present context, coteachers and colearners. Our learning (with respect to genetics in general and dihybrid crosses and how to teach them) stands in the foreground of this research. This case study is therefore an example of continuing (lifelong) learning about subject matter and subject matter pedagogy, both topics that are rarely, if ever, made thematic in science education research.

This case study is also an example of how knowledge arises from a dialogue between people and about important matters of praxis; our praxeology exhibits all the characteristics of the dialogic nature of all knowledge.[3] It should therefore not surprise our readers that we chose to write our case study in dialogic form, making our writing reflect the process by means of which we learned and came to know.

The Lesson of the Dihybrid Cross

In the first part of the lesson, Stephanie had asked students to conduct an investigation. This investigation took longer than planned, so Stephanie did not want to start the second investigation. On the spot, she decided to review inheritance and the use of the Punnett Square. When this part was done, she handed over the lesson to Bert, who was willing to teach about dihybrid crosses. The lesson unfolds, ending in confusion, for which, because of our commitment to *co*teaching, all coteachers bear responsibility.

As Bert walks toward the front of the classroom, he announces, 'First of all, dihybrid cross, without even looking, this is gonna be a nine-three-three-one ratio.... When you do a dihybrid cross that's a genetic law: 9-16th, 3-16th, 3-16th, and 1-16th.

---

3   On the dialogic nature of knowledge, see Bakhtin, 1981.

Let's take a look at the genotypes of a dihybrid theory. We are talking about eye color and hair color. If this follows the pure law of dominance, what would this individual look like?'

Natasia is the first student to respond, 'Brown hair, black hair and brown eyes'.

Bert acknowledges her contribution and continues, 'If two parents basically had the same genes, for this ... let's say we cross both of these'. He turns to Stephanie and asks, 'Have you gone over what the square will look like for a dihybrid?' Bert goes on after Stephanie responds that this is the first time they have discussed dihybrids in the class.

'You have to account for all the possible gene combinations', Bert continues. 'So what you are going to do is, you are going to set up a Punnett Square, do you see that?' He begins to draw a square subdivided into smaller boxes as in Figure 6.1a. 'That instead of just being four blocks is now going to be...?' 'Sixteen', Natasia suggests, and Bert continues, 'Sixteen blocks. So, let's set up a Punnett Square....'

At this point both Ken and Stephanie suggest with somewhat subdued voices that Bert should let the students figure out how to complete the square. At first, Bert does not react, continues to work on the square, writes 'BbHh x BbHh' on the transparency, and subsequently notes 'BbHh' at the beginning of each row and column of the square (Figure 6.1b).

Bert continues, 'What's the cross going to be? It's going to be this, large H small h, OK?' Bert records each letter in the square

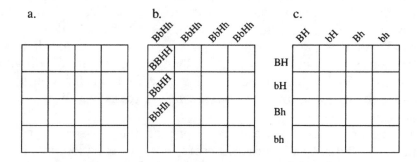

Figure 6.1. Consecutive stages of the drawing projected against the front wall by means of the overhead projector. At some stage, Chuck realizes that he 'made a mistake' wipes off what he had and begins a new 'Punnett Square'.

that he is currently working on, leading to four-letter combination in each of them (Figure 6.1b). 'So what do you have to do as far as separating the genes?' He then invites the students, as previously suggested by the coteachers Ken and Stephanie, 'You try it, and I will go over on the overhead with it'. There is a pause, which Bert then fills by asking, 'What are possible combinations that you can have?' There are no responses from the class and Bert continues, 'Let's just take the large Bs'.

Together with the students, Bert begins to write four-letter combinations into each square. He asks, 'What can you have this large B hook up with?' One student calls out, 'Everything', and Natasia suggests, 'The other large B'. Bert continues, always writing down the letters that he utters, 'A large B with a large B. What else? A large B with?'

In the background, Ken explains something to Stephanie that Bert cannot hear. His hands gesture something written horizontally, then vertically. Bert continues, with single- and double-letter responses from the students, to fill his square. A little later, Stephanie suggests a different way of finding the solution. 'Right, but one way you can do it is, because the allele ... the allele on one side of the condition and then the condition on the other, and then you bring this together and cross'.

Bert acknowledges Stephanie's contribution with a 'Yeah' and continues. After completing the square with the four-letter combinations, he explains, 'Since this is the genotype possible combinations of one parent, the other parent would have the same and you bring it down here and then you recombine them'. He suggests that students should do that on their own and then gives them a hint for checking their work: 'If you do it right, you can always check this block right here'. Bert points to the bottom right square and continues, 'Because there you are going to get a homozygous recessive. One-16th, in other words, when you combine, you get the answer in the 16th block, small b small b, small h small h'. Natasia suggests, 'We already know that' but Bert does not seem to take note of this comment. At this point, a quick exchange between several coteachers brings about a turn in the unfolding lesson.

At first, Ken asks, 'Can't you write the hair across the top and the height down the side to get the same?' Bert immediately and without looking up from drawing another square answers with an extended 'No!' Michael enters the exchange and explains, 'You have to have one parent on the top and one on the side'. Natasia comments, 'I know...' and begins to work out a square in her notebook.

Bert, who has continued to write, acknowledges an error: 'You know what? Oh, I am sorry. I am screwing up. It should just be, basically, I am giving you four different letters for the genes and it should just be one letter. I am already thinking of the answer. Here we go'. He wipes the earlier square off the transparency and continues, 'It's large B large H, large B small h, small b large H'. He sets up a new Punnett Square as in Figure 6.1c, and writes two-letter combinations next to the beginning of each row and column. As he writes he mutters, 'Large B large H, large H small b, small b large H, small b small h. Now you recombine them in the block. I screwed up. I am sorry. Now you can recombine them and get the answer'. Several students suggest that they had told him this before and that they already had it right.

Bert fills the new squares with four-letter combinations that arise from combining the letters at its corresponding row and column beginning (Figure 6.1c). He asks, 'Do you see how I recombine them. You know what I did? I didn't separate them. The mistake that I made when I put this on the overhead was that I didn't separate the genes that go into the sperm and the egg. So you couldn't get double combinations in there. So what we have now is basically what is going to be in the egg cell or the sperm cell, depending on the . . . when you are male or female and the possible genetic combinations'.

As the lesson comes to its end, Stephanie asks students to complete the square for homework. We (Ken, Michael) begin to talk about our respective ways of doing the dihybrid cross. Ken then walks over to Bert and shows him the solution that Ken had constructed during the lesson.

Talking Punnett Squares and Dihybrid Crosses

Our cogenerative dialogue session began before the two students who had volunteered to participate arrived from lunch. On this occasion Michael, who had cotaught the lesson that had just concluded, joined Stephanie, Bert, and Ken. As the four entered the staff room they continued their discussion about the dihybrid cross that had begun in the classroom immediately after the lesson. Now, standing next to the chalkboard where he sketched his own solution, Ken argued in favor of his suggested method. Stephanie and Bert disagreed and Michael explained to Ken that, although his method worked out mathematically, it made little sense from a scientific point of view.

Michael:	[*To Bert*] No, Ken's right. It works because you put in all the genes. It just mirrors the genes rather than ...
Stephanie:	You get the combinations but not the cross. You get the two effective combinations, but not the cross.
Bert:	You know you're right on this when it comes down here that you get the two ... You can't do it....
Michael:	[*To Ken*] You're right. Mathematically it will come out the same....
Bert:	Oh, will it?
Michael:	You know why? Because what he does he just transposes the two genes
Ken:	I told you it is mathematically correct. I didn't know if it made any sense scientifically...

The transcript shows that not merely the subject matter pedagogy was at stake, but the very understanding of Punnett Squares. Everyone acknowledged that the two different ways that Ken and Bert had proposed yielded the same result, all genotypes and their frequencies of the cross between two dihybrid parents. But the initial reactions were different. Bert acknowledged the sameness; Stephanie suggested that while you get the right combinations, you do not have the representation of crossing (parents). What was open at that moment was why and how it worked. Michael made a first proposal in suggesting that there was a simple transposition of the genes from the two sides of the Punnett Square. Michael proposed that the two results were the same because of a 'transposition'. We do not know what exactly this implied or what he meant. But, as we show below, further inquiry into the topic by the coteachers in various situations brought out a possible answer to this question of 'transposition' and the implied symmetry in the two ways of setting up a Punnett Square.

A little way into the cogenerative dialogue session, Bert raised the topic of the (bungled) dihybrid cross; he wanted to know from the students present how to better teach the topic. He was genuinely concerned about understanding what he could have done in the situation that both identified as having involved 'mistakes'. The following brief interaction occurred between Bert and Natasia:

Bert:	Basically when I did that dihybrid cross, what would you have done? How would you have changed that?
Natasia:	The way you made the dihybrid, with the mistakes...?
Bert:	Yeah, with mistakes.
Natasia:	Well that's good. I been ... the easiest way is to make four boxes of four.... One big Punnett Square and make four individual Punnett Squares in it. Simple!
Bert:	Oh, then you would have recombined all the blocks from the four different Punnett Squares? Yes. OK. That's one way.

Here, Natasia provided yet another approach to conceptualizing the task of finding all possible crosses that none of the teachers present had brought up. Although we did not pursue her explanation at greater depth at that point in the discussion, it is important to note that a student contributed a potential pedagogical strategy to teaching dihybrid crosses by means of the Punnett Square.

The Punnett Square episode was sufficiently problematic and raised so many questions that it became the topic of a number of exchanges between Ken, Michael, and Stephanie, some focusing on the content, some on the form of representations, some on other ways of presenting the lesson. As a result, we all ended up having a better understanding. Our understanding increased, not only about how to teach dihybrid crosses and how to use Punnett Squares (subject matter pedagogy) but also about the subject matter as we came to construct what some cognitive scientists call a 'deep structure' of the domain.

Two Reflections on the Dihybrid Lesson

After the lesson, we reflected on our personal experiences. We shared these reflections with each other, and then began a new cycle of (email) conversation about the dihybrid cross, the Punnett Squares, and the ways to teach these topics.

Ken: I thought that the students were not following Bert's lecture. I had been scanning the class and watching what Bert was doing. Essentially he was wrong in what he was doing. Rather than say that he was wrong, I suggested that the students might be able to work it out. Perhaps I did not say it convincingly—but my sense was that the students heard it and so did Stephanie. I think Bert did not acknowledge what I said because he was challenged by the problem and probably was thinking 'Darn it—this is not working out! What am I doing here?' He was not prepared for doing this since Stephanie had dropped it on him.

At one point, Stephanie seemed to suggest that the students might try it too. A little later, Bert finally suggested that the students should work on the problem, but he did not give them time to do it—but by now he was obviously confused. At some point thereafter, Stephanie and I discussed what Bert was doing and I showed her what he might be doing. Natasia also made a suggestion but I think she needed space to figure it right out. I am sure she could have done it.

Stephanie seemed to suggest what I now refer to as 'my method'. Bert then (again) said the students could try it—but again he continued to talk and lecture. He was still puzzled as he walked away but he said, 'You know what, I might just set this up for them'. At that point, I suggested to him to do it my way—and he said 'No'. Michael suggested that you have to have one parent along one side and the other parent on the other side. Bert saw his problem and again said—no it is me that is screwing up—he continued and continued to screw up. Shortly before the end, there is some evidence of coparticipation as Stephanie walked up to Bert at the overhead and Natasia was obviously working out her solution to the Punnett Square aloud too.

Michael: The lesson had its own dynamic and, though we had really interesting coteacher interactions just prior to the 'Dihybrid' episode, there were things we could have improved in this part of the lesson. We bungled the lesson together with Bert. Now after the lesson, I am thinking that it would have been interesting to bring out all the different understandings of how the cross should be conducted and represented. But there did not seem to be time;

the lesson was like a runaway truck and there was little that I could do to divert it from where it was going. As the lesson unfolded I thought that Bert did not use a conceptual approach to inheritance. Rather, he was focused on combining letters and what the outcome would be when like gene combinations were counted. I thought about algebra and physics. In particular, I thought about the difficulties that many students have when asked to deal with notations that refer to generalized rather then specific entities. His focus was on getting the combinations, the fractions he had mentioned repeatedly. I failed to create space (room to maneuver) for myself in order to change the situation.

Both Stephanie and Ken made suggestions for going about the task differently. In the first instance, Bert acknowledged Stephanie's proposal ('Yeah') but it is unlikely that he engaged with the content of her statement, for it appears to be different from what he said. Or he interpreted it as basically saying the same as he had said before. In Ken's situation, Bert simply said that it was not possible to have one expression on one side of the Punnett Square, the other expression on the other. However, there was no discussion of why it could not be done. Bert knew, without having to think about it, that the convention is to have one parent's genes on one side, the other parent's genes on the other. However, none of us articulated that during the lesson.

Why did we, the other coteachers, not engage Bert more forcefully in changing where the lesson was headed under his lead? Stephanie and her coop Bert have a good relationship and share in the teaching. However, the fact that she did not pursue the difference between her own approach and what Bert presented shows that there may be more to that, for example, in terms of the power relations that still exist. But there are also other issues. For example, one teacher might not want to put another in an embarrassing situation. This certainly would be the case for me, especially because I also felt I was a guest in this classroom.

Continuing Conversations and Reflections

For us (and later for Stephanie), matters were not settled with the conversations about teaching dihybrid crosses and using the Punnett Square as a tool to find all possible combinations. Having been coteachers in the situations, we continued to reflect on particular lesson episodes, especially those that gave us an intuitive sense that we could learn for our professional practice more generally. Rather, as with many other topics that were taught by one or both, we engaged in continuing conversations about the subject matter and subject matter pedagogy and exchanged reflective notes that we made as part of our personal inquiries. We both had access to the video of the lesson and the subsequent cogenerative dialoguing. We frequently directed each other's attention to specific instances in the episode videotape to talk about their relevance for learning about teaching.

Initial Exchanges

FROM: Michael
RE: Punnett Squares
I was thinking that reflecting on learning subject matter and making use of our exchange as a form of learning among coteachers would be something quite useful for others.

FROM: Ken
RE: Punnett Squares
I would suggest (in favor of the less scientifically correct way to think about it) to take each attribute, one at a time. For example, let's take hair color. There are four combinations possible if fertilization occurs between a hybrid male and a hybrid female. The possibilities are 'HH', 'Hh', 'hH', and 'hh'. Write these possibilities across the top of a Punnett Square with hair color on the top and eye color on the left side. Now we can write the results for a hybrid cross involving eye color in the far-left column. These possibilities are 'BB', 'Bb', 'bB', and 'bb'. The cells within the square now show the possible combinations in a dihybrid cross for (eye color) x (hair color). Intuitively this seems very straightforward and it might be a first step toward understanding what is going on here.

You will notice in the video that I suggested that the students be left to work it out for themselves. I wish Bert had followed that advice because I know they would have been better off had they done it. I am certain that some would have done it one way and others would have developed other successful strategies. Then we could have spent some time talking about the merits of the different approaches.

The suggestion you made in class and later during our debriefing makes good sense and it is more scientifically grounded in one particular way. That is, we should be consistent in having the genotypes for the mating partners as rows and columns. Then the columns and rows are the gametes.

TO: Ken
RE: Punnett Squares

My sense is that there is nothing wrong with your approach and it is just a matter of convention to have the parents on the different sides rather than the different gene combination in the egg cell.

There may be an issue of going from the simple case, for example, crossing parents for one trait only, to the case you are describing. Let's take eye color 'B' (brown) and 'b' (blue). When you cross a mother 'Bb' with a father 'Bb', then it might be confusing to construct a Punnett Square in the way you do, unless you said something like 'take the dominant gene on one side and the recessive on the other'. But then, you run into problems with cases such as 'Bb' x 'bb', because the second set of alleles does not have a dominant allele. So, and given that you write a cross using 'x', it makes sense to have father and mother on different sides.

I am sure, if you let kids work it out, many other ways of looking at it would come out. What's of ultimate importance is finding the crosses. But because beginners are often caught up with the question 'how do you do it' and getting just one recipe rather than many different ones that they have to decide among, it makes sense to consistently use parents as the dimensions on the Punnett Square.

The other concern is one of constructing an internally consistent system. From this perspective, it makes sense to have parents on the sides rather than traits.

During the lesson, I did not receive your suggestion to let students work it out with the strength that you suggest it here. That

		BB	Bb	bB	bb
	HH				
	Hh				
	hH				
	hh				

		MALE			
		BB	Bb	bB	bb
F					
E	HH				
M	Hh				
A	hH				
L	hh				
E					

Figure 6.2. Two different ways of finding the genetic makeup of the offspring given that both parents are dihybrid.

is, I did not take your comment as a strong suggestion for changing the method. If this was the case I might have expected you to make a much more forceful suggestion of letting students work it out and then having them compare the results. Or I might have expected you to engage in a quick exchange with Bert on the sidelines to organize this part of the lesson. I also thought that Stephanie—but perhaps in a different part of the transcript—was suggesting to Bert that the students should work it out.

I think that they should have worked out not just the filling in of the boxes, but the setting up of a procedure for finding all possible crosses and the relative frequencies on their own. Subsequently, they could have discussed the benefits of the different approaches that they had come up with. In the end, Bert could have still articulated why scientists or teachers prefer one way over all the other possible ways of finding all possibilities from the crosses.

TO: Michael
RE: Update on Punnett Squares

I am attaching an Excel file (Figure 6.2) with my two alternative models for the dihybrid cross. Both need explanation, but the first one was what I intended to tell Bert about when he got himself confused in class. Later in the praxeology session I developed the second one following up a comment you made in class. You said, 'You have to have one parent on the top and the other on the side', or words to that effect. I made a sketch to see what you might have meant. Here I did much the same thing but for the female and male separately. The advantage of this is that it reflects the possible combinations (contributions) for the genes in a gamete. I am not sure if it is viable but it seems so. It is more difficult for students to grasp the second situation because in the Punnett Square the gametes need to be repackaged. For example in (2, 3) (r, c) we have 'Bh' and 'bH'. The repackaging leads to 'Bb' and 'hH'. I think that Table 1 (Figure 6.2, top) is not as good as Table 2 (Figure 6.2, bottom).

TO: Ken
RE: Update on Punnett Squares
Thanks for the spreadsheet. I know that you were thinking about Table 1, for you asked during the lesson whether we cannot have 'eye color across and height down', and from this I knew that you were looking at the possible combination in the fertilized egg.

Your second table corresponds to what I had produced, for it puts the possible combinations of alleles in the sperm on one side, in the egg on the other. For comparison purposes, I reconstructed the different ways to solve the problem of the dihybrid crosses as they were suggested during the lesson. I am attaching it as a figure (Figure 6.3).

Your comments about the repackaging are interesting, for I hadn't thought about which aspect might be difficult for students. Now after your comment, I am thinking that 'all possible combinations' for the sperm/egg cell may be the first trouble spot, and then the one you are referring to, sorting alleles in the fertilized egg may be the other.

When I think about it, I have never had an explicit explanation or diagram which said 'all possible combinations of alleles in sperm...', 'all possible combinations of alleles in egg...', and for the crossings, 'all possible combinations of fertilized eggs'.

Some teachers might just go for the letters. They probably do not think about the potential difficulties that students might have. Also, they may not provide students with more opportunities to go back and forth from phenotypic information to genotypic in-

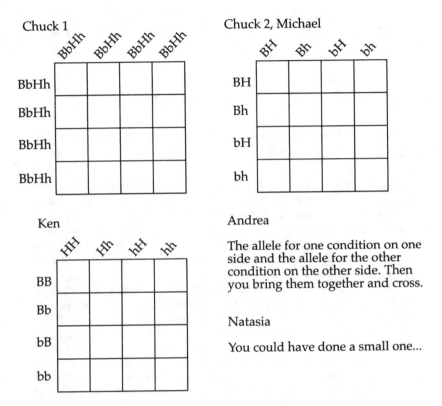

Figure 6.3. Comparison of the different solutions for finding all possible gene combinations in the offspring generation.

formation, and so forth, as was required in the example I made up.

Personally, I had not thought about the fact that it might be difficult for students to arrange the four letters that would end up in each cell, I mean, that the 'repackaging' might be difficult. This, from a learning perspective, would have been an interesting case. We could have compared it with the work that Dennis Newman, Pam Griffin, and Michael Cole described from their analysis of fourth graders who were asked to find all possible combinations between pairs of cards or colors or something like that.[4]

---

4   Newman, Griffin, & Cole, 1989.

I am thinking right now that Natasia might have thought about doing it your way, first finding all the genotypes for hair and eye color, then finding all combinations possible for the genotypes.

From Michael's Reflective Journal Entry, May 30, 2000

As I am going over my notes from the lesson in Stephanie's class, I find the following from Chiew's half of the class:

> I am working at the elbow of Bert in my attempts in helping her [a female student] construct a Punnett Square. My task is unsuccessful for two reasons. First, the student seems to be reluctant to construct me as a teacher and is continuing to seek help from Chiew although I am offering to answer any questions. Second, the student does not understand what is meant by the task and does not really listen to my explanations of how to find all possible crosses.
>
> When Bert enters Chiew's classroom, the student calls Bert, who approaches her. I am staying right there to listen to how Bert teaches the student to help her understand. He begins talking about crossing a heterozygous and a homozygous dominant individual. At that point, the student says, 'Why do you give me that big talk with words that I don't understand?' Bert explains again and goes into the mechanics of setting up the Punnett Square and putting the letters along the sides.
>
> The student acquiesces but I am walking away with the sense that she still does not understand. Bert asks her to 'do all possibilities of breeding the F1 population given that the parents were 'GG' and 'Gg'. That is, the student is to find the genotypes and phenotypes of the F2 population. A recollection flashes through my mind. In the book, *The Construction Zone*, the authors show how 'finding all possible combinations' was not an instruction that students followed or did not follow, but the description of a situated achievement when it actually happened (among the fourth graders).

Given these observations, I am now thinking that there are probably students in our class experiencing difficulties understanding. The big words, 'homozygous recessive', 'homozygous dominant', and 'heterozygous', in the context of many other foreign words—in the root language that students bring to class—make for a discourse that is strange and incomprehensible to (some) students.

I am doing what I understand the task to be on a little sheet of paper (Figure 6.4).

I want to find out what you get in F2, and which proportions, when you cross a 'homozygous dominant' and a 'heterozygous' parent. I begin by doing a Punnett Square for F1. Then I am doing 'all possible combinations' of crosses given the F1 population containing genotypes 'GG' and 'Gg'. I then do the three Punnett Squares to the very right. I realize the combinations of F1 crosses will not occur with the same likelihood. Off the top of the head, I am thinking 25%, 50%, 25% and write these down the left side. I copy the percentages on the right side. I then wonder what the genotype proportions will be in F2, and have the idea that 50 is double 25, I add another Punnett Square next to the '50%' one. I then count out all items 'GG', 'Gg', and 'gg' to get 9, 6, and 1.

These considerations bring me back to Bert's lesson where he insisted that you would get 9, 3, 3, and 1. I am thinking that there is probably an underlying structural similarity between the dihybrid cross and finding out F2 given parental genotypes.

I become uncertain about the relative frequencies of F1 crosses and go back to the Punnett Square at the top right of the figure. I am drawing the little subdivided box containing 'GG' and 'Gg'. As I draw the two arrows on top of the box, symbolizing first and second pick of an individual, I realize that it is like rolling the dice with two sides, a coin throw. There are twice as many possibilities for an uneven pairing than for the same sides to show up; that is, head-head and tail-tail have half the possibilities of head-tail combination (which could also be tail then head).

At this point I have the sense that I 'got it' and consider my search terminated.

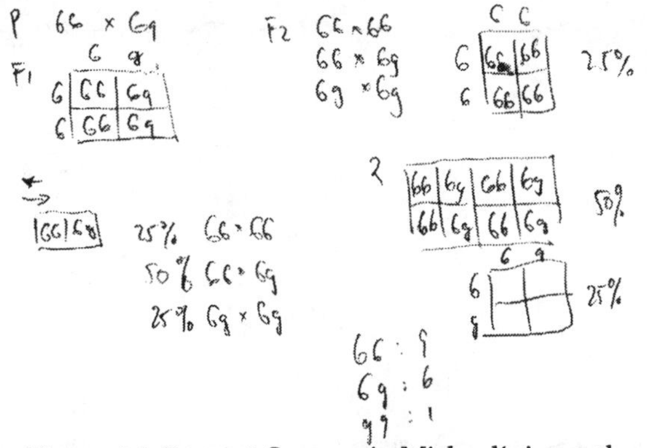

Figure 6.4. Punnett Squares in Michael's journal.

Unfolding, I learn, rather than having a logic that emerges. The crosses and counts are not self-evident and straightforward unless one has overlearned and is very familiar with the topic. I evidently do not have the answer to the problem but engage in finding one that is satisfactory to me, or as happens sometimes, one that I will abandon if my search doesn't lead to a satisfactory answer.

As I am looking back over my own process, I see that there are likely to be a number of challenging steps for students, steps that I engaged in intuitively but which would have to be articulated for the students. Or, which the students have to discover for themselves in their own actions.

The big problems are likely to arise in the second step, finding all combinations of crossing, and then finding the fractions of possible allele combinations in F2.

*

As I am looking back over my notes, I realize that I could make a 4 x 4 square, put 'GG' and 'Gg' on top and on the side. I then think that it would be like four small Punnett Squares and wonder if I would get the same numbers as I had before. I take out a sheet of paper and actually do it. I get the square in Figure 6.5.

As I am writing out the F1 genotype combinations, I realize that it will be in the relation of 9:6:1 for GG:Gg:gg; I do not have to count but intuitively know that this is the case. (This is similar to Bert's 9:3:3:1, but because I only have two alleles, the '3' and '3' are the same in the present case.) I think it works because there is a 50:50 chance that the father is 'GG' or 'Gg', the same for the mother. That is why the Punnett Square will provide the same answers, because I get all possible combinations from the population, that is, I get twice as many 'GG' x 'Gg' as I get 'Gg' x 'Gg' and 'GG' x 'GG'.

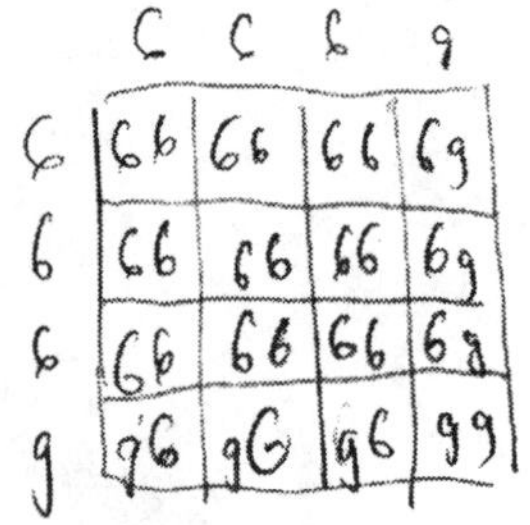

Figure 6.5. Punnett Square in Michael's journal involving a thought experiment.

I feel that I learned something in genetics that earlier this morning I had not known. It is a satisfying feeling to find the underlying structure that is isomorphic. That is, there is an underlying pattern that makes things regular in the way they appear, and it is satisfying to find these patterns. When things make sense, there is a sense of gratification.

I am thinking about Ken and the way he earlier constructed his Punnett Square. He was really satisfied with the way he could cross hair and eye color; it made sense to him in the way he had achieved it. When I talked to him, I remember that it was satisfying to know why the two different ways lead to the same number. That is, I knew the structural properties (perhaps deep structure) that would make the outcomes of the two approaches similar. All of this reminds me of a case in the history of physics where there existed at one point two approaches to quantum mechanics: the wave equations proposed by Schrödinger and the matrix mechanics by Heisenberg. It took some work, two years (Wolfgang Pauli or Dirac?), to show that the two approaches were equivalent.

What I am describing here has likeness with the genetics we are dealing with, though perhaps in the reverse way. On the surface there appear to be differences, that is, there are different ways to get the same results, predictions. In fact, what we can do is construct a similarity at another level, which then allows us to commute between the two different approaches, and we know why despite their apparent differences they will lead to the same results.

TO: *Michael*
RE: *Punnett Square*

I read over the analysis that you provided in your Reflective Journal (May 30) and what you have written in your email message. The vignette is very fresh in my mind because Stephanie and I discussed this yesterday afternoon while we watched the videotape a couple of times. I want to take a moment to stand back and reflect on how far we have come.

I can see a lot of learning and increasing generalization that come from our interactions that have occurred since that lesson and particularly in your journal notes. First, beginning with the initial understandings in the classroom we all began to better understand the different solutions to finding all possible combinations when we talked about it in our praxeology session. Your initial reflections (when you were working at Bert's elbow) already provided you with insights for subsequent parts of the lesson. Then you, Stephanie, and I continued our interactions and articulated why the different approaches yielded the same results. That is, we elaborated what researchers sometimes call a deep structure of the domain. Second, we similarly developed a deep understanding of the pedagogical issues involved in teaching dihybrid crosses and the use of Punnett Squares in science classrooms.

When I look back at our process, I can see a continuous spiraling evolution in which we take earlier understandings and develop them through analysis and further reflection.

Michael's Reflective Journal Entry, June 2, 2000

From the beginning, I was interested in why the different approaches worked, and today, I set out to follow up on this. My hunch was that there is some underlying symmetry, perhaps two processes that are commensurable so that you can do first one action then the other without a difference in the result. That is, I was looking for two operations (matrices in quantum mechanics) that are commutative (commutative property of addition in mathematics). So I conceptually unpacked both approaches by reconstituting them from 'first principles', that is, laying out all operations. This led me to the diagrams and notes in the figure (Figure 6.6).

Because I was thinking of the symmetry and two steps (there were 'literal' images in the back of my mind of the quantum mechanical operator and also of differential operators), I immediately began numbering my steps. I wanted to be able to show that the two steps are reversed in the two approaches. In a second step, I wanted to show that these two steps are commutative.

Ken's approach basically constructs all possible pairings of genes for hair color, then all possible eye colors, which can be done with the Punnett Square. Then he uses a 4 x 4 Punnett Square to 'find all possible combinations'.

Ken

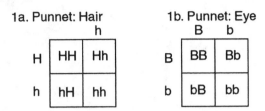

1a. Punnet: Hair

	H	h
H	HH	Hh
h	hH	hh

1b. Punnet: Eye

	B	b
B	BB	Bb
b	bB	bb

2. find all pairings, each with each,
   use a square.

Michael

1. Find all pairings for each parent

	B	b
H	BH	Hb
h	hB	hb

parent 1, 2

2. then cross (find all pairings)

Figure 6.6. Michael's analysis of different approaches to the problem of 'Finding all possible combinations'.

I then construct my own approach, which is to 'find all pairings for each parent', meaning all possible allele combinations that would be in a chromosome passed on to the offspring. 'Then cross' means that all found possibilities are crossed, each parent on one side of the resultant Punnett Square.

I realize that the Punnett Square really is nothing else but an accounting device to 'find all possible combinations'; that is, there are two steps where you find 'all possible combinations'. These two steps are commutative. To make this even more explicit, each allele could be marked as coming from father or mother. Because the F1 generation will have one allele from each father and mother, the overall task asks us to find all possible combinations of placing one allele from each parent for each color.

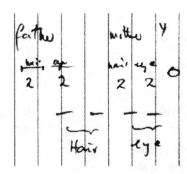

Figure 6.7. The representation that allowed the recognition of 'commutativity'.

Now I think I have an even better understanding of the underlying structure that makes the two approaches commensurable. In
the following diagram (Figure 6.7), I wrote out what the child gets
in terms of alleles (lower part), that is, there are four slots to be
filled, two by the mother and two by the father. Two slots have to
be hair color alleles and two slots have to be eye color alleles.

If I want to find all possible combinations, I get two possibilities for a hair color allele from the father on the first F1 slot and
two possibilities for an eye color allele from the father on the second slot. The same pattern comes from the mother, for the third
and fourth slots in F1. So that I end up with 2 x 2 x 2 x 2 = 16
possibilities. Now it doesn't matter which way I arrange the slots
on the bottom, all that happens is that the 2s in my multiplication
will change their slot. But we know that multiplication is commutative so that it does not matter which place each multiplicand
takes, the final result will always include 16 different combinations of two different alleles from each of two different parents.

I think that here the arrangement, the physical arrangement of
slots for parent (see father) and child helped me in this 'break-
through'. The arrangement at one level is by parent, attributing
hair and eye to parent. The second (lower) arrangement of slots is
by trait, but also contains a total of four slots, two for each trait.

TO: Ken

RE: Further learning about Punnett Squares

I am still thinking about why it works conceptually and have worked out a solution, which I have attached to this email as 'Reflective Journal Entry (June 2)'. There has to be some underlying symmetry, something that arises because you do it twice, and then it does not matter which you do first and which you do second.

I am just now going back over your notes. You said 'I am not sure if the science is always correct in what I have written'. I am certain that what you have done is *intrinsically* correct, as I showed there is no difference between the two approaches at a conceptual level. It may not be consistent with what biology teachers attempt to teach, the rote adherence to particular procedures, but it is fundamentally correct in yielding the results you are supposed to get.

As I go back over the process of thinking through the lesson and the problem, I feel a deep satisfaction that I know something that I didn't know before. Also, I feel satisfied because it is not just that I acknowledge that the two methods yield the same result. Rather, it is the fact that there is a way that I can see the fundamental similarity between the two approaches, based on some 'abstract' scheme that is consistent with other schemes that I know.

It is perhaps only over a lifetime that science teachers come to such realizations because they might not take the amount of time that I spent here in coming to grips with this problem. But I have a sense of deep understanding, which I often get only after having taught something many times over and being not only familiar with it but also in the position to answer all the different student questions that could come up about the topic.

I am pleased with our process because I have the sense that I could teach the subject and would have alternative pedagogical approaches to teaching the subject matter. I could do this, although I have not taught genetics in close to 20 years. Then I was a beginning teacher and the classes consisted of grade-nine students who had genetics as part of their general science course. I know I would teach genetics differently now than I did during those days. I would now set up problems of the type, 'find all possible combinations' and then let students find them. Then engage them in a whole-class conversation and talk about the different approaches that they may have come up with. So I feel I also developed a pedagogical content knowledge in the process of working through the problems following our lesson.

Metalogue: Teaching and Learning About Punnett Squares

Michael: Where does this lead us with teaching and teacher education? I think that coteaching provided a starting point for us to learn about the content of genetics in ways that we probably would not have if we had taught by ourselves.

Ken: That is certainly the case. If I were to teach something like this myself I would have prepared from a book because for me this is quite out of field. I have taught genetics as a teacher but the last time was in 1973, and even then my knowledge was based on what was in college and high school texts at the time. In this particular vignette our roles were not as clearly defined as they were when Stephanie was at the front. I think that is possibly due to Bert being handed the reins. He burst forward and set himself up as in charge. Had it been Stephanie who taught, I would have stepped forward if the confusion had unfolded as it did with Bert. Then I would have done it with hair on the top and eye color on the side. Then there would have been confusion!

Michael: We probably did not make the best out of the different approaches in our praxeology session, but certainly our present interaction (yours and mine) allowed the two of us to come to new understandings. If we had to coteach again, the lessons would reflect this learning.

Ken: Our cogenerative dialoguing was very good in many aspects. The issue of the dihybrid cross came up twice. In the beginning I was writing on the chalkboard and the three of you took a strong view that what I did was mathematically OK but of limited use scientifically. I knew the answer was right but wanted to be sure that what happened was conceptually solid. So, I just took your word for the fact that my approach was just a way to get the right answer. During the cogenerative dialoguing when Bert raised the issue directly with the students I did not take the chance to say more because I had decided the issue was dead. If we had

had our most recent discussions prior to the dialogue I would certainly have asked Natasia what she had in mind for the four small Punnett Squares.

Michael: I feel that reflecting on my own process of doing the Punnett Squares also allows me to reflect on possible difficulties students might face and at what point these difficulties would arise. But I am certain that if we were to engage in a conversation with you and other coteachers in this lesson, I would learn even more. It might turn out that what I have been doing up above is not consistent with the canon. In which case I would have to reconsider and learn even more.

Ken: I too learned a great deal from the coteaching, the conversations after, and then the subsequent conversations with you and Stephanie. I am very conscious of the folly of teaching such ideas algorithmically. What we want students to understand is really about relationships between phenotypes, genotypes, and the complex arrangements that can arise from sexual reproduction. However, it can all be systematized and patterns can be seen in the data. I think these are the most important aspects to be learned. I do not see anything so particular about this dihybrid cross against other forms of dihybrid cross that can also be done. Stephanie and I worked through many (perhaps all) crosses involving two alleles and involving homozygous dominant, homozygous recessive, and heterozygous examples. She explained to me that these are not typically done in biology classes because they are too straightforward. My own impression is that they should be done.

Ken: The situation you described in which students were asked to generate the possible distribution of traits in the F2 generation resulting from interbreeding among F1 associated with a 'GG' and a 'Gg' got me thinking back to Natasia and her comments about four little Punnett Squares. If you do this problem on a 4 x 4 Punnett Square each cell represents four possibilities. Working it all out results in 36/GG, 24/Gg and 4/gg. Maybe this is what Natasia meant when she talked about Punnett Squares within Punnett Squares. If so I am not sure how she would set it out. I have set it out in several ways that are not all that meaningful.

Michael: Cogenerative dialoguing and reflecting on the deeper aspects of the kinds of things we are teaching allow us to come to better understandings of the subject matter and subject pedagogy. Now here I participated as a researcher-coteacher, and the participation has allowed me to understand an aspect of genetics and genetics teaching in new ways. This is also an aspect of professional development. That is, we are science teachers who have changed our understanding of genetics and pedagogy, but such learning is seldom made thematic in the science education research literature.[5] This development can influence the preparation of new teachers.

Ken: Yes. I think this is a good example of how we can build deeper understandings of the science subject matter. Of course we could have done precisely the same thing if we had selected some aspect of African American psychology, for example, verve, to build into the enacted curricula. In that case the discussions would have led to a deeper understanding of African American psychology and the ways in which curricula can be designed and enacted to be culturally appropriate. In any event, as a new teacher, I am sure Stephanie benefited a great deal from the praxeology and various Internet and face-to-face interactions.

Michael: How to better prepare future teachers in terms of subject matter is one of the challenges that science (like math) educators are struggling with, and that was one of the key issues in some of your earlier research grants.[6] It is possibly not by taking more courses, but by engaging in the same kinds of activities as I have done here that we come to better understand the subject areas that we are supposed to teach.

Ken: This is a very significant realization I think we both have come to. I did not think too much about cogenerative dialogue as a way of developing deep understandings about science subject matter.

---

5   For an exception, see 'Autobiography and Science Education', special issue of *Research in Science Education*, 30(1).
6   E.g., Roth & Tobin, 1996.

Another Recursion

Six weeks after the lesson, and after having reflected on the content and pedagogical content of the lesson on dihybrid crosses, Stephanie and Ken watched the episode again to permit possible further learning to occur.

Ken:	Given what the kids know, what is the best way of getting from a monohybrid cross to a dihybrid cross? I mean, from our perspective now where we have had maybe six weeks to distance ourselves from this episode?
Stephanie:	Well, the advantage I feel of doing the cross is that they can actually visualize the coming together of the alleles.
Ken:	When you say the cross, you are saying 'Using the Punnett Square'. So there [makes a cross over the Punnett Square] is a cross. Is that what you mean? They are coming together?
Stephanie:	Yes, because you have a pair on this [horizontal] side and a pair on this [vertical] side you are actually in a position of seeing an allele from this [horizontal] parent matching up with an allele from this [vertical] parent.
Ken:	What caused you to make that move? Is it just the way you've been taught, to have a parent on the left and a parent on the top?
Stephanie:	That's right.
Ken:	So how would you set that out in this example for someone like Natasia who understands it fine? Or, I'm a physicist, just teach me how you would do it in this scenario that we're just talking about now with a parent on each side....
Stephanie:	Well, this is the part that's confusing, the part that Bert had trouble with and the part that I had trouble with too is.... You have to account—and this is the part that I bet there is a better way, if I really sat back and thought of it—because it is the part that is confusing. I think that you have to account for all of the possibilities. So, the possibility could be to have the dominant, so a big H and a big B. Now that I'm thinking this through, it is all coming clear now. What had not been taught is that this should really be taught alongside sexual reproduction because what actually needs to be seen here is that these are within gametes.
Ken:	These are possible gamete combinations?
Stephanie:	These are possible gamete combinations. And in biology it usually varies; sexual reproduction can be taught in a to-

tally different unit, like way down the road, when it comes to human physiology, even though at this point mitosis and meiosis have been taught. Not a lot of time is actually spent on, you know, 'Here are the eggs and sperm and these are the possible combinations that come together'. So maybe something actually more visual in terms of showing that. Because this just looks like letters, just letters, you know, coming together, combinations. This is more like math. So you can have this combination.

Ken: That's a critical pedagogical move; to relate that to gametes is really important and so the other thing you need there is whether you're talking about the mother or the father. And I don't think that was ever made clear in Bert's efforts to do the Punnett Square.

Stephanie: Right. And one reason for maybe not is... because they are both about the same. You know what I'm saying?

Ken: Right. But as a pedagogical move? Don't you want to say we are, just by convention, we are always going to put the father across the top or we are going to put the mother across the top whatever convention you are going to have?

Stephanie: I think that definitely would have helped to make it more personalizing. It would make it like 'This is a human being crossed with another human being' rather than 'These are letters being crossed with other letters that would lead to this ratio', as Michael has pointed out earlier.

Readers will notice that the conversation was quite equitable. Both Ken and Stephanie met in order to pursue what we have learned from talking about, analyzing, and reflecting on the episode. Ken, though he had been Stephanie's methods professor, did not come down on Stephanie for not having prepared an alternative lesson that she could have substituted for the planned investigation, a plan that had to be abandoned because of lack of time. The purpose of the conversation was to extend the praxeology and build our understandings of what was taught and how it might be better taught in the future. In fact, Ken and Stephanie were both attending a course on African American psychology.

Ken had thought about another way of doing the Punnett Square and was not convinced that letting students figure out their own approaches would not facilitate their learning of dihybrid crosses. Stephanie first recited a way of using Punnett Squares to figure out the result of crossing different parents—it is what many teachers including Ken and Michael do with all but a few areas of special expertise. When Ken asked Stephanie how to teach the dihybrid cross, she articulated the difficulties in teaching this. As she attempted to articulate how to teach dihybrid crosses she began to realize ('it is all coming clear now') that the context for teaching dihybrid crosses should be different. Stephanie began to articulate that one should assist students in understanding the provenance of the gametes from egg and sperm rather than teaching the Punnett Square. Punnett Squares 'just look like letters' and become 'more like math'. Here, she moved to a new level of understanding subject matter pedagogy.

Ken articulated the process of placing parents at the two sides of the Punnett Square as a convention, which Stephanie elaborated by suggesting that this fact allows us, teachers, to reconnect to students' experience of crossing human beings with human beings. Ken and Stephanie continued their conversation, which allowed them to develop their understanding of the particular contexts that might help students to construct an understanding of Punnett Squares.

Here, further learning about teaching Punnett Squares occurred not because a teacher said that the learners had to acquire new understandings or because there was an external pressure (grades, professional development requirements) but because of an interest in further understanding how to improve the teaching of mono- and dihybrid crosses.

*

In our experience, there are many areas that we know because at some point in our lives we were forced to rote-learn something that we did not understand. As engaged and professional teachers, we uncover such moments and develop them. This development benefits us, in that we come to better understand subject matter and subject matter pedagogy. In this, our own learning comes to benefit our students and their learning, the true object of the activity in which we engage on a day-to-day basis.

Coteaching, the associated cogenerative dialogue sessions, and the subsequent face-to-face and email interactions provided us with many opportunities to learn subject matter and subject matter pedagogy. Our learning process documented here exemplifies the tremendous learning that coteaching/cogenerative dialoguing affords—as we have documented for other teachers in other forms elsewhere. Because of our strong commitment to changing teaching praxis by participating in praxis, our own learning has to be a core aspect of our participation in the everyday activity of teaching school science. Commitment and partiality therefore characterize our approach, but the partiality is accounted for in and legitimized by our theoretical framework and its associated first-person methodology.

CHAPTER 7

Coteaching/Cogenerative Dialoguing: Research as Classroom Praxis

So far, we have presented coteaching/cogenerative dialoguing as a way of teaching and learning to teach. In this chapter, we articulate these activities at a meta-level, which allows us to conceptualize teaching and researching within a common framework. In the process we outline activity theory and describe coteaching/cogenerative dialoguing in terms of this meta-theory. Then, in order to articulate the roles of researchers in our paradigm, we return to the genetics lesson that we cotaught with Stephanie and Bert. We use learning environment research as an example of the type of academic research pursuits in school classrooms because we have engaged in it ourselves and in the process have changed significantly in the way we have done research during our careers.

Over the past two decades, learning environment research has become a firmly established form of research on teaching and learning.[1] Whereas after its initial conception researchers mostly used questionnaires, recent studies enact and recommend the use of a range of observational and interpretive methods.[2] Questionnaires and interpretive methods enhance each other in the sense that interviews are used to probe in greater depth what individual students and teachers have to say about their classrooms and the resources used to support their learning.

---

1   Fraser, 1998.
2   McRobbie, Roth, & Lucas, 1997.

Each methodological approach makes use of a particular set of constructs, developed by researchers with or without prior interpretive research that probes the way in which people understand their relationships to the contexts in which learning occurs. As theories of teaching and learning change, so do the constructs, and with them, the learning environment questionnaires, which frequently make use of combinations of old (proven) and new scales. Each construct and the methods used to research learning environments 'reduce the complexity of what happens in classrooms, and focus on selected aspects of student and teacher actions and interactions'.[3] As researchers point out, however, each theoretical frame with its associated set of constructs constitutes only one window into learning environments. Because observation and theory are tightly related, neither can be foundational in the comparison of competing theories.[4] The choice of theory, and therefore the range of observable phenomena, will reflect the values of researchers and their educational praxis.

In this chapter, we propose a different way of doing classroom research grounded in a theoretical framework that has as its basic value the primacy of human agency. This agency, or power-to-act, includes the capacity of individuals to participate in creating their lived-in worlds rather than merely being determined by them. We subscribe to a fundamental belief that researchers can select the form of inquiry they find appropriate to explore the puzzles that underpin their research on learning environments. Accordingly, in this chapter, we do not participate in the pervasive critique that adherents of the theoretical framework we are using have launched against the use of questionnaires, surveys, and experimental research.[5] Rather, we elaborate on our approach to research on learning environments which, among other approaches, contributes to overcoming two persistent gaps in education, between educational theory and teaching praxis and between the praxis of research and the praxis of teaching.

Over the past decade, we have developed *coteaching* not only as a form of teaching but also as a way of learning to teach, doing research, supervising new teachers, and evaluating teaching in

---

3   Tobin & Fraser, 1998, p. 624.
4   Kuhn, 1970.
5   Holzkamp, 1991a.

classrooms (see Chapter 8). Coteaching is based on the fundamental idea that practices can be understood only from the perspective of the participating subject,[6] thereby requiring researchers to coparticipate in teaching in order to understand it. This first-person perspective provides us with a radically different view of classroom events and the classroom environment, a view that readers may want to explore for themselves.

In this chapter, we exemplify our theory-oriented work at two levels. First, we cogenerate theory together with teachers and students, with whom we have already shared classroom experiences, for the purpose of improving the practices of teaching and learning. Because of the equitable relations between participants, this is 'open theory', a democratic process of generating understanding and explanation. Second, we simultaneously theorize the activity systems of teaching/learning and researching at a meta-level, which allows us to account for the presence and interaction of researchers with the phenomena researched. Because of the particularities of human practices (e.g., meaningful and mediated subject-object relations), only first-person (subject-centered) perspectives allow us to recognize salient meanings and motivations that subjects (teachers, students) deliberately use to ground their actions.[7] Activity theory allows us to account for the mediated nature of human activities and therefore to counter those theoretical approaches which reduce humans to reactive and externally determined beings. Our framework therefore explicitly accounts for the fact that human beings participate in the shaping of their learning environments rather than merely reacting to a set of given conditions. The framework allows us to understand the mediational effect of the researchers' presence on the situations they research; that is, researcher-researched interactions cannot be neglected and have to be theorized together with the object of the research. We begin by articulating activity theory and use it to frame our *coteaching/cogenerative dialoguing* paradigm at a meta-level. We then provide a concrete case study of learning

---

6   Markard, 1993.
7   In this chapter, 'subject' connotes subjective level rather than the 'human subjects' of (quasi-) experimental research. We are interested in learning environments as they are constituted and experienced by each individual at the subjective level.

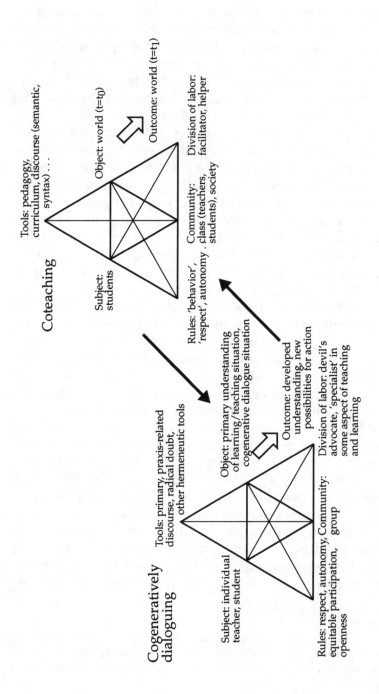

Figure 7.1. Activity theoretic articulation of coteaching/cogenerative dialoguing. All relations between pairs of concepts are mediated by a third concept.

environments within the *coteaching/cogenerative-dialoguing* paradigm.

Activity Theory, Teaching, and Classroom Research

We practice *coteaching/cogenerative dialoguing* as a method to deal with the problems created by a separation of theory and research from teaching. Here, we articulate *coteaching/cogenerative-dialoguing* practice in terms of practice-oriented and practice-relevant activity theory. Activity theory and the associated subject-centered (first-person) research approach are based on the assumption that it is inherently futile to attempt to understand human activity independent of contexts and that human practices can best be understood from the perspective of praxis.[8] Human beings and their environment, including researchers, are theorized as part of a fundamental unity. When we consider learning environments in terms of activity, we simultaneously theorize research and its object (e.g., the praxis of teaching and learning), thereby removing the gap between theory and the praxis that research seeks to explain. Teaching, learning, and researching are regarded as constitutive parts of daily classroom praxis.[9]

Activity Theory

Social science research generally focuses on what people do and, given certain external conditions, how they participate. In this way, human cognition, beliefs, attitudes, and so forth are theorized independently of the external world, which itself is taken as the source of external stimuli that bring about responses. However, this approach to human knowing has been criticized because the contributions that human agents make to constructing and structuring their environments are not included in an integral way.[10] Activity theory is explicitly based on an assumption that humans are co-creators of their (learning) environments, agents of

8   Leont'ev, 1978.
9   Roth, 2000.
10   Lave, 1988.

change with the power to act. Hence, activity theory regards learners as active creators of their learning environments rather than as passive reactants in a learning environment.

In most theoretical approaches, the unit of analysis is the individual human subject who engages with an object. In contrast, activity theory takes into account the context in which subject-object relations occur. Activity theory is conceptualized in terms of six primary elements: subject, object, tools, community, rules, and division of labor. Because the subject-object relationship is the primary concern in an activity it is necessary to consider at the same time the effects on the subject-object relationship of the co-mediational relationships involving the other four elements.[11] For example, if the student is the *subject* and learning science is the *object*, then salient *tools* might be communication, pedagogy, and curriculum. These tools are not independent entities; they are shaped by the social and cultural factors that characterize a *community* (e.g., school, classroom), such as its *rules* and the *roles of participants*. In learning activities, these elements and the mediated relations in which they are situated constitute the learning environment. In this way, activity theory simultaneously and dialectically articulates the human subject, its learning environment, and the (mutually constitutive) relations between both (Figure 7.1). In classroom research, if the student is the *subject* of the activity and her primary *object* is (an aspect of) the world (Figure 7.1, top right), then the purpose of teaching is to assist the student to change her relation to the world and thereby to provide her with an increased potential to act in the world. This increased potential to act is the *outcome* of the activity. In this process, *tools,* including pedagogy and subject matter language, mediate the student's relation to the object (i.e., the world). That is, the relation between the subject and its object is *mediated* rather than being of an immediate nature. What makes activity theory non-reductionist is that subject, object, and tools also participate in other mediated relations. For example, the society (*community*) mediates the relationship between student (*subject*) and pedagogy (*tool*); that is, because tools have cultural-historical origins, the activity of teaching and the associated learning environments for students are con-

---

11   Engeström, 1987.

nected to and are mediated by factors from within and outside the schools.

Learning environments are constituted by the mediated nature of the student-world relation (i.e., the primary relation) and the other possible mediated relations that set the context of the primary relation. For example, the relationship between student and teacher is mediated by pedagogy (tools) and also by the rules of interactions between them. 'Learning to speak out' would be a dimension of the 'rules' that mediate the relation between students (subject) and teachers (community). 'Learning to learn' is a dimension of the mediation of the subject-community relation by pedagogy. 'Learning to communicate' is a dimension of the relationship between students and other members of the class, that is, mediation via the rules. Hence, this approach to learning simultaneously takes account not just of different nested and hierarchical levels of environmental units, but also of the essentially mediated nature of all these levels.[12]

Activity systems embody internal and external contradictions that interfere with and impede the motives of the activity. For example, in urban schools, we often detect a contradiction between the language inner city students currently master and the middle-class language used by their teachers; there is therefore a contradiction between the subject and the tools. Contradictions are not inherently bad. Rather, in activity theory, contradictions (dilemmas, disturbances, paradoxes, and antinomies) are the driving forces of change and development.[13] These contradictions become central to our approach, because, once understood—not only in terms of lived experience but also in terms of their structural origin—they can lead to the articulation of actions and change.

Activity theory allows us to frame the contradictions between being a teacher and being the object of research on teaching. In research on teaching, teachers and the learning environments of their classroom are the constituent *objects* of the research activity system. As objects (objectified subjects), they are made accessible to analysis in various forms of representation including questionnaires, scale scores, interview transcripts, and videotapes. (Teachers and other individuals often fear of becoming the 'lab

---

12 Engeström, 1999.
13 Il'enkov, 1977.

rats' or 'guinea pigs' of social research.) Simultaneously, teachers experience themselves as objectified subjects in research and as subjective actors in the teaching activity system. There is a fundamental contradiction between these two activity systems, which teachers often perceive as conflict-laden relationships between two types of experience. There is the lived experience of being a *subject* and the simultaneous experience of being an *object* of research (i.e., *objectified* subject). Thus, theory-building research and teaching are different activity systems not only because of the difference between their system-constituent objects but also because of the contradictions in the experience of the participants in both activity systems. Because this form of research inherently remains external to the primary activity, teaching, we believe that it is a major obstacle to significant and lasting change.

Coteaching

From an activity perspective, coteaching provides an ideal context for learning by providing a 'zone of proximal development' in which the collective achieves more than any individual alone.[14] This zone of proximal development arises from the dialectical relation between social and individual development and is defined as the 'distance between the everyday actions of individuals and the historically new form of the societal activity that can be collectively generated'.[15] Coteaching therefore enables (new) collective actions that span a zone of proximal development. These collective actions become, as part of ongoing praxis, part of the individual action repertoire and therefore enlarge the action potential of the individual teacher. The individual member makes a contribution to the development of the community, and thus indirectly to her own development and learning process. Learning is therefore an integral and inseparable aspect—and one of the characteristics—of the praxis of teaching and learning.

Coteaching as an activity system is depicted on the upper right in Figure 7.1. The central object of coteaching is the same as

---

14 On the notion of 'zone of proximal development' see, for example, Wertsch, 1984.

15 Engeström, 1987, p. 174.

in traditional teaching; so are many of its tools and many of the rules that mediate the relations with students. However, there are relations and mediations that do not exist in the traditional situation, because of the newly introduced division of labor at the classroom level that has a horizontal (democratic) rather than a hierarchical character. It is evident from our figure that new relations between students and teachers are possible. These are often experienced by the individuals in our research as possibilities for better student-teacher personality matches, multiple opportunities for expressive means (tools), or teacher opportunities for attending to different aspects of the lesson (organization, telling content). This division of labor often 'changes the classroom dynamics' and leads to different student behaviors, which are concrete expressions in immediate experience of the changes that have occurred in the activity system. Thus, coteaching leads to new mediational forms that modify the learning environment.

As coteaching researchers, we are involved in the everyday praxis of teaching and therefore directly experience the learning environment. We are no longer removed from teaching but a central part of it. A crucial question for us is how we get from the primary understanding of praxis, that is, in terms of immediate experience (understanding), to a generalized, structural understanding. In our work, this is achieved by engaging a dialectical interaction of understanding, experienced in practice, and explanation, achieved by means of critical analysis. Understanding is a prerequisite for all theorizing; but only explanation-seeking critical analysis wrestles with the hidden presuppositions and common-sense ideology that surround us. These explanations enable *generalized* understanding and therefore give rise to new action possibilities and, ultimately, to change.

Cogenerative Dialoguing

Discussions constitute an integral part of our practice and include all participants (or their representatives) involved in classroom praxis (Figure 7.1, left). These include students, new teachers, teachers, university supervisors, and researchers. Max Eldon and Morten Levin refer to such talk about praxis as *cogenerative dia-*

logue.[16] The intent of these sessions is to use current understandings to describe what has happened, identify problems, articulate
problems in terms of contradictions (generalization), and frame
options that provide us with new and increased choices for enacting teaching and learning. That is, these sessions can be understood as a new activity (and learning environment) that takes the
classroom learning environment as its object of inquiry. To assist
us in making these sessions productive and equitable, thereby explicitly modifying this learning environment, we have developed a
heuristic that allows us to check whether the interactions that occur are consistent with some general goals (Table 5.2, p. 196). As
Table 5.2 shows, rapport, inclusion of all stakeholders, respect for
different forms of experience, and equitable participation are central tenets of these sessions regardless of a person's experience or
knowledge along one dimension or another (e.g., being a methods
professor or having 30 years of teaching experience). This heuristic
is therefore a tool to monitor the practical functioning of this secondary learning environment.

Our description so far has shown that all individuals participate in teaching and learning; in our original research on coteaching, no 'fly-on-the-wall' observers were allowed to participate.
Such a first-person methodology harbors dangers in that existing
understandings could be reified and thereby become ideology.
That is, when we use only immediate descriptions of the context,
we are likely to remain stuck and re/produce ways of perceiving
and acting in a particular context. So, while we need our immediate experience in terms of the immediate concepts that correspond
to them, we also need to engage in a critical analysis to come to an
understanding that makes salient the fundamental structures of
the condition that we find ourselves in while coteaching. This critical analysis requires our personal understanding of praxis but also
a 'radical doubt' or 'suspicion of ideology' to overcome the possibility that we might remain ideologically stuck in our current understanding.[17]

On the level of immediate understanding, we can come to understand conflicts as they appear at first sight. But immediate

16 See Eldon & Levin, 1991.
17 On the notions of 'radical doubt' and 'suspicion of ideology' see Bourdieu,
    1992b, and Markard, 1984, respectively.

understanding does not automatically increase one's action potential. This action potential lies at a very personal level, always being a question of 'What is my room to maneuver?' and 'How can I enhance the options I have?' Arriving at explanations, and implicitly at new understandings, puts a person in a new improved situation characterized by increased room to maneuver. All participants operate out of their own initial frames using their primary discourses to describe aspects of their praxis. In so doing they communicate at a level where frames can be analyzed and altered, and new frames can be generated. Paolo Freire advocates dialogic relations within a community, providing its members with opportunities 'to name the world in order to transform it'.[18] Cogenerative dialoguing therefore leads to locally relevant theory about praxis: praxeology.

Activity Theory and First-Person Research Methodology

In our work, activity theory goes hand in hand with a 'practice of (research) method' developed by the critical psychologists of the Berlin school.[19] The basic category in critical psychology is 'power-to-act' which irreducibly connects an individual and an environment, a fact that has to be accounted for in general models of human action. What must be central to any research effort in this spirit is the development, for each particular case, of a language and procedure that allow an understanding of the existing conditions in a *generalized* form not only by the researcher but more importantly by the subject herself. This development is directed not only toward understanding but also, and more importantly, toward creating new and *concrete* action possibilities, which lead to the removal of existing contradictions within the individual subject or the systemic relations. The development of new, concrete (rather than idealistic) action possibilities are therefore the motivation for doing research on learning environments. This replaces the identification of perceptions, for example, in the form of 'preferred' learning environments. Preferences often do not lead

---

18   Freire, 1972, p. 136.
19   This school was founded by Klaus Holzkamp, 1983b; for English texts on critical psychology see Tolman, 1994, or Tolman & Maiers, 1991.

to useful actions because, as the popular adage goes, 'the (pre-ferred) actions are *possible in theory* but *not in practice'*.

On a concrete level, we are obliged to ask how to articulate a specific praxis as part of the research process. Out of this proc-ess, it should be possible to capture the conditions that enable an extension of power-to-act, that is, the conditions an individual creates to increase the opportunities for him/her to maneuver. These conditions for the extension of action possibilities are there-fore understood *out of* praxis itself under the inclusion of the re-searcher and the inclusion of the particular researcher identity. Because meaning relations that give rise to action are always per-sonal, research questions are framed from the perspective of the person (*subject*) rather than from a third-person perspective (ques-tions *about* people). We assume that one can understand the con-ditions and in particular the room to maneuver only because we participate in praxis—or more strongly, we assume that to under-stand practice, we must participate in changing it.[20] This is so be-cause the room to maneuver during practical action is a charac-teristic phenomenon of praxis, subject to particular constraints of time and the level of experience of the practitioner. Conducted in this way, learning environment research becomes emancipatory to researchers and teachers because it brings about change in prac-tices that become *the* testing ground of theory. *Coteach-ing/cogenerative dialoguing* is our response to the gaps between re-search praxis and teaching praxis and between theory and prac-tice.

Classroom Research in an Urban Science Class:
Practice of Method

In our work, *coteaching/cogenerative dialoguing* arose in response to problems in the praxis of teaching. (As we described in Chapter 4, Michael began coteaching because his participating elementary teachers wanted to innovate but felt that they did not have suffi-cient science background to teach novel engineering curricula.)

---

20 Marx & Engels, 1970, in the last Thesis on Feuerbach suggested that philoso-phers were generally concerned with understanding the world whereas the real issue of research is to be able to change it in desired directions.

Since we engage in a practice of method, we provide a concrete example from our research. This example, which takes us back to the biology lesson that we cotaught with Stephanie and Bert and the associated cogenerative dialogue (see also Chapters 5 and 6), serves to show yet another dimension of our coteaching/cogenerative-dialoguing paradigm as it unfolds in the daily praxis of our work.

Coteaching Biology

The grade-10 biology class started with students constructing answers to the daily question designed to get them started and to refresh their memories of what they had learned previously. While Stephanie was preparing the materials for the upcoming student investigation, Bert talked to students about an article on the cloning of cells that had appeared that very morning in the newspaper. Ken picked up and expanded the topic. Stephanie then commenced the lesson. As the lead teacher she had planned a student investigation for the first part of the lesson, designed to assist students in learning about the scientific method, control of variables, independent and dependent variables, and so forth. Throughout this part of the lesson, the four teachers interacted with individual groups of students, sometimes standing at each other's elbows, and at other times working on their own with individual student groups. For the second part of the lesson, Stephanie had planned another activity, in which students were to apply what they had learned by constructing mobiles based on a scientific method of inquiry.

The first part of the lesson lasted longer than originally planned because we allowed more time to adjust to students' needs as they became apparent during the lesson. Accordingly, Stephanie and Bert replaced the second planned activity with an activity on genetics that first reviewed the monohybrid cross and then extended to the teaching of a dihybrid cross. Midway during that part of the lesson, Stephanie handed over the lead to Bert. Although the lesson was now in a whole-class forum, the different teachers still provided each other with space to enter into the ongoing conversation.

The following excerpt comes from the first part of the lesson when students investigated different variables that influenced the fall of a slice of bread spread with jelly to test the hypothesis 'bread always falls jelly side down'. The camera records the events at two different places, the front and back of the classroom.

Back of Classroom

Stephanie: OK, that would be another independent variable. How about height?

Natasia: I am not, if height is a variable then I can't change the amount of jelly. But I can do it with a lot of jelly up in the air [holds hand high up]

Stephanie: You are really doing two independent variables, and what we are going to do is, we are doing it simpler. We are going to do two separate experiments, each with one independent variable.

Natasia: No, this is not what I meant. See [moves toward Stephanie, about 6 feet from her].

Michael: How often did you drop it?

Natasia: Like this [holds her hand above her head] one time.

Michael: How sure are you that this one time it...?

Natasia: I am not. I was just testing. [Turns toward Stephanie.] I am making these two charts, and then testing the height three times.

Stephanie: OK. Perfect. Two different experiments. So you need to specify which one you are going to control, and then vary the height.

Natasia: You are using your left hand and then your right.

Stephanie: But that is not what you are changing, you are changing

Front of Classroom

Ken: [Stands next to the teacher's desk. Two students to the right of him are still sitting in their seats.]

Ken: [Approaches one of the two students, still in her seat, almost looking as if bored or not knowing what to do.]

Ken: [Touches her arm.] Are you ready to start?

St: Heh?

Ken: Are you ready to start?

St: Yeah, I am just [gets moving].

Ken: You needed a pep talk, did you?

Ken: [Walks on to the next student in her seat.]

height. You are not changing
the hand. You are changing
the height [moves away
from the two groups of stu-
dents].

Stephanie: [Moves next to Ken and the
second student still in her
seat.]

In this episode, we observe several elements characteristic of coteaching (see also the items in Table 5.1, p. 189). Michael, who despite his experience was a newcomer in *this* classroom community, followed Stephanie around to learn about appropriate ways of interacting with *these* students. However, being in a coteaching learning mode allowed him to interact with the students. Thus, when it became evident that Natasia had done only one trial of tossing the bread from a certain height, Michael posed a question that brought this to her attention as she walked toward Stephanie. As a physicist, he had not been satisfied with obtaining only one data point in a case where the outcome measure was a dichotomous variable. Thus, Michael utilized a moment of transition to ask a question that Natasia answered appropriately.

Michael—who in a traditional sense would have been designated as a 'researcher' watching the class and taking notes, subsequently used to write field notes and reports—adopted a different role. He was a participant and, as the lesson progressed, he interacted with students in increasing ways, assisting them in learning about experimenting and subsequently about genetics (i.e., he mediated their relation to the world; see Figure 7.1, p. 246). That is, rather than presuming that standing back gave him a privileged perspective, he participated in order to get the practice perspective.

While Stephanie and Michael interacted with two groups of students doing their investigations at the back of the classroom, two other students were still sitting in their seats. Ken, although Stephanie's supervisor, did not sit back and observe, and later admonish her about having failed to see these uninvolved students, but rather approached the students to involve them himself. That is, his role was not to judge the activity in the classroom from the outside but to actively participate. As a coteacher, his primary duty (within our shared understanding of coteaching) was to contribute to making this the best learning environment possible. He would later contribute his own perspectives on the events, such as lack of student involvement in the present situation, during the cogenerative dialoguing. As it turned out subsequently, the two students had been a concern of Stephanie for some time, because they seemed to have difficulties in following the lessons.

Cogenerative Dialoguing About a Biology Lesson

After the lesson, the four teachers (Stephanie, Bert, Ken, and Michael) and two students (Natasia and Shawan) met for a cogenerative dialoguing session. In this session, the most important issue to be raised and covered was how to deal with students who have learning problems. That is, although Ken had initially stated his observation of students sleeping or not being involved, Stephanie had reinterpreted the events in terms of the learning problems of the uninvolved students. This became very clear when Michael asked Stephanie about the critical issue arising from the lesson that they had shared:

Stephanie: Even in that small of a class, with the levels being so different, I feel like there are always two students left behind, who I am not giving enough attention to, and these are the students who need more attention. But because the other students are so much more boisterous and outgoing, I am always drawn to them. You know, 'What are you doing?' 'What is the independent variable?' And then I turn around and see that there are two students who are still sitting at the table, not doing the work. So, that's just a class of 15, or there were only 11 today. So when there is a class of 30, 33, and the gaps are even bigger, like how do I get my attention around to all of them? That is difficult.

Here, Michael had asked Stephanie to articulate an issue. He thereby took on a mediating role between Stephanie, the subject, and understanding the lesson, the object of our activity (i.e., a division of labor in the activity system [Figure 7.1, left]). Michael therefore encouraged Stephanie to talk about the lesson from her perspective and therefore to articulate it and evaluate it from her perspective. This is a starting point for one person, but has the potential to be picked up by others and become a topic for the group. This was a real problem that was picked up later again, and in fact was provided with some solutions including suggestions by the students. Michael pursued the issue further by asking Stephanie whether and how she started dealing with the problem she had identified. But Bert was the first to answer:

Bert: You mean, addressing the weak students? I mean you have the aides coming in. And we also have the grouping, we can do group activities....

Stephanie: One thing that I have found, and it has worked very well in the next-period class, because I have the weirdest division between students who work very, very fast and students who work very slow. And what I did, I buddied them up. And I was worried about that at first, because I was worried about, the poor students you know, they have to be buddied with somebody else, you know.... But they enjoyed it. And I spoke with the students, who are sort of the tutors, and I said, 'Don't go around bragging, 'Oh you need help, I need to help you'. Take your time, don't do the work for them'. And they like it, because they feel like they are teachers, and the other students just actually look forward to the help. So a student walked in the other day and said, 'Oh no, what do I do?' you know, 'My buddy is not here'. And when she comes in the next day, she goes 'Oh thank you. Thank God, she is here'. So that worked well. I was worried that it would place a stigma, and certain things, but they enjoyed it.

Although Michael directed his question to Stephanie, Bert entered the conversation and asked for clarification. Stephanie then addressed the question by offering an example from her own experience. Here, she provided a specific example of what she had done to deal with the problem of students being behind. The fact that this technique had succeeded provided her with the confirmation of a workable aspect of practice.

Michael, together with Stephanie and Bert, elaborated on the issue of using the buddy and tutor system by contextualizing it in terms of the learning that occurs as part of teaching. All three were in agreement that teaching subject matter actually assists them in better understanding the very subject matter. Thus, the potential problem Michael had raised—a fear that those who teach, tutor, or help others are held back—was resolved. In a more encompassing picture, teaching was reframed as a way of learning.

Ken:	Lots of variability, Stephanie finds this a challenge. We all find it a challenge. How do we deal with that challenge?
Natasia:	Have the people who catch on fast work together with those who don't catch on fast.
Ken:	And you don't think that the people that...
Natasia:	No, I mean like mix them together, like half, like me Jeanine, and a couple of other students in one group. Because some don't catch on as fast as others.... And let the ones who catch on faster help the ones that don't catch on as fast.
Ken:	What do you [to Shawan] think about that?
Shawan:	When I am in a class like where she is the only person who catches on like this [snaps fingers], like there is not everyone as fast.
Stephanie:	She is like super fast but not everyone else.

Natasia interrupted Ken to contribute to the conversation. This is unusual for students and in fact her contribution would, in most circumstances, be construed as undermining the power of teachers and university visitors.[21] Natasia suggested group work as a solution to a problem raised by Ken, but then Shawan provided an example in which this solution might not work. Natasia's suggestion was consistent with the literature in education that supports the use of heterogeneous grouping practices. But Shawan raised a potential problem with this model, if there was an insufficient number of students in the class to assume the leadership needed to provide sufficient expertise in each group.

In the following situation, Natasia and Shawan further developed enablements and constraints to learning in groups, and discussed having one or more of them participate as a peer teacher:

Michael:	What about if you had her [Natasia] taking on one group and then each, Ms. Stephanie and him taking on another group of four and another group of four? So in this way, you divide the class into 13, 14, groups of three?
Shawan:	So a teacher takes on...?
Michael:	Natasia one group, and each of them one other group.
Shawan:	That's good, but some of the kids might get a little disruptive.
Natasia:	Some kids will do that anyway.

---

21 Lemke, 1990.

Shawan:	So when she ... she is explaining the lesson to 'em and everything, but they go aaaah, they won't listen to her, they go, 'she's just like me, I won't listen to her'. And then they are tuning her out.
Ken:	And you think that they are just being disrespectful?
Shawan:	Yeah. Or, as many people is ... get the teacher for whatever she taught to help them better understanding. And Ms. Stephanie's case, she would teach the kids that don't catch on that fast. And then tell the kids, they should listen to what they are saying, because when Natasia is finishing, you know ... cause she's gonna ask them, you know, what they learned from what the teacher was saying. That's the way, to me, they would get dumped on, so they got to listen to her now, cause she's gonna ask us.
Stephanie:	But on research reports, you catch on and so you could help other students [to Shawan]. Every student has something that is her favorite.

Stephanie pulled the discussion together in the sense that she suggested how this could be organized across different activities and content areas where the different abilities and competencies of different students become important. She used a specific example in which Shawan had excelled to exemplify for the student what she meant, and to suggest that Shawan could take a role in assisting other students. So, although Natasia had been in the foreground as the central student in the genetics class, Stephanie pointed out that Shawan had excelled in another domain, where her own role would change from someone being helped to a helper. Both students agreed with this assessment, not only in its content, but as grounded in their lived experience of having helped other students as part of the class activities.

Metalogue

Michael: I was reflecting on the cogenerative dialoguing sessions. In our collective effort, we, students and teachers, enact practices that are consistent with the practices included in learning environment instruments you have used in the past including such dimensions as 'personal relevance', 'critical voice', and 'shared control'.[22] For example, in this one lesson we find that students are provided with opportunities to learn about the world outside the class. There was an activity in which they investigated the claim that slices of bread always seem to come to land on the jelly side; also, Bert and you brought up an issue relating to the current curriculum that had appeared in the news that very day. But more so, I find that being able to talk face to face about these issues and to enact personal relevance, critical voice, and shared control is a form of practicing solidarity rather than keeping the control of the lesson with the teacher who might administer a questionnaire.

Ken: This activity was a splendid example of how Stephanie, in particular, is able to connect not only with mainstream goals for science education, such as pursuing inquiry, but also how she is able to enact the curriculum in ways that are culturally relevant for her African American students.[23] For example, of nine psychological dispositions that Boykin attributes to African Americans (i.e., as part of their *habitus*), Stephanie incorporates at least six of them (e.g., verve, affect, communalism, expressive individualism, oral tradition, and social time perspective) into this one lesson. Stephanie enacts a curriculum that allows her African American students to get involved and thereby to accomplish what might be described as mainstream goals. I regard the incorporation of those African American dispositions as critical components of the learning environment because it is what possibly makes the lessons so inviting to her students (all of whom are African American).

Michael: We can see that students not only have a critical voice but that Stephanie changed her practice with the input from students and later assessed these changes as being of a very positive nature to the learning environment. Overall, it struck me how well the student participants articulated pertinent issues even though they represented the broad spectrum of students. Some of them were failing or had poor attendance records, and yet they made incisive and justified critiques, gave understanding comments, and proposed viable alternatives for ways of changing the learning environment.

---

22 Constructivist learning environment scale (e.g., Tobin & Fraser, 1998).
23 In Chapter 5, we present Boykin's, 1986, work on African American psychology more extensively.

Ken: *Cogenerative dialoguing* sets a context for change in the learning environment, if not within a week, certainly within the next month or couple of months. The conversations were very rich, detailed and persuasive. I can see this as a way of building credibility with students too. If you show a willingness to listen and act to improve their learning, I can see this being a major factor in establishing rapport with students and gaining their respect too.

Michael: What is most important to me is the radical openness that all parties bring to the cogenerative dialogue. It seems as if nothing is sacred and all participants contribute enormously to maximize learning in both environments (classroom, cogenerative dialogue). Even traditional hierarchical relationships between students and teachers have been abandoned. Thus, neither Natasia nor Shawan were afraid to voice preferences that were not consistent with those declared by their teacher. But they not only voiced alternative preferences, they also articulated rationales for them.

Research, Praxis, and Democratic Reform

In this chapter, we propose classroom research as a form of praxis in which teaching and research are different aspects of one overarching activity system intended to assist students to learn. Coteaching, constituted from a teacher perspective by its components of teaching and learning to teach (cogenerative dialogue), is a recursive process in which the same individuals engage in two different but functionally dependent types of activities—which we have theorized in terms of activity theory. As part of the research praxis of coteaching, cogenerative dialogue is based on the following central tenets. Common experience is the foundation for participation; all concerned (or their representatives) must participate; everybody needs to be active, contributing to the dialogue; all participants are equal at the outset; and participants' experience must be treated as legitimate, even if it may not be shared. In fact, the research can assist participants to develop the range of actions available to them, requiring that they understand the constructs.[24] If we attempt, for example, to derive an individ-

---

24 Holzkamp, 1984.

ual teacher's understanding of the learning environment by drawing on abstract constructs (e.g., the constructivist foundations of
'cooperative learning'), then he may feel disempowered since he
may not recognize his own situation and action possibilities in
such constructs. Furthermore, constructs that generalize 'common'
attributes rather than derive from and emphasize common historical origins always fail to capture what is concretely shared between people and things.[25]

The a priori selection of categories that might have salience to
the learning environments experienced by different types of participants is unlikely to be fruitful. We have participated in research in which this issue has been recognized and learning environment categories have been selected at some point during the
study when the research has been in progress for sufficient time
for the participants to have a grip on what is salient. We envision
discussions of a cogenerative type yielding categories that then
can be explored within a classroom using a variety of methods.
What might be different in what we are proposing is the inclusion
of students and teachers as equals at the table at which a decision
is made as to what is salient. As these discussions progress we
foresee situations emerging in which there is recognition that different people at the table are better able to contribute to one another's learning in different ways and in different domains of
learning. We think this is what makes the cogenerative dialogue
form such an exciting contribution to our work. The domains in
which the students could be helpful in teaching us are not necessarily predictable a priori.

The researcher as coteacher loses power and privilege in many
senses. One privilege that is lost in the cogenerative discussions is
the power to focus the discussions in particular ways. For example, a researcher as coteacher might find the discussion focused on
his teaching practices and the ways in which he might change to be
a more effective teacher. And in discussions of values and practices it might be the researcher's beliefs that are marginalized and
the emerging consensus within a group could be for very specific
changes to be introduced prior to and during the next lesson. We
cannot assume that the privilege of a researcher, often enshrined in

---

25   Il'enkov, 1982.

a priori questionnaires that measure perceptions of learning environments, can withstand discussions of the type that we have described in this chapter.

Despite (and perhaps because of) loss of researchers' privilege, the generalizations lead to local theorizing and lasting change in teaching practices. This is so because the mediations of individual possibilities by the generalized possibilities that exist in the society are made central. Our *coteaching/cogenerative-dialoguing* model therefore constitutes a way of walking the walk of 'learning environment research' and teaching. Here, all stakeholders who participate in a lesson (or their representatives) participate in conversations that are democratically structured. At issue is not the agenda of a more powerful agent, but the improvement of the situation in which all individuals are, although differently located, participants.

Participation is a necessary but insufficient condition for the success of learning environment research as an aspect of praxis. Participation in all phases (while undertaking participatory action research) is necessary, though knowledgeability is likely to be heterogeneous and distributed. Participation must be 'full' in terms of being legitimate or a form of 'codetermination' if it is to be empowering. Participants create new understandings of the learning environment in their own terms through a learning process that plays out as a dialectic between lived experience and critical analysis. Different individuals are not merely consulted in each phase of knowledge production; rather, they participate as co-producers of knowledge.

Our model of cogenerative dialoguing does not require *every* individual (such as every student) to participate in discussions about the classroom learning environment. The size of meetings if every individual were to participate would be prohibitive; rather, the stakeholders have to be legitimately represented. For example, different studies in the Scandinavian work context have shown that the participation of the entire organization is not required to improve the work environment, but that it is sufficient to have representatives of workers, unions, and management participate.[26] Initially, participants may have little expertise in empow-

---

26 For example, Ehn, 1992; Eldon & Levin, 1991; Onstenk, 1999.

ering forms of participation, that is, little expertise in making cogenerative dialogue itself a productive learning environment. Here,
our heuristics in Table 5.2 (p. 196) provide a framework to begin
and fine-tune interactions. We have found it useful to speak to
participants about the possible forms of participation before and
after a cogenerative dialoguing session, thereby sensitizing them to
a full range of possible types of interaction.

Traditional models of the individual and her environment are
based on the presupposition that individual beings and their environment can be theorized independently, and any interactions between the two are treated as add-ons. Learning environment research within such a perspective reifies the division between the
human subject, its context, and the notion that the (material, social) environment determines human actions. The 'learning environment' is thereby theorized as a box in which individuals find
themselves, and in respect to which they react.

From an ontological perspective it makes no sense that we
separate 'I' from 'we' or 'we' from 'it'. However, historically there
has been a tradition of people undertaking research from the side
and in a relatively nonparticipatory manner. They have identified
some interesting trends, outcomes, and implications. We assume
that they will continue to do this. In our own early research, we
used to separate the observed situation from the research, although we knew that the presence of researchers and the participants' knowledge that they are being researched affected in non-
negligible ways the research itself. Activity theory forces us to account for the researcher in the overall picture; that is, research
from a perspective that accounts for all the mediated relations
that constitute the context for an activity system necessitates that
we account for our own interactions with the participants. In this
way, we account for our own subjectivity and partiality, which
are often obscured in other paradigms. As our Figure 7.1 (p. 246)
shows, we explicitly articulate our simultaneous involvement in
teaching and in research on teaching and therefore incorporate the
effect of research on its object. We regard this approach to research on learning environments as contributing fresh insights into
teaching, learning, and the improvement of learning environments.
The approach addresses the problem that much of the research on
learning environments is built around a single theoretical frame-

work and its associated methodology. We do think many researchers in our field of learning environment research do what they do out of habit. It is time for the conversation about methods and the associated conceptualizations to be undertaken in a serious manner. Our suggestions here might be one way to proceed.

Credo

A school is a lousy place to learn anything in.[27]

We began this chapter with the statement that theory choice is based on values. One of our central values is the practical relevance of our work to the daily work of teachers and students. We chose activity theory because it is interventionist in its methodological approach. Seeing humans as creators of their learning environments, activity theory aims at assist learners in reconstructing these environments in practice 'so that people are not just objects or subordinate parts but *regain their role as creators*'.[28] We therefore endeavor to enact an activity-theoretic practice (of method) to build and sustain learning environments conducive to growth. Contrary to Howard Becker's line, which begins this section, we believe that schools can be exciting places to learn for students, (new) teachers, and researchers alike. Through our research activities we are committed to and personally invested in making a positive difference to the learning environments of schools in which we conduct our research.

Historically, as a result of a division of labor, educational researchers (and theorists) were able to separate themselves from daily praxis and retreat into the confines of the 'ivory tower'. In the society at large, there are many prejudices about the idealistic nature of theory, ivory tower thinking, and the irrelevance of university-based research to everyday life. Antonio Gramsci rejected the idealism of intellectuals who thought that practices and worldviews could be changed through rational analysis and critique.[29] He did not want intellectuals to work for their own sake

27   Becker, 1972, p. 85.
28   Kuutti, 1999, p. 373, our emphases.
29   Gramsci, 1971.

but to enter into a practical relation to society that contributes to a change in the cultural context. We feel that we are practically involved in the everyday affairs of education like Gramsci's 'organic' intellectuals.

Our methodology breaks with past traditions, taking us (researchers) into the front lines of the daily work of schools and, thereby, assisting in bringing about change. Our choices to undertake research in this way are based on our values and commitments. With Gramsci, we believe in the unity of understanding and changing of praxis and its political dimension. Whereas previous historical developments brought about a division between educational theory and educational praxis, and a physical movement of the former out of school, *coteaching/cogenerative dialoguing* returns university-based researchers to their historical origins to become significant partners in educational praxis. Thus, we ask ourselves about the extent to which our work in schools has emancipatory practical value to those whose lifeworlds we share. If the practitioners (the supposed beneficiaries) were to view our research and theory as idealistic, resulting in impractical outcomes, we would deem our effort to have failed.

Michael: Much of my research has been conducted from a position as the teacher—both the research on learning and the research on teaching. Although some of this early research was conducted with another teacher and involved a lot of collective planning and even coparticipation in teaching, we never thought of our activities in terms of coteaching. It was only when I became a professor that I started to engage explicitly in coteaching as a method of doing research, all the while contributing to the science learning of the students in our care. Coteaching/cogenerative dialoguing has had a tremendous impact on my own teaching and my understanding of the teaching of others.

Ken: My beginnings in classroom research began in 1973 with a study of teachers using an extended wait time to improve the achievement of elementary science students. This was a quasi-experiment that distanced the researcher from the researched. Gradually I became aware of more qualitative ways of exploring teaching and learning, and since the mid-1980s I have moved along a continuum toward more participatory ways of engaging research. The impetus for making changes in my ways of being a researcher is partly ethical and increasingly epistemological. On the one hand I view research as an activity that is necessarily transformational to the settings in which it is situated and on the other I feel like you, that to know teaching and learning it is necessary to coparticipate in the environments under study.

Michael: Coteaching/cogenerative dialoguing allowed me not only to view my own teaching more critically, through the views of others who wore the same shoes, but also to understand my own experience of teaching more deeply. That is, the paradigm allowed me to develop both my immediate understanding and my explanations of teaching in ways that brought about changes in teaching. It was through coteaching that I came to understand not only my teaching but also teaching more generally in the particular way that I do. I have also come to experience my relation to the students in my care in a different way, moving from the remote position of the authority of the teacher to the involvement of someone who experiences teaching as an act of solidarity.[30]

Ken: It turns out to be a little different for me. When I began to coteach with Mario it was more a case of him handing his class over to me and I had the task of making it work out in a context of the radical breakdown of my *habitus*. My dialoguing with you and one or two colleagues enabled me to reconceptualize the problems I was experiencing in terms of *habitus* and then to gradually set about creating new *habitus* through my teaching, reflective conversations with others such as you, and coteaching with Gale and Cam. Eventually Mario began to coteach as well, and over time he became my principal coteaching colleague. The bottom line is that change was slow and resulted in moderate successes in my teaching of the students in *Incentive*.

Michael: For me, coteaching had profound implications for the way I view and understand classrooms. Even if I pretended that a non-partial, objective view on classrooms was possible at all, coteaching would have immediately taught me that teachers perceive and experience themselves differently than the dispassionate researcher sitting on the sidelines. When I coteach, subject to the particular temporality of never-stopping events, what I experience

---

30   Roth, 2000.

is different than when I simply observe a classroom. Thinking about what I would have done if I had been a teacher and thinking about what I actually did being the teacher turn out to be quite different. It is different to tell a teacher that he should have dealt with a student who acted up at one point in a particular way and to get in the face of the same student, feeling the possibility that he might knock you out.

Ken: It is a reality check. Teaching is very different now than when I was a full-time high school teacher for the last time in the early 1970s. Not only that, teaching in urban schools is a very different proposition than teaching in the suburbs. The who, where, and when make a big difference in teaching and learning. Advice from the side must be cautiously offered. One issue that must be kept in mind about approaching students is that it depends a great deal on who does the approaching as well as when and where the approach takes place. There is a tendency for people on the side to assume that because they could do it someone else could do it similarly with the same postulated outcomes.

Michael: I have often thought about the comment of our colleague who, judging the events at City High School from the sidelines, suggested that the students needed to take a shower and clean up. I cannot imagine that anyone truly concerned with assisting these students in learning science could make such a remark. It struck me as a comment that might only be possible when research is conducted from the outside, where there are no stakes, literally removed from what is going on.

Ken: Whew. How disrespectful of him! Each day as I walk to City High I see homeless people asleep on the footpath, catching whatever warmth they can from the underground rail system. One day I know the sleeping individual will be one of my former students. I am ashamed of my failure to make a dent in the social fabric of this country, which sustains a system of inevitability that propels students like those at City into the streets, reproducing the poverty that our colleague viewed with deprecating eyes. In this, as in most other cases, the view from the inside is much more compassionate and less replete with deficit-laden solutions to complex problems.

CHAPTER 8

Coteaching/Cogenerative Dialoguing as Evaluation Methodology

In this chapter, we reflect on coteaching/cogenerative dialoguing as a fresh epistemology for the evaluation and supervision of teachers. Rather than making evaluation a process external to teaching, with its tendencies to objectify teachers and teaching, coteaching/cogenerative dialoguing makes evaluation part of the everyday work of teachers, students, and supervisors.

> Today is my big day. Mr. Ernst, the person from the Ministry of Education who will evaluate my teaching and determine whether or not I will receive my Ontario Teacher Certification, is coming to my classroom. Although I have already nearly 10 years of experience, I am tense. I am thinking about whether the lesson I have planned will meet the expectations of the evaluator. I hope that my students play the game—I have prepared them in that I told them how important this visit is to my own career.
>
> During the lesson I do not teach in my normal way. Not only am I over-conscious about what I am doing but I am also aware of my desire for Mr. Ernst to have a favorable impression of my teaching. I planned an activity on the computer, where students can explore the motion of physical objects by conducting their own experiments. Although I would have done this activity anyway, I am concerned that Mr. Ernst will think I have staged it for his benefit. In a sense the lesson is staged because I thought more than I usually do about the activities, their legitimacy in terms of my epistemology, and the extent of their fit with the provincial curriculum guidelines.
>
> When students have problems understanding, or when they get stuck, I immediately think about the effects of their difficulties on my evalua-

tion. I am sweating, which I never do while teaching—this event brings back memories of an unpleasant experience when, in a similar evaluation in a different school and province a student publicly announced my sweating and trembling to the class. 'You're sweating and shaking. Are you scared because of the person watching you?' Despite my tension and fears, the lesson eventually comes to an end. I am relieved that the lesson is over, but I am still worried about how Mr. Ernst has perceived what has happened and how the evaluation has come out.

It turned out that Mr. Ernst was very pleased and remarked to the school administration that he had observed an exemplary teacher; he began to advise other principals and teachers to visit my classroom in order to observe exemplary lessons. Even though all of my teaching evaluations have been positive in this way, and supported with commendations from my various superintendents, my level of anxiety is high each time I am evaluated. Although I have always taught the lesson as I would have done anyway, I have never lost the sense that these occasions were little more than dog-and-pony shows.

In this autobiographical account of personnel evaluation from the perspective of a teacher (Michael), we notice several important aspects that frequently are not taken into account in the supervision and evaluation of teachers. It is clear that the presence of the evaluator (the observer) changes the situation (of the observed). No longer is the primary goal of teaching to afford student learning. Instead, the principal goal is for the teacher to demonstrate effective teaching to an external evaluator who is trained to decide what is and what is not effective teaching. Not surprisingly, many teachers are uncomfortable with the idea that an outsider can validly assess the effectiveness of their teaching in a classroom that is normally shared only by a teacher and her students. In the context of such evaluations, many teachers plan and enact special lessons contrived to show their effectiveness in specified competencies, to teach in ways that are convincing to an external evaluator. In such circumstances, teaching is often enacted in ways that are mostly deliberative and conscious and thereby markedly different from the teaching that occurs normally.

From the teacher's perspective the goal of the activity in the above vignette is to obtain certification rather than to foster the learning of his students. The teacher enacts teaching to demonstrate his effectiveness and an external evaluator comes to a decision by comparing the narratives and scores constructed from the observation with some standard. In this way, the decision is based on comparing one representation against another (sometimes nonarticulated theories of teaching competencies). In the construction of the data on which the decision is based, a material record is constructed. This record stands for the individual teacher and his actions. That is, the teacher first becomes objectified in the record of his teaching effectiveness, on the basis of which a comparison is conducted with performance standards or benchmarks, which then supports a decision to certify or to not certify. That is, the decision to certify or not is abstracted from the individual subject and his teaching. When evaluation involves teachers who are already tenured, a negative outcome may lead to a recommendation for (compulsory) professional development. This 'professional development' is to be achieved in terms of taking further coursework, by working with a coach, mentor, or other person. In any event, an individual teacher is constructed in terms of deficits, to be overcome through additional professional education that frequently is disconnected from the praxis of teaching.

In this chapter we describe a radically different approach to the evaluation of teaching. Through coteaching we are able to merge the usually separate activities of professional development, supervision, evaluation, and research. In coteaching, several traditionally differently located individuals (teachers, cooperating teachers, student teachers, supervisors, evaluators, researchers) coparticipate as teachers. Shared experiences are evaluated in activities in which the coparticipants (including students) reflect on the teaching-learning activities. Within a context of enabling learning, the focus is not on the performance of only one teacher but on the performance of all coparticipants. Accordingly, coteaching constitutes a change in the unit of analysis of teaching, which we study in terms of all the elements that are considered in an activity system. In respect to teaching, the activity system considers teachers and students (subjects), reproduction of society as the motivation of the activity, tools (such as pedagogy, curriculum, material resources), community, rules of interaction in classrooms and schools, and the division of labor (the different roles of the individuals involved in schools).

Activity Theory and Traditional Personnel Evaluation

In the previous chapter, we introduced activity theory, which describes human activities in terms of sets of mediated relations each constituted by a triad of entities. However, the salient elements accounted for in activity theory and the ensemble of mediated relations are not the only characteristic features of an activity system. In each activity system there are also contradictions. These contradictions constitute primary forces of change in an activity system, in that participants attempt to remove them.[1] However, participants may internalize systemic contradictions and adapt their actions to work around them. For example, in software and tool design, participants often work around known bugs by adapting their practices to meet their goals while bypassing the bugs.[2] In the example of teacher evaluation, a teacher may deal with the contradiction of having to perform by setting aside his concerns about focusing on the needs of students and switch instead to the demonstration of teaching competencies that are deemed effective. In so doing he can be regarded as working around contradictions by staging an event that looks like authentic teaching but which is focused more on his own performance than the learning of his students. Systemic contradictions also may be internalized and thereby personalized, leading to stress and more serious psychological disorders.[3] While teaching in urban schools, for example, teachers often will work around a persistent problem of inattentive and disruptive students, focusing not on controlling disruptive students but on mediating the learning of those who want to learn. In this case the workaround involves tolerating known inadequacies with the interests in mind of those who want to learn (in a manner that is analogous to Tyrone's advice to teach only those who want to learn [see Chapters 1 and 2]). Workaround strategies such as these can be stressful and lead to burnout and even withdrawal from the teaching profession. In other school-related examples, teachers can assume responsibility for deficiencies in the system. For example, to overcome shortages of

---

1   Engeström, 1994.
2   Bannon & Bødker, 1991; Orr, 1998.
3   Dreier, 1993.

material resources teachers might purchase equipment and supplies out of their own pockets.

As the introductory vignette shows, teachers often experience supervision and evaluation as stress. From the perspective of activity theory, evaluation usually involves an outsider applying a set of culturally and historically developed criteria during an arranged observation of teaching. The evaluation usually incorporates additional 'anecdotal' information together with artifacts provided by the teacher or other stakeholders. For example, a teacher may provide as evidence of her effectiveness a videotape that shows her teaching in different contexts, a reflective journal that includes evidence of her reflective practices, and a portfolio containing artifacts of work selected to show the achievement of her students. Similarly, a school administrator might submit written records of formal evaluations undertaken in the past semester and a summary of the results of a survey of students' perceptions of their learning environment. These artifacts, which can be weighed to inform a final decision, reflect implicit and nonarticulated theories and assumptions. Equipped with a variety of data, the evaluator examines various aspects of classroom life and compares the performance of teaching to established benchmarks. In this way, the entities and mediated relations of the learning activity system are objectified in and through representations (e.g., scores based on comparisons with benchmarks on an evaluation form and/or a narrative account of teaching) that can then be used to support an evaluation. Thus, a complex system of activity and contexts is reduced to a set of attributes that represent the quality of teaching in ways that are regarded as objective. The process of evaluation leads to the production of records that stand for teaching performance. Invariably these records are 'de-subjectified' or 'de-populated'.[4] In this way the evaluation process objectifies the teacher, who is (socially) constructed as 'competent', 'in need of professional development', or 'ineffective'. In an interesting analysis of group decision making, Hugh Mehan shows that evaluations in which the voices of those most concerned are not included in equitable ways can lead to objectified (social) attributions and inequities for some of the individuals be-

4   On the notion of 'de-subjectification' see Dreier, 1991; on that of 'de-population' see Billig, 1994.

ing evaluated.[5] Mehan shows that inequities emanate from hierarchical relations between participants and the socially mediated legitimacy of their knowledge.

Some of the contradictions of teaching arise from processes of evaluation. Given the stakes involved, a teacher to be evaluated puts on a performance, a staged event that is not authentic because of the presence of the outside evaluator and a manner of teaching that is more conscious than normally is the case. In some cases this might be associated with deception and resistance, actions that are typical of hierarchical relationships and teachers' feelings of powerlessness. An example of this would be a teacher staging an inquiry lab activity when the usual approach involves the students completing activities from a textbook. Teachers can experience negative emotions due to contradictions associated with hierarchical power relationships between teacher and evaluator and with being constructed without a meaningful and sufficient voice. Evaluation and the hierarchical relations in the school and school system, which have an effect on the employment status of the teacher, are contradictions that may be internalized by teachers as disaffection and isolation. What can be done where such contradictions exist, to alleviate disaffection and stress? Is it possible to create an authentic system of evaluation in which teachers have a meaningful voice in evaluations of their own performance and which consider the sociocultural contexts in which teaching and learning occur?

Critical psychologists, whose theoretical foundations lie in activity theory,[6] suggest that it is not sufficient to deal with contradictions at a personal level. Rather, participants have to recognize contradictions as emanating from sociocultural conditions that have to be removed in a collective manner so that participants can experience life as subjective, satisfying, and free of fear.[7] In order to achieve this, evaluation necessarily requires a methodology in which all stakeholders (i.e., teacher, students, and evaluator) pursue and fulfill common interests and fulfill common goals. If an evaluation is undertaken by an external evaluator, her experiences of teaching and learning are radically vicarious since evaluation

---

5   Mehan, 1993.
6   Leont'ev, 1978.
7   Holzkamp, 1984.

from the side provides no direct access to the action possibilities available in the unfolding moments that comprise teaching and learning.[8] Instead of experiencing first-hand the possibilities of enabling learning, an evaluator must infer what might have been done and how learning might or might not have been shaped by what was or was not done by a teacher or students. When it is conducted in this way, evaluation is an activity that involves judgments from the side using criteria considered to have salience in the setting. Even though the evaluator may be secure in her knowledge, we regard this as false security. How can it be known that a particular action will produce a postulated social outcome? Or, how can an evaluator know if actions she recommends a teacher to undertake are feasible in the unfolding circumstances of praxis? Even in the best of circumstances the recommendations of an outsider can only be regarded as one possible narrative of what might have occurred or what might be desirable. Even though an evaluator's rendition takes into account her knowledge and expertise it includes only a distant and vicarious experience of the teaching and learning that are the objects of the evaluation. We maintain that an alternative way of evaluating teaching is likely to be more productive than the traditional 'outsider' approach described here. Not only does our alternative approach involve insider perspectives but also the focus of an evaluation shifts from an individual to a group of coparticipants. In our approach, one individual would no longer bear the brunt of performance evaluation. Instead, the process would involve cogenerative dialoguing over experiences shared during coteaching. The conversations are necessarily grounded in what is experienced and thereby incorporate participants' experiences of salient sociocultural factors including (but not limited to) the interchanges of the social and cultural capital of teachers and students. For nearly a decade we have studied teaching, learning to teach, research, supervision, and evaluation as unified activities. In the following section we articulate what we have learned from our research.

---

8   Holzkamp, 1983a, 1983b.

Coteaching as Epistemology and Method

In the model of coteaching, learning is explicitly made the primary goal of the activity. Two or more teachers divide the labor and teach at each other's elbows in order to facilitate student learning. As the events of the classroom unfold there are more teachers to deal with them in ways that afford the learning of students. Our research conducted in and as part of teaching praxis evidences significant learning by all participants involved, teachers and researcher-teachers. Interestingly enough, this learning often occurs in nonconscious ways, and teachers realize only much later what and how much they have learned while working together with one or more colleagues. Also, it is possible that most of what is learned remains beyond consciousness.[9]

Our fundamental condition for research, supervision, evaluation, and learning to become a teacher is coparticipation. All individuals—new teacher, (regular, cooperating) teacher, researcher, supervisor, or evaluator—participate in teaching so that they share symmetrical mediating relations between students and their knowledgeability. That is, as a teacher collective, we do not condone the involvement of individuals who construct themselves as outside observers looking at teaching and learning rather than participating in it. Praxis has its own constraints; most importantly, praxis unfolds in time and therefore has local coherence whereas evaluation seeks global coherence, which is nearly always irrelevant for practical action. There is no time-out for practitioners, forcing them to enact their knowledgeability rather than standing back, as theorists and outside evaluators are able to do, to consider and elaborate all (theoretically) possible forms of action.[10] These constraints of the temporality of praxis and the praxis-related limitations in the action *Spielraum* (room to maneuver) are available only to participants in praxis.

Coteaching experiences are coordinated with meetings during which coteachers and students debrief, make sense of the events, evaluate what has happened, critically reflect on their understanding, and construct local theory and new action possibilities. In our earlier form of coteaching, the teachers involved met later in

---

9   Bourdieu, 1992a; Dewey, 1933; Lakoff & Johnson, 1999.
10   Bourdieu, 1990.

the day (after class, during recess, after lunch, at the end of the school day) to discuss the shared experiences. In our recent work, as is described earlier in the book, (ideally two) students also participate in these meetings to make sense of what has happened, construct generalizations, and expand action possibilities.

Coteaching is based on an equitable approach to teaching, and on articulating differences between teachers in terms of their different life histories and experiences. The meetings are also based on a strongly participatory approach, in which all participants, including students, have opportunities to make sense, contribute to the interaction, ask questions, articulate issues, and so forth. In order to guide our meetings, interactions, and types of issues to be addressed, we developed the heuristic that we first presented in Chapter 5 (Table 5.2, p. 196).

This approach necessitates new ways in which the traditional roles of new teacher, (cooperating, regular) teacher, supervisor, researcher, and evaluator are understood and enacted. Because the approach is symmetrical in the classroom, traditional forms of critique by one individual (e.g., supervisor) of another individual (e.g., new teacher) lose legitimacy. For example, in a traditional situation a supervising university professor might admonish the new ('student') teacher for not having attended to sleeping students or for having wasted time in a transition from one activity to another. In coteaching, if the supervisor observes a sleeping student or notices that the transition wastes valuable learning time, he is morally obliged (an obligation that is shared and therefore socially mediated within the coteaching group) to act. This does not prevent him from raising the salient issue during the subsequent meeting.

Teaching and Evaluation in Praxis

Coteaching

Episode 1. The new teacher, Stephanie, had planned two activities on scientific method, a core area for the citywide standards and an associated standardized test, for this 90-minute lesson. However, as the first lesson unfolded, Stephanie noted that students, in order to draw maximum benefit in terms of their learning, required more time than she had planned. When the activity was finally completed, Stephanie realized that there was not enough time left in the period for students to complete the second activity. She and her supervising teacher (Bert) decided that they would first review what they had done so far in genetics. As she prepared the overhead projector she realized that she had used up the only available transparency earlier in the day and therefore sent a student to get it cleaned. There was a long moment of suspension: 'nothing' appeared to happen. The videotape showed Stephanie walking to the door, as if looking for the student who had left the classroom. Ken, sitting among the students, (impatiently?) drummed on the desk and suggested to Stephanie that she might quicken the pace of the transition. He then encouraged the participation of Keesha who had her head down on the desk. Soon afterward, the student returned with a clean transparency sheet and Stephanie began the review of Mendelian genetics.

Episode 2. In this second episode, we are in the middle of the review of Mendelian genetics. Stephanie writes pairs of letters on the transparency and asks students to name (scientifically) various gene combinations that she writes down as 'BB', 'Bb', and 'bb'. Stephanie then asks Keesha to demonstrate what characteristics an offspring would have based on a given gene combination of the parents.

Stephanie:	Excellent, little 'b', little 'b', so we got homozygous recessive [*makes a note on the acetate*]. And what is the last condition?
Several Ss:	Heterozygous. Little 'b', big 'B'...
Stephanie:	Heterozygous, awesome. Homozygous recessive means that there are two recessive genes. Keesha, come around.
Bert:	A good way of remembering this ... someone just said phenotype, genotype, and you gave the correct answer. An easy way of remembering this is ... just think of the first letter. A 'p' for physical expression, for physical appearance. A 'g' for the genes. So if you ever get confused, genes, genotype, physical expression, phenotype.
Stephanie:	[*Keesha has arrived at the overhead projector.*] All right, Keesha is going to put this on the overhead for us.

As Keesha has to walk a considerable distance to get to the front of the classroom to construct the Punnett Square, there might have been a lengthy transition. As Keesha walks to the front, Bert uses a moment of transition as a 'teachable moment' and volunteers information that will assist students to remember how to relate the scientific terms of 'phenotype' and 'genotype' to their more familiar language. Bert, in effect, builds a bridge between two forms of language, one that the students bring to class and another that is appropriate in the context of formal science.

Rather than sitting in the back of the classroom, constructing an evaluation that he subsequently gives to Stephanie and then uses to evaluate her teaching, Bert moves in and teaches. Rather than admonishing Stephanie later for a long transition, he sets an example of how periods of transition can be transformed into moments for additional teaching and learning.

Episode 3. As we discussed in previous chapters, Stephanie completes her review and seems ready to enact a transition to the next part of the lesson. Michael raises his hand as a sign that he wants to contribute to the ongoing lesson. Stephanie provides the space for him to coparticipate and engage students in a conversation about a real-life genetics problem.

Michael:	I wonder if anyone can figure out a little bit about my family? So, I have blue eyes and my wife has blue eyes. I was wondering whether you can figure out, what color my son's eyes are?
Natasia:	Blue eyes.
Michael:	Why would they be blue?
Natasia:	You have blue eyes, she has blue eyes....
Stephanie:	This is a good question.
Natasia:	She has blue eyes and you have blue eyes, you all must have recessive genes.
Stephanie:	OK, let's think about that [*begins to write*] let's list the possible ...
Natasia:	Make them have all the different combinations....
Stephanie:	Excellent, excellent. A good point. [*Turns to Michael*] I am glad you brought that up. Natasia has a good point. Let's list all the possible genotypes. OK. He has blue eyes. Question. So phenotype is blue? So what are the possible genotypes he may have?

Voiceover (Michael): Earlier in the lesson I attempted to help a student in the other half of the class working out a genetics problem. I was not successful for she did not understand me. I thought her failure to understand was partly because she was not used to me and did not construct me as a teacher. But I waited to see what Bert would do and to learn how to teach students like these. He began to talk to her using words such as 'heterozygous dominant' and 'homozygous dominant'. She stopped him saying, 'Why you giving me big talk with words that I don't understand?' So I realized that students might find it difficult to relate to the topic and I wanted to add to the lesson by bringing in a very practical example. This example and the one I provided right afterward, which brought a quite different perspective to genetics, seemed necessary to make the lesson more concrete and palpable to students. It was quite interesting that Stephanie later used an example from her own family modeled on what I had contributed earlier in the lesson. That is, she appeared to have learned this and immediately enacted a relevant practical example from her own family. Rather than waiting until I could talk to her about being too abstract and about using more practical examples, I enacted such an example right then and there, when it was most appropriate.

Cogenerative Dialogue

Case 1: Transitions. During the discussion activity (praxeology) in which we make sense of the lesson that we had experienced together, Ken raises the issue of the long transition from the first activity to the moment when Stephanie finally begins the lesson. He asks whether Stephanie had overheard his comment. With Stephanie's response, the topic of transition becomes the topic of the conversation. Stephanie accepts the responsibility for the delay.

Ken:	What did I say?
Stephanie:	'I am falling asleep. Keep going'.
Ken:	That's right, I said, 'come on, come on, come on, you are driving me nuts. If I were a student in this class, I would be falling asleep'. How can you work your way through

	periods like that? I know you had plan A, which was to do whatever. And you didn't have time left to do plan A, whatever... And so you had to switch to plan B, but the transition was ...
Stephanie:	Right, it was long....
Ken:	It was really long. And I was next door to someone who was battling.... Maybe she is one of those who go to sleep in every period, who knows. But she was battling to show any interest at all. So what she needed, I would say, is a fire lit under her. How could we have...? I mean, I don't have any answer.... But we didn't need a long transition there.... Because the kids had done the jelly, they were moving into something else, you had to wash the transparencies....
Stephanie:	Well that was the problem. I mean the problem was, I had to decide. Like I had planned that we make mobiles and stuff, with the scientific method. And I realized that there would not be enough time. And I had all that stuff laid out. So I thought we could get into genetics and do a dihybrid cross. And a student had written all over the acetate, as they were supposed to, and we had to wash them all off.
Ken:	That's good, but ... so? It was down time ...
Stephanie:	Maybe get a discussion going, like have a question or something like that....
Natasia:	Sometimes she lets us ... just to sit and relax for a few minutes. But you can't, like sometimes it is too long, and like ...

Case 2: Real-life Contexts. In this episode Natasia raises the issue that her interests are not being met, in opposition to the claim made by Bert that he focuses on students' interests. However, there appears to be a deeper concern about the relevance of the subject matter to real-life situations. In the following excerpt from the cogenerative dialogue, Natasia makes an important contribution to the evaluation of the learning environment.

Bert:	With the students in the class, I have always had a good relationship in terms of maybe what they like to see taught, or techniques, you know, or what their interests are, so you always have that openness.
Natasia:	My interests are not met!
Michael:	What is that?
Natasia:	Because you can actually do DNA research in the zoo.
Stephanie:	She is dying to go to the zoo. She is talking about it every day.

Natasia:	I do. I really do.
Ken:	There is the new primate exhibition.
Natasia:	Yeah, and you could like, multicolored, like the hair color of the monkeys. This is stuff like DNA, right?
Stephanie:	Doing crosses and things like that.
Natasia:	So I always thought we could make a trip to the zoo. Right?

Natasia makes more than the claim that her needs are not being met. She provides a practical example of the zoo as a site where the current curricular topic, genetics, could be contextualized. She elaborates this issue after Ken mentions the primate exhibition that is being staged at the moment. Natasia suggests that they could investigate monkey hair color, which is a function of inheritance and DNA.

This episode is interesting from the perspective of the relations that are enacted in cogenerative dialogue sessions. Traditionally hierarchical relations, here between a student and her teachers, are flattened in the sense that Natasia can provide constructive criticism without fear of reprisals. Her claim contradicts her teacher's perception that he is in tune with and meets students' interests.

Metalogue 1

Michael: Episode 1 is really quite unusual in terms of our research and our commitment to the principle 'don't blame others if you don't or can't take care of the situation yourself'. But the issue then came up in our cogenerative dialoguing. This episode really stands in contrast to the other episodes that are more characteristic of what we do. If someone notices something that can be improved in the lesson, s/he will immediately attempt to make this improvement. Thus, in Episode 2 Bert makes use of a transition to provide students with a mnemonic that can help them to remember the words 'phenotype' and 'genotype'. In Episode 3, I contribute an everyday example in which the somewhat abstract talk about 'little and big Bs', 'homozygous' and 'heterozygous' individuals, and 'genotype and phenotype expressions' is brought to a concrete level. Both examples therefore encourage the learning of students and coteachers alike.

Ken: I can see where you are going with your argument and I agree that my actions in the classroom and the cogenerative dialogue are probably a throwback to earlier times and roles. A critical issue in coteaching sessions is to deal with the events as they unfold in real time. These classes are so event-full that it is not possible to be everywhere at once and resolve all issues of which you are conscious. We just pitch in when and as we can with the goal of improving the learning of students. Then, during the cogenerative dialoguing we all should feel comfortable in raising issues of which we are aware. This is not an occasion for self-congratulatory remarks, but an opportunity to learn from our discussions of shared experiences.

Michael: When the long transition came up, your critique and our reactions did not contribute to making us collectively responsible. Stephanie was in a defensive mode; Bert and I did not contribute. Natasia contributed interesting insights on what can be done and suggested that a long transition can give students a needed rest. But these comments did not redistribute the responsibility for the long transition. Really it should have been a critique of our collective teaching rather than just of Stephanie, for we were all responsible.

Ken: That is a good point. I am glad that you raised the issue because I can now be more conscious of the goal of collective responsibility. This is a critical goal of cogenerative discussions that may have been below the surface of consciousness for me.

Why do we do what we do? I cannot say for sure why I chose to raise that point at that time. It is complex so let me unpack it as best I can. First, most of our teachers, new teachers and resident teachers, have problems in teaching through an entire 90-minute period. Typically we start late and finish early, and in every transition students exhibit what I describe as the 'urban shuffle'. Transitions and activities take about three times as long as I believe they should. During these long transitions, particular students are bricoleurs and use the time to pursue some of their own goals. Some lose interest, and others put their heads down as happened in this class. So, the length of transitions is an issue of which I am conscious and about which I am concerned. I would like all teachers to work together to redress the urban shuffle. In addition to that issue is a concern that, until today, Stephanie was not happily participating in coteaching. Prior to today Stephanie looked somewhat exasperated when one of us stepped forward to coteach. I had spoken to her about it and she understood the desirability of providing coparticipants the space to get involved. I guess I was sensitive to her previous reticence and chose not to enact another activity while the transparency was being cleaned. Finally, I had no way of knowing that this would work out the way it did. I think the best way to go into cogenerative dialoguing is with a conviction that any issue can be set on the table without judging or assigning blame. I do believe in your point about collective action and collective responsibility. I am not concerned that Stephanie accepted responsibility for the long transitions. I am only too aware that I have long transitions when I teach and the urban shuffle is characteristic of all classes in the building. Bert too experiences this problem. By raising it I have put it on the table for discussion and reflection. I expect it to come up again and again. It is not essential that we deal with each issue fully on the day that it is introduced. What would be most unfortunate would be if Stephanie were to feel diminished by me raising the issue and suggesting that she was to blame.

Michael: I think that we can take this case to yet another level and frame the situation in terms of the larger activity system and the relations that mediate the classroom events that we experienced. That is, we can come to understand that event as the result of a structural contradiction that was personalized and attributed to Stephanie. In a traditional evaluation model, she might have been blamed for the long transition period. It is not surprising, then, that Stephanie framed the problem in terms of the transparencies that had been used previously and now needed cleaning. This is a framing in terms of immediate understandings. However, we need to step back and realize that insufficient numbers of transparencies (or lack of an acetate roll...) really is a structural problem, one that arises from inadequate funding for urban schools. What we need to do at this point is to ratchet up the analysis and look at the problems not in terms of our own deficiencies, but as larger structural problems. Now, what are our options in this situation? How can we transform the structures in order to have access to sufficient resources so that the particular problems are not internalized (e.g., a teacher having to buy these resources out of her own pocket, or internalizing the contradiction in the term of stress, etc.).

Ken: We can also look at this in terms of students enacting roles that are consistent with their ways of being in out-of-school contexts. It goes beyond there being a shortage of material resources, a problem that might be addressed at the level of a science department, school, or school district. My experience is that the nature of participation is a reflection of the students doing what they are able to do and needing scaffolds to do some things that we want them to do. How can we assist students to build a sense of urgency into their participation? I do not see students being impatient because there is insufficient time to get done all that they want to do in 90 minutes. Instead I see even the best of students shuffling through the activities. What is needed to sustain an inquiry-oriented learning environment is probably much the same in suburban and urban schools. However, for the most part the teachers are from the middle class and know how to provide appropriate scaffolds for students from social backgrounds that are similar to their own. I think we all need to focus on how to recognize the social and cultural capital that our students possess, so that we can provide appropriate scaffolds to enable them to approach learning in a more energetic and sustained way. As we discuss in Chapter 5, Stephanie is much better able now to enact science curricula that take account of the dispositions of our students. Even so, there is more to be done and the enacted curriculum supports only minimal levels of learning for most students.

Michael: With our changed approach, evaluation really comes to focus on student learning rather than on teacher performance. An evaluation will be largely positive when the participants have both the sense and the evidence that learning is fostered whereas it will be negative if the needs of students are not met. However, because these cogenerative dialogue sessions are built into co-teaching, change and ongoing improvements are built into the activity system by design. We do not need the anxiety-ridden situation where external evaluators come into a classroom but we would rather have evaluation as part of the process, conducted by the stakeholders themselves.

Ken: As we enact cogenerative dialogue there is a tacit agreement to honor each person's voice and endeavor to learn from what is said. There is an acknowledgment that the purpose of the dialogue is to assist us all to learn better how to teach students like these students in this classroom (and those participating in the cogenerative dialogue). The basis for successful cogenerative dialogue is mutual respect and rapport among the coparticipants. The explicit goal is to learn to teach in a particularized way through coparticipation in conversations on shared experiences.

Coteaching and Teacher Evaluation

Michael: Some years ago, an article in the *Review of Research in Education* suggested that the 'social relationships of education—the relationships between administrators and teachers, teachers and students, students and students, students and their work—replicate the hierarchical divisions of labor'.[11] I think that coteaching significantly changes these relations. With the leveling of the relation between (new) teacher and supervisor, coop teacher and evaluator, previously existing hierarchical relationships are undermined and re-enacted in the form of cooperation in the service of a (societal) motive: assisting students in their learning. While teacher-student relationships do not have to be inherently asymmetrical, they are still perceived and enacted in this manner even in our coteaching classroom. However, we are taking steps to overcome this contradiction by including students in cogenerative dialogue to construct local theory (praxeology).

Ken: Eli Anderson[12] speaks about the currency of the streets being respect. In this school it is important to know this. If a teacher does not show respect for students and expect respect from them (by earning it through her actions) then it can be very difficult to teach effectively. So, when you speak of a symmetry in the relations between the teacher and students I see this as primarily involving mutual respect for one another while appreciating that the student and teacher have somewhat different roles that will evolve continuously and recursively in the contexts of schooling. I have been impressed in almost every cogenerative dialogue by the helpful and mature conversations involving students. I can

---

11 Pinar & Bowers, 1992, p. 165.
12 Anderson, 1999.

think of only one instance in which a student used the setting to show his contempt for teachers and teaching. My interpretation of this student's actions is that he endeavored to humiliate the teachers and thereby gain the respect of a peer who was involved in the session.

Michael: Making supervision and evaluation a central part of an activity system rather than an activity that comes from the outside to objectify and disenfranchise the primary stakeholders seems to me the crucial move that is made in our coteaching model. It reminds me of what is happening in a range of European projects, Dutch and Scandinavian, which are generally described as 'labor friendly' and democratic.[13] Even government organizations recognize the need for first-person perspectives in the evaluation of the social projects that they fund.[14] Mutual learning is organized in terms of quality circles where, with the goal of improving performance, coworkers and experienced colleagues discuss problems arising from the work process on a daily basis. Sometimes, existing hierarchical levels of supervision and evaluation are reduced and, within working teams, structured pay is linked to improving skill levels and coaching capabilities. That is, in these approaches, individual and collective learning become the central by-product of doing the day's work.

Ken: So what does this all say to the issue of assessing teacher performance? This is a hot issue now and has been historically. Rightfully society demands well-qualified teachers who do their utmost to foster the learning of their students. Coteaching has the potential to blur the traditional boundaries of evaluation and professional development. It seems to me that something that is closely analogous to formative evaluation occurs in coteaching when an event occurs and one of the coteaching partners participates in that event using what Dewey has referred to as a habit, a nonconscious way of enacting teaching. An event occurs, and a coteacher acts, using her *Spielraum* in such a way that student learning is made possible. All coteachers experience what happens, some consciously and others in nonconscious ways. The direct experience of the teaching of others can lead to the adapta-

---

13   For example, Ehn, 1992; Eldon & Levin, 1991; Henderson & Kyng, 1991; Onstenk, 1999.
14   For example, Nissen, 1997.

tion of a teacher's teaching *habitus* such that when a similar event arises in the future the teacher deals with it appropriately and without a conscious awareness of either the event or the associated teaching actions. On some occasions the actions of a coteacher will not be expected and for that reason they are noticed. These noticed actions could then be foci for discussion in praxeology sessions and set a context for the building of a new teaching *habitus*.

Conclusions

The application of activity theory to the evaluation of teaching began with a vignette in which Michael was assessed by an outside evaluator. He described how the event became staged, in that the focus shifted momentarily from promoting the learning of his students to one of ensuring that he demonstrated teaching competence. The contradictions that are made visible by our analytic approach were manifest in this case in terms of his stress in dealing with them. We have then shown through our examples how coteaching can set a context for ongoing evaluation in which the focus is on teaching with the intent of enhancing the learning of the students. The goal becomes one of learning to teach students like these at this time and in this place. In earlier chapters we have shown how coteaching is an ideal context for learning to teach. Here we have shown that coteaching also provides evaluation of teaching in a collective sense that is analogous to embedded formative assessment.[15] The evaluation associated with coteaching can inform the praxis of all coteachers, not just new teachers. However, there is still a need for summative evaluations of teaching. Can this teacher teach this class in these circumstances? The certification decisions that affected Michael in the first vignette are going to be necessary to ensure that we get the best teachers to teach our students. So, to what extent does our research on coteaching shape our perspectives on summative evaluation? We hasten to say that we are not advocating a methodology that will meet every emerging contingency. Coteaching is not offered as a

---

15   Black & William, 1998.

master narrative that operates as a panacea for all problems of teaching and learning. However, we do see applications of coparticipation to summative evaluations. We cannot condone from the side, 'external' evaluations as legitimate practice. Instead we see advantages in coteaching for a period of time so that first-hand experiences are obtained of the teaching of a teacher for whom a summative evaluation is needed. Then, recognizing that those who are empowered to make such decisions need to make them, we see cogenerative discussions as setting a context in which the voices of all stakeholder groups can discuss events and phenomena deemed salient to the decisions that are necessary. The forum of the cogenerative dialogue sets a context in which power relations can be equalized and actions about which there is a conscious awareness can be discussed with a focus on the extent to which any individual's teaching is viable for this class at this time.

With the proposed epistemology of evaluation, we expect changes in the way teachers and students take responsibility for the teaching and learning processes. Examples of changes that are possible have been observed in different European countries where labor process evaluations have changed from external evaluations (often conducted by more powerful managers) to self-evaluations conducted by each team of workers. The evaluations within the group involve all members in more equitable ways. Middle managers formally responsible for monitoring and increasing productivity have been eliminated and some of the salary savings are redistributed within the group among those who best scaffold learning and productivity within the group. As a result, the workers themselves have become more productive and have assumed control of the activities in which they are involved. In a similar way, we may expect students and teachers to take greater responsibility for the quality of the processes in which they are involved. The former evaluators and their roles may be abandoned in favor of a variety of different coteachers, whose roles nevertheless remain focused on fostering student learning and improving learning environments. We can even envision that a particular coteacher remains with a class for a number of lessons to participate in promoting the changes that have been identified as necessary within the group.

Michael: When educators think about quality of teaching, they focus perhaps too much on summative evaluation as an index of ability. We have to ask the questions, 'Who gains from summative evaluation?' 'Is summative evaluation necessary or are there other means of assuring quality of education?' 'Who should be involved in the evaluation process?' and 'How should the process be structured?' Do existing forms of evaluation take account of the learning potential of the individual teacher? I am thinking of the learning potential that is enhanced when teachers have opportunities to work alongside peers for a while. As for teaching, I cannot imagine why there should be summative evaluation for the purpose of making decisions once an individual has been accepted into the profession. So there may be a question of summative evaluation at the end of the formal educational experiences at the university, which would assist potential employers to make a decision about whether or not to hire a teacher. But then, we might ask the question why such decisions about the competence of a teacher are not made by those directly concerned and in the context for which they want to hire the individual.

Ken: Your position on summative evaluation is stronger than mine. Teacher evaluation is a critical component of the accountability systems being instituted by school districts and local school boards. Schools want the best teachers for their students and have a right to expect teachers to teach in ways that are appropriate for the students in the context of school and district policies. What we have proposed is a somewhat radical set of ideas that move the locus of evaluation decisions away from the tradition of experts operating from the outside to a more inclusive process that involves insiders engaging in coteaching and associated cogenerative dialogues. Our recommendations do not exclude experts or deny the value of summative evaluation. We want all stakeholders to be involved as insiders because many of the extant contradictions are eliminated by what we propose. Having said that, I do not expect that our proposal to use coteaching and cogenerative dialogue will be feasible in all situations that might arise. We are not suggesting a method that is good for all situations that might arise.

Michael: The potential problems residing in more traditional evaluation processes are embodied in the following case from my own work as a department head. One of my teachers was put on probation by our school administration, which had a history of letting teachers go at any time of the year with little notice. I asked for a chance to work with the teacher. We planned lessons together, participated in each other's teaching, and discussed what had happened during the shared lessons. By the end of the year, the school administration decided that there had been sufficient growth to warrant a continuation of the teacher's contract. We continued to collaborate over the subsequent two years, and he became a highly competent science teacher. If the administration had fired the teacher as it intended to do, it would have lost a teacher who subsequently showed and realized great learning potential.

Ken: This is a good example of evaluation leading to an appropriate and effective form of professional development. I do envision many situations in which schools and school districts have to choose which teachers to hire and/or retain. In those situations, in which decisions must be made, there is a possibility that coteaching and cogenerative dialogues, as we have described them here, can offer a methodology that might provide the kinds of data that can inform the decisions to be made.

Michael: I also believe that in addition to the kind of changes that we can envision, a change to coteaching/cogenerative dialoguing will entail benefits (and also new constraints) that we cannot yet foresee. I would expect, though, that some of these benefits are going to bear similarities with the kind of changes in the industrial workplaces that I talked about earlier. In the Scandinavian countries where these models have been tried, the benefits to the collective have become more important than those that might accrue to individuals, especially those with power to make important decisions.

EPILOGUE

Looking Back—To the Future

We bring this book to a conclusion by highlighting issues that arise from our researcher-teacher experience reported throughout the text. We understand this activity of looking back as also one of looking forward. It is through our practical experience that we can envision concretely possible futures for teaching and learning to teach. There is therefore a dialectical tension between the past and the future it enables. The reader may notice that there are other dialectical tensions, too. For example, the dialectical tension that links notions central to this book—praxis and praxeology, immediate understanding and distancing explanation—is reflexively embodied in our respective voices, which are drawn to the particular and the general, respectively.

From *Habitus* to Collective Responsibility

Michael: I had been teaching for nearly 15 years before I seriously began to investigate coteaching, particularly the coteaching situations in which I was involved. When I did start to look at my teaching, aided by the refraction of experiences through the views of others during cogenerative dialoguing, I became aware of the tremendous role of the nonconscious parts that are involved in my own teaching and that of others. It was at that point that I came to understand that I was not simply following sociocultural or cognitive rules but that in every act of teaching, I mustered a practical wisdom accumulated throughout my career.

Ken: Researchers and other scholars have focused on those aspects of teaching about which teachers are conscious and about which they can talk and write. Even though John Dewey[1] talked about habits as practices that are beyond the consciousness of actors, there has not been a serious effort by educational researchers to study teaching habits. There have also been few efforts to apply the ideas of Harold Garfinkel,[2] who articulated everyday common practices in much the same way that Dewey wrote about habits. Our thinking on teaching *habitus* has been shaped by Pierre Bourdieu's[3] theories. These theories draw attention to the significance of not just understanding that much of teaching occurs as *habitus* that generates practices but also of understanding the critical need to connect the theories to the experience of teaching. We have shown here, through numerous examples, how cogenerative dialogue has the potential to draw attention to salient aspects of teaching in which changes can be contemplated. Our approach sets out a methodology whereby we can bring together the parts of teaching that can be and have been made thematic with those parts that are grounded in praxis, as has been experienced by a collective consisting of several coparticipants.

Michael: Here, I see an interesting dialectical tension between praxis and praxeology, which I would like to bring up later. But go on.

Ken: What seems critical, as we look back on what we have written in the book and how this might be interpreted by readers wanting to make some changes, is the necessity to do more than just teach together. It might be said that teaching together with others is a necessary but insufficient condition for effectively coteaching. The cogenerative dialogue, as it has evolved (as distinct from how we might have practiced and described it previously), must contain some essential components. The first component involves the inclusion of multiple voices in cogenerative dialoguing. It is one thing to bring different stakeholders to a table and quite another to hear the voices of each.

---

1   Dewey, 1933.
2   Garfinkel, 1967.
3   Bourdieu, 1990, 1992a.

Michael: I cannot imagine cogenerative dialoguing other than as a democratic forum for all voices, a place where theory is open to be constructed in a collective effort resulting in a collective product. But becoming a collective product requires that participants are willing to listen to and understand others and accept the fact that there are multiple ways of perceiving and experiencing any event.

Ken: It has to be apparent to all participants that others do not only hear but are also willing to understand and act on what they hear. We found it useful to use the heuristic for cogenerative dialogues to sensitize participants about how they might participate. But we need to go beyond that. During the cogenerative dialogues it is imperative for each of the participants to speak and be heard. All contributions should be resources for the learning of all of the participants. If this is to occur, it is necessary for respect and rapport to be pervasive and for each participant to be simultaneously a learner and a teacher. Speaking is not enough. Whereas it is important to describe events in terms of everyday language and experience, it also is necessary to take every opportunity to infuse into those descriptions what we already know ...

Michael: Something hermeneutic philosophers have always insisted upon.[4]

Ken: ... which may be relevant theory and research. This will then allow all participants to lift their game in terms of what they understand about the nature of teaching here with these students at this time. The here and now and the everyday commonplaces of teaching need to be critically interrogated, bolstered with relevant theory and research, in a way that is intelligible to all participants. In this way the cogenerative dialogues can 'push the envelope' of what is known and practiced. What concerns me therefore is that cogenerative sessions might not have sufficient critical edge. We do not want to get into the self-congratulatory mode of only discussing what seemingly works well. Issues of equity and social justice need to be brought to the table in the same way as do those aspects of teaching that impede learning.

Michael: For this very reason, I am thinking about the necessity to engage radical doubt and critique of our own ideology, so that

---

4 Gadamer, 1975.

we do not get trapped in immediate understanding. A number of the authors we cited throughout the book, including Paul Ricœur, Klaus Holzkamp, and Pierre Bourdieu, therefore advocate critically interrogating our immediate understanding by means of hermeneutic analysis.[5] In this way, we establish a dialectical relationship between the immediate understanding that we need to arrive at any sensible explanation of our situation, and the explanations (local, critical theory) that we construct in the process of cogenerative dialoguing. Because of the different social and experiential locations that participants bring to the table, we can play different roles that lead to better explanation and elaboration of understanding.

Ken: Focusing on learning and collective responsibility makes it possible for roles to be refined continuously and for collective planning to occur with respect to the next lesson that is to be taught. Whereas each person should commit to particular roles and associated responsibilities, it is paramount that no one person sees herself as the key to making or breaking the next lesson. It should never have been the case that I attributed long transitions during the lesson on monohybrid crosses to Stephanie. It was not her fault or responsibility any more than it was the responsibility of Bert, you, or myself as teachers, or of Natasia as a student.

Michael: But we, as others, have to accept that change does not come easy even if these are changes in our own practices. Taking on collective responsibility when our *habitus* has been formed in a sociocultural context that prizes individual responsibility will take some time.

Ken: There is institutional culpability, too. In a cogenerative dialogue there needs to be an emphasis on collective responsibility, a stronger sense of the collective 'we' rather than the individual 'I', and a realization that institutions are essential to the success of any science education program. Why was it necessary to send a student out to wash a transparency? Was it a case of planning or is it a case of a pervasive shortage of the tools needed to support teaching and learning? Collectively, decisions need to be made about what the collective 'we' can do and what institutional support can be expected.

5   Bourdieu & Wacquant, 1992; Ricœur, 1991; Holzkamp, 1991b.

Michael: Which really means that *being-with* is not simply a state into which we are thrown without our wishes but that we have a moral responsibility toward the Other, teacher or student, to make teaching and learning work as a collective endeavor.

From Subjectivity to Society

Ken: The accounts of teaching and learning in cogenerative discussions are first-person narratives of lived experience. Because of the extent to which experiences are shared, it should be the case that one person's renditions are of interest and relevance to all participants. As we learn from what is said there need to be commitments about how roles will change to address emergent problems that are associated with the curricula as they are being enacted.

Michael: This, to me, is a critically important aspect of our work. The first-person perspective that we take on teaching and learning to teach as researchers, supervisors, teacher educators, and evaluators allows us to get a better handle on the experience of teaching in the *here* and *now* of particular settings. From the perspective of all of these roles, the views that become salient are not those of disengaged individuals (who have no stake in the primary activity, re/production of society through the education of students) but those of concerned and caring individuals who contribute to a common good.[6] As we can ascertain from years of research from different paradigms, viewed through the eyes and experience of participants, classroom events look and are different. What has not been sufficiently appreciated is that to understand teachers, we need to understand their perceptions and experiences; change of praxis is possible but it has to appear necessary and intelligible in the experience of the respective teachers. It is for this reason that a first-person perspective on research, supervision, and evaluation makes so much sense to practicing teachers. Advice that appears idealistic and possible only in theory rather than in the practical context that teachers face in their present situation contributes little to promote teacher develop-

---

6   Concern and care are central (ontological) concepts in *Being and Time* (Heidegger, 1977), the foundational work on practice and commonsense activity.

ment, change in the learning environment, and ultimately improvement in the learning opportunities provided to students.

Ken: From my own perspective the research that has been possible through coteaching has been rich in terms of my own learning as a scholar and teacher. As a scholar I have had to come to grips with the intersection of the micro and macro aspects of sociology in my own classroom. The face-to-face interactions that define microperspectives in sociology also defined my lived experiences as a teacher in *Incentive*. I struggled with the humiliation of being ignored day after day. I was fearful most of the time that I could not control what might happen at any moment (I did not feel safe). I agonized over how to start a lesson, how to get students to participate, how to keep them active, and how to redirect their attention when they drifted away from the assigned activities. I also agonized over how to evaluate what they had learned or over how to respond to their responses and actions. As I taught I was ever conscious of the microelements of interaction, and my teaching *habitus* carried me through lesson after lesson. I planned sedulously to improve the learning environments and to gain higher quality participation. I attended to the goals of state, district, and school to the extent that I considered it ethical to do so. But above all I never lost my focus on what I was there to accomplish. I was driven to improve the learning of the students.

Michael: But everything you did was always and already mediated by existing societal structures, schooling and its institutions, that you were subjected (and therefore reacted) to and, simultaneously, contributed to re/producing. That is, the micro-sociological events were inherently mediated by macro-sociological realities.

Ken: The macroelements of sociology became apparent to me in my regular discussions with Gale, Cam, and Mario. Imagine my disgust when I realized I was a cultural dope, trapped in the whirlpool of re/producing social practices and status. I had the highest expectations for my students and myself. I planned that way and when I came to the class I taught like a dope. I knew to get the students involved in problem solving and planned to do so. I knew to take them to the computer lab regularly and did so. I knew to take them outside and to get them involved in a form of science that was relevant and that would connect to their interests. I also knew that I had to listen to the students and learn from their voices. The problem is that when I enacted the curriculum I could not do what I planned. My goals may have been necessary but they were by no means sufficient. To be blunt and rather self-critical for a moment, I did not know how to teach these students in this place at this time. But it is not really a case of not knowing how to think, write, and talk about what had to be done. That was not a problem for me, even though there was a need for me to study and learn more about social and cultural knowledge pertaining to the students I was to teach. No, the knowledge I needed is highly contextualized. I needed to know how to teach *these* students in *this* classroom with *these* tools at particular times. I got better at it, especially with the help of Tyrone and Gale. I learned from *being-with* Mario as he began to coteach and I suspect I learned from coteaching with Cam. But at the bottom line there was a fundamental problem that I could not address and it had to do with the organization of the school.

Contradictions and Societal Mediation

Michael: In our work in the schools, coteaching/cogenerative dialoguing has turned out to have a tremendous potential for teaching and learning to teach. One drawback of what we have done so far appears to be that we have not succeeded in bringing coordinators, principals, and district people into the experience. I see this as a drawback, because at the classroom level you can go only so far. If the more encompassing levels in schooling are not involved, I expect that teachers and their students will begin to incorporate and adapt to the contradictions that exist at the systemic level. Perhaps, coteaching/cogenerative dialoguing involving students may never get off the ground even at the classroom level because the local culture mediates against it. However, I cannot see how real change, involving new ways of acting, can become possible unless we do not construct our situations simply in immediate terms, but we come to understand our contradictions in generalized terms. An example of going from immediate understanding to generalized understanding was when we constructed the long transition between two activities as that of lack of resources (transparencies) rather than teacher inability to promote rapid transitions.[7] That is, if we come to understand our limited action potential as a restricted form of a more general action potential. This process of coming to understand is achieved through a critical hermeneutic analysis of each individual situation.

Ken: In an endeavor to make City High School a safe and caring place in which teachers and students became a community, there were major organizational changes put into effect. The students were moved to the same part of the school and used a small number of classrooms for their entire program of study. Similarly there were restrictions on the number of teachers they would have for their four years of high school. These social arrangements addressed a significant problem of safety and the necessity to have schools that were caring places where students felt they knew their teachers and other students. Unfortunately, the creation of a new social structure led to the demise of some very significant institutions. Principal among these and of great significance to my teaching is that there no longer is a science department, a head of department, or specialized science rooms and facilities. When I looked around for the marble chips they were not there and I could not expect them to be there any time soon. Simply put, there was no structure to support their appearance. If I were in a room especially set up for science I would expect to find equipment and materials in that room to support a curriculum.

Michael: And this is where we need to begin our critical analysis. Noting what would happen 'if', when we really have no means to satisfy the condition, is not unlike recommending change to teachers that they recognize as a possibility 'only in theory'. We need to ascertain more than the lack of resources that would change the situation. Our critical analysis ultimately needs to construct the situation as a contradiction at the level of society and then identify practical avenues for removing the contradiction.

Ken: Yes. I was caught in the sense that there was no structure in the school to support systematic ordering and maintaining of equipment and materials. Nor was there a structure to inventory, store, disseminate, reclaim, repair, and restock materials. Teachers quickly learned that they should create their own collections of

---

7   See Chapter 8.

supplies, and major items of equipment were stolen, lost, or broken. The ordering of materials and equipment became uncoordinated and local. Materials in storage became old, chemicals deteriorated, some of them becoming unsafe, and dirty glassware and dust-filled apparatus became commonplace. The science laboratories on the third floor of the building were converted for uses in social studies, English, and computers and in many cases they were simply closed, with the water and gas being turned off. Over a period of 30 years the science program was disassembled and became uncoordinated as individual teachers decided what would be taught when, where, to whom, and by whom. When I came to *Incentive* to teach science it was Mario who decided what to teach. He was assigned a former art room in which to teach and as a new teacher in the school he scrambled to locate a small collection of materials and out of date textbooks. What he needed he bought, and although there was a budget to support more spending he did not know what to buy nor did he have the time to create major orders. The absence of a department took away the chance for him to interact easily with other science teachers, and isolation was a problem.

Michael: The problem is that in this way, Mario enacted a workaround, and he therefore internalized problems that really needed to be understood and dealt with (acted upon) at a different level. No teacher will be able to keep up providing those means that are really aspects of a collective responsibility, a responsibility of a just society that is truly interested in the common good for all its members.

Ken: But in this particular situation, the details are highly significant when taken as contextual factors that affected whether or not I would be able to effectively teach these students science in this place. It is apparent that I experienced a breach in what I had expected to happen and my *habitus* was not fitting well with the *habitus* of the students. However, it is also apparent that my opportunities to adapt my *habitus* and learn to teach were radically mediated by the social structures of the school....

Michael: Such a recognition is a first step to understanding and seeking solutions at a more general level rather than internalizing the contradictions that existed at the school, school board, and societal level. But go on....

Ken: Irrespective of what I could do or planned to do I was part of a community that was organized in a particular way, in which the division of human and material resources constrained what was possible. It took extraordinary efforts on my part to plan and prepare so that I could better use the cultural capital of students and build social capital by earning their respect. To build social capital I had to learn to show less disrespect for my students and learn how to interact with them. My goal in building social capital was to convert it to cultural capital in the form of their increased learning of science. To the extent that social and cultural capital are fungible commodities, I can envision how greater efforts from me as a science teacher could lead to improved learning environments. In addition, if others were to systematically coteach with me and accept a communal responsibility for the enacted curriculum and the associated learning environments, then I can see how significant improvements could occur.

Michael: Because coteaching/cogenerative dialoguing involves colleagues, it would address some of the problems that continue to plague teaching including isolation, the feeling of being burdened by the responsibility that comes with decision making, or the lack of opportunities to develop while doing the job. All of these problems contribute to burnout and, for some, to dropping out.

Ken: If students were to make similar accommodations it is apparent that a productive learning community could have grown within the *Incentive* SLC. But could it have been sustained? Would my professional life have been less stressful? How would the remaining contradictions be dealt with? My point in raising this issue is that without significant new institutional arrangements it seems impossible for any group within a school to effect lasting change.

Michael: Coteaching/cogenerative dialoguing can assist teachers and their students to realize the emancipatory potential in making collective decisions to get the most out of their involvement in the activity system of which they are constitutive parts. Teachers and students will begin to sense that they are shaping agents of their situation rather than cultural dopes who merely react to external constraints and according to given patterns.

Ken: Tyrone helped me a great deal. He's a smart kid who can read and think through complex issues. Yet at the same time, I couldn't seem to help him get off the street. Tyrone continues to hear a calling from the streets. He was moved to *Incentive* because he did not fit into the institution of schooling. He resisted his being in *Incentive* and recognized it for the sham that it is. He dropped out, preferring instead to hang out with his 'homies' in the streets. He entered Twilight School, which is fast-tracked to graduate students who cannot keep themselves in school for a variety of reasons. But he could not make it there either. Tyrone is smart enough to learn and accomplish but he chooses to follow what he thinks is fair and reasonable. He will not succumb to oppression and in his resistance he fuels the re/production cycles. Like others in his family, Tyrone will live a life on the edge.

Michael: Which is but one of the societal contradictions that mediate the work we do in schools. But there are other, more positive cases such as the kid from *Incentive* whom we met last night, and who is currently enrolled in a theater arts program at a local university.

Ken: Definitely. Also I see hope for Tyrone. At present he is back at school again, this time in a charter school for dropouts. He is still in grade 9 and is unlikely to accrue the credits needed for high school graduation even in this charter school where he is learning a building trade. He works in the community for 50% of the time and still could graduate in a relatively short time compared to what it would have taken in *Incentive* (which was also designed to allow students to compensate for earlier failures and to graduate on a 4-year schedule).

From Dialectics to Lifelong Learning and Change

Michael: I see tremendous potential in the pairing of coteaching/cogenerative dialoguing. This pair of activities is associated with a dialectical pair of knowing, praxis (practical wisdom in teaching) and praxeology (discourse about teaching). As all dialectical pairs of concepts, that of praxis/praxeology embodies contradictions. Knowledge about teaching, even if it is praxeology constructed by teachers themselves, is never equivalent to the practical wisdom that is enacted by teachers in praxis. However, as the Russian philosopher Evald Il'enkov has eloquently argued, the contradictions embodied in dialectical units are driving forces for change and development.[8] Therefore, teachers anywhere along their career trajectory of legitimate (peripheral) participation have access to an increased potential of growth and development when afforded the possibility of participating in the complementary activities of coteaching/cogenerative dialoguing. That is, these complementary activities lead to a dialectical unit of two forms of knowing that, because of the contradictions they embody, lead to a continued professional development. In our paradigm, this development begins when individuals enter the profession and continues throughout their career.

Ken: Coteaching offers teacher preparation a great deal. We have found that with few exceptions our new teachers prefer to be assigned for their field experiences in pairs and when the arrangements do not permit it they feel disadvantaged. Already most of them see the potential of collective teaching with another new teacher. Cooperating teachers begin to regard the new teacher as a principal resource to support their own learning to teach. The role of the cooperating teacher is adjusting and there is little doubt that there is no longer this perception that the cooperating teacher is the principal resource to support learning to teach. The inclusion of students in cogenerative discussions has increased the awareness of the significant roles that students can have as teacher educators.

Michael: Actually, I see it as a failure of current schooling not to include students to a greater degree in matters that concern them. From the perspective of society, schools are the institution in which it re/produces itself. Coming generations are educated to take their own constitutive parts in society and, thereby, to guarantee its survival and evolution.[9] Including students in creating appropriate learning environments for themselves and for their teachers is only one way in which students realize their power to act. But involving students will change the roles of those who currently participate in education.

---

8   Il'enkov, 1977, 1982.
9   Holzkamp, 1983a.

Ken: I agree. Speaking for my colleagues in science education as well as speaking for myself, it is apparent that our roles are radically altered. Just as Peter Grimmett has reformed his methods courses to be responsive to the unfolding events in the field, so too have we changed our methods courses in radical ways.[10] For many years, we have situated the methods courses in the school. Now we teach the methods in school time. Three times a week we meet for methods in a science lab at CHS. There we participate in activities that are very much like cogenerative dialogue sessions. The three of us who supervise new teachers and undertake research on learning to teach science in urban schools all participate in activities that are planned to deal with pre-identified issues (on Monday), connecting theory and research to practice (on Wednesday), and emergent issues (on Friday). Often we involve high school students in these activities and always we connect overtly to the teaching and learning that is going on in the building. At 9:15 a.m. we finish our methods classes and all head for the SLC to which we have been assigned....

Michael: Do all of you participate in coteaching?

Ken: Coteaching that includes the three supervisors is now routine and so too are cogenerative dialogues as we have described them throughout this book. These dialogues occur at least once a week and also involve the cooperating teacher. It is becoming a rare event for me to sit down in a one-on-one situation to discuss a new teacher's teaching. In fact I do not recall it happening. I often meet with new teachers in one-on-one situations but these usually are to discuss issues pertaining to programs of study or personal matters. Marked changes have occurred in the way teacher education is practiced, and the signs are that the students are learning to better teach these students in this place. What is equally apparent is that what we are doing cannot be sustained without an institutional commitment and reorganization. The pull toward traditional structures is apparent throughout the teacher education program even where coteaching has been enacted. There is a pervasive tendency to observe and evaluate from the side, meet separately with students to tell them about the evaluations of their teaching, and not schedule or participate in the cogenera-

---

10   Grimmett, 1998.

tive dialogues. Except for science and mathematics education, the methods courses are still relatively unconnected to the field experiences. Accordingly, the institution of coteaching has been appropriated and enacted within an institutional frame that is resistant to change. Just as it is difficult to initiate and sustain change in *Incentive*, so too is it difficult to initiate and sustain changes of the type we have described and advocated here within our academy.

Michael: There is another threatening aspect of our model of coteaching/cogenerative dialoguing for our peers. Some university colleagues might think that our coteaching/cogenerative dialoguing will make them and their research superfluous. While I agree that it will lessen the interest in the kind of research that objectified teachers and had relatively little impact on classroom practice, I believe that there would be an increasing demand for professors who engage in the way we do. In our paradigm, a diversity of voices is acknowledged as a way to resist getting stuck in immediate understanding and ideology. As long as we recognize differences as having their source in societal mediations and cultural-historical differences in individual experiences, and as long as we do not privilege some voices at the expense of all others, diversity contributes to the production of local theory and enactment of change. And changing the situation to make it better is exactly what we have been after throughout this book. For example, in one of the schools where I worked, we began with one pair of coteachers who worked together over a 3-month period. Other teachers were freed up for one or more lessons to participate in coteaching and cogenerative dialoguing. We subsequently cotaught with some of these participants, thereby assisting an increasing number of teachers in the school to learn from working with peers (including graduate students and professors). Over a 3-year period, considerable changes in teaching science at that school could be observed. This is to say that a small team involving one or two professors, two graduate students at a time, and a nonacademic research assistant responsible for data collection and transcription had a tremendous transformative potential on teaching science in one school. I see little reason why, over time, given the (underused) potential of professors and under/graduate students in education as participants in coteaching/cogenerative dialoguing, more systemic change would be impossible.

Permit me a change of topics to pick up on one of your ideas that I wanted to pursue—lifelong learning. If we begin to think about teaching and learning to teach as a lifelong endeavor which begins with an individual's enrollment in a teacher preparation program, coteaching/cogenerative dialoguing sets a context in which this continuity can be achieved. An individual would participate in teaching from early on, always with a sense that she is contributing to achieve what motivates education—student learning. Much like the navigators on Edwin Hutchins' naval vessels,[11] teachers would move through different roles as part of their career cycle—new ('student') teacher, regular teacher, cooperating teacher, supervisor, and, perhaps later, university supervisor, methods teacher, or researcher. Stephanie, who was coteaching with Bert, might have, during the following year, been hired to teach at City High School, and she, like Mario, might become a cooperating teacher for the next generation of teachers at her alma mater. Eventually, she might become an SLC coordinator and participate in coteaching activities, including cogenerative dialoguing with the intent of contributing to the evaluation portfolios of all participants.

Ken: I agree with you. Coteaching is a practice that has the potential to blur boundaries between teacher preparation, professional development for resident teachers, and lifelong learning for all participants, including university people in all of their different roles. If we take the time to enact coteaching throughout a school we might expect to see radical improvements in enacted curricula as learning communities grow around to accord with communal agency. Will the changes be evolutionary or revolutionary? There is a part of me that wants to opt for the evolutionary track because I am essentially afraid of revolution. But there is another part of me that acknowledges that it will take a revolution for coteaching to fulfill the rosy image we have of it. We advocate a change in the way teaching is conceptualized and practiced, we advocate a change in how new and resident teachers learn to teach, we advocate a change in the roles of stakeholders in learning to teach, evaluating teaching, doing research on teaching, and even designing the curriculum. That is a lot of change to occur and if it is

---

11 Hutchins, 1995.

somehow phased in, my concern is that the roles and rules that have traditionally mediated schooling will continue to operate and appropriate coteaching—mediating its enactment in such a way that schooling remains much as it was. So, in the final analysis I have a both/and feeling about the future. Coteaching has the potential to do much for education. Yet to be successful we must address the contradictions that permeate the existing institutions and mediate collective agency. If coteaching is to be systemically enacted and sustained, thence to fuel a transformative science education, it is necessary to create new institutions to identify and remove contradictions from the activity system in which teaching and learning coexist.

Michael: Some readers may object, suggesting that coteaching/cogenerative dialoguing is simply not financially feasible. Apart from rejecting such an argument on the grounds that our children are our greatest assets and the most worthwhile to invest in, I think that we have not thought about realizing the unused potential that lies in the sheer number of university students enrolled in teacher education. It should be evident that university students, considered as legitimate participants in the teaching of K–12 students, contribute in essential ways not only to their own learning but also to the professional development of the resident cooperating teachers. If some or all of them were to be involved as legitimate participants in teaching throughout their program—in continuing internships or as part of cooperative education arrangements—we would tremendously increase the number of teachers in the classroom. As you have been remarking for some time, new teachers have to be recognized as a transformative element rather than as a necessary evil that disrupts normal school functioning and to whose presence some regular teachers object.

Seen in this way, we also expect the role of supervision and evaluation to change. Whereas there may still be particular events in the lives of teachers, such as graduation and receipt of diploma, these may become rituals along a trajectory. This trajectory is envisaged as being continuous rather than discontinuous. Discontinuities are currently encountered, for example, as a change in legitimacy (e.g., 'getting one's own class') or form of learning (from book theory versus from experience). Evaluation and supervision are then of and by a teacher (and student) collective, interested in maximizing student learning. As in the workplace situations in Holland and Scandinavia described in Chapter 8, individual teachers may then be characterized not in terms of individualistic properties—as 'satisfactory', 'competent', or 'exemplary' teachers based on the knowledge exhibited in formal evaluations. Rather, individual teachers may then be characterized (and rewarded) in terms of their contributions to the learning potential of the group (teachers and students).

Dialectical Postscript

As we were nearing the end of our project, reflecting on the implications of our work, we came to realize the Janus-faced nature of our outlook toward the future:

On the one hand,
we resent the implication of being cultural and social dopes, that is, being subject to external social and cultural forces without the ability to exercise free will. We do not like to think of our agency as an impotent one. Yet as we look forward and in particular look at the pervasive problems in science education, we can only fear that all of us involved in science education are destined to be social and cultural dopes. How can we be sure that our efforts at cultural and social production through the aegis of science education will do more than fuel the savage whirlpools in which cultural and social re/production are conceived? We have little confidence that any well-intentioned group acting alone will do more than re-create the social and cultural system that we are trying to improve.

On the other hand,
we believe that coteaching/co-generative dialoguing is a form of praxis that engages key stakeholders in meaningful ways that are oriented toward learning. Systemic enactment of coteaching in schools offers the potential of ongoing professional development, the design and enactment of socially and culturally relevant curricula, and improvements in the quality of learning environments, educational research, and evaluation. In the enactment it is as well to remember that co-participation is a requisite for all participants. If a collection of individual 'I's can become 'we', develop communal agency, and assume corporate responsibility for student learning then the future for science education and its transformative potential are realizable.

Learning until the End

Our project has been one in which we learned until the end. When
we worked out the details of coteaching and the associated cogenerative dialogue we were in a position of not knowing exactly
what roles were to be enacted by supervisor, cooperating teacher,
new teacher, and students. We knew that we wanted power dif-
ferentials to be minimal and that all would come to the table to
speak and be heard. We realized the potential of this being a forum in which all participants could learn more about teaching and
learning. But at that stage there was much still to be learned about
just what could be accomplished through cogenerative dialogue.

As we wrote the chapters of the book we searched for ways to
enrich our discussions through a hermeneutic process in which different theoretical lenses brought different issues into the foreground. The application of activity theory and critical psychology
to coteaching and cogenerative dialogue necessitated a significant
effort on our parts to identify and work through the various implications. It might well have been the case that we would have come
to the same point through the application of different theoretical
frameworks. However, activity theory/critical psychology produced a rich yield of implications. For example, the issue of a
teacher becoming better educated and enacting more appropriate
curricula activities while assuming responsibility for what happens in the classroom is a romantic idea that does not hold up
under the lens of activity theory. Unless something is done to resolve the contradictions of the societal mediations that lead to the
underfunding of urban high schools and the absence of necessary
institutions and associated roles, there is little chance of initiating
and sustaining change. Similarly, activity theory draws attention
to the necessity of examining the micro- and macro-sociological
effects that link interactions between coparticipants in classrooms
with the specter of social and cultural production-reproduction
cycles.

Perhaps even more salient was the realization as we undertook our final rewriting of the chapters that activity theory emphasized the significance of individuals shedding their individual
agency to embrace a communal responsibility for teaching and

learning. We had not fully considered this as a possible outcome of coteaching and cogenerative dialoguing. For that reason it was not an aspect that we had emphasized in our discussions about what was happening. Although we cotaught with shared responsibility in mind, it was not something that was ever discussed and negotiated. Similarly, in cogenerative dialoguing we tended to view the chief purpose as to improve the quality of teaching (with the ultimate goal of improving learning) and regarded the new teachers and the resident teacher as the key stakeholders. We did not view our own learning to teach and to research as essential ingredients in the development of communal agency and in the concerted effort of the 'we' to promote student learning. The writing of this book has brought our awareness of this to a critical level and we can now use our deeper understandings to improve the quality of cogenerative dialogue and subsequent coteaching.

With our deeper understanding comes an emerging focus for research. Just how do individuals with agency evolve to become 'we' with communal agency? Who should be involved in cogenerative dialogue and how often? We have discussed the inclusion of delegates from the students in a class. When we suggest to students how this might be enacted we usually talk about having two quite different students, one of whom stays on for some time while the other changes so as to include more students over a period of time. How does this relate to the development of a community with agency? These and other research questions emerge as we enact coteaching and begin to see its potential. While we recommend the use of coteaching, we are excited about the contexts that will be created in which research can be undertaken with the purpose of improving the learning of students, while those who teach learn how to teach better with these students, in this place, at this time.

GLOSSARY

Activity theory. A non-reductionist way of understanding human activity. It assists researchers in considering not only the relationship of a human being to the object of its activity but also the ways in which tools, rules, community, and individuals' roles mediate this relationship. Furthermore, activity theory acknowledges that internal (psychological) and external (sociological) factors do not simply determine human activity; rather, human beings (subjects) actively shape the contexts of their contributions and the ways in which they contribute to their activity.

Being-in/with. In a phenomenological approach, being-in the world and being-with others are the fundamental a priori conditions from which human understanding, knowing, and learning have to be thought. As human beings, we can never think about these issues other than as beings who always and already find themselves in a physical world and in a social context.

Cogenerative dialoguing. After coteaching a lesson, the various teachers and student representatives talk about their experience with the purpose of understanding the different experiences and of improving the learning environment for all participants.

Coteaching. In coteaching, two or more practitioners work at each others' elbows to get the day's work done—assisting students to learn. Coteaching differs from team teaching in two important ways. First, in team teaching two or more individuals usually split the work, each taking on the aspect with which they are most familiar. Team teaching is conceived of as drawing on the strength of each person and of making the work easier by dividing it up into manageable parcels. Second, our coteaching is associated with a particular epistemology grounded in sociological phenomenology.

First-person methodology. Practical activity is characterized by particular constraints of time; in teaching, as in many other activities, taking time out to reflect on all possible ways of looking at the situation and considering all possible ways of dealing with it is not an option. Therefore, to understand activities such as teaching, researchers need to see and experience them through the eyes of the practitioner. They need to be participating, in person, in the activities and to be subject to the same temporal constraints as the practitioner. Putting oneself in the position of the practitioner, and participating in activities with the intention of doing the practitioner's job is therefore a first-person research methodology.

Habitus. We see the world around us and do the things we do without really knowing why. We can say that there exist dispositions that make us see and do things in particular ways. These dispositions therefore structure our perceptions and actions. However, because these dispositions have been formed through our experience in and of the world, they have themselves been structured by outside forces. We refer to such dispositions as *habitus.*

Hermeneutic phenomenology. Hermeneutic phenomenology is an approach to human knowledge that focuses on the dialectic of two aspects of understanding. There is immediate, primary understanding of the world (as it appears in the form of phenomena), which is often unarticulated and arises from praxis. This primary understanding is the precondition for any more advanced abstract understanding, which arises from a critical (hermeneutic) analysis of primary understanding. Thus, primary understanding is developed by through explanation-seeking hermeneutic analysis; but this form of analysis is only possible because we already have a primary understanding.

Incentive. City High School is divided into small learning communities, each representing a stream focusing on specific themes such as sports, health, or mathematics and sciences. *Incentive* is our pseudonym for the lowest stream.

Metalogue. A metalogue is a conversation in which the results of previous conversations or previous texts become the topic of an inquiry. In other words, a metalogue abstracts from and seeks generalizations from earlier conversations and texts.

New teacher. Traditionally, individuals who are enrolled in a university or college program intended to prepare them for the work of teaching are referred to as 'student' teachers while they are out in the schools. Consistent with our epistemology, which views learning to teach as a continuous trajectory from the beginning to the end of a career, and which rejects the notion that learning ends with the reception of a diploma, we refer to these individuals as new teachers.

Non-teaching assistant (NTA). As the term indicates, NTAs do not assist in teaching but assist in the running of the school by monitoring hallways to prevent fights, getting students to their classes, and so on.

Praxeology. The concept literally means talk (Gr., *logos*) about action (Gr., *praxis*). We use this term to refer to the local knowledge about teaching and learning created by participants (teachers, students, new teachers, researchers, supervisors, and evaluators) in the process of talking about their shared experience in the context of cogenerative dialoguing.

Small learning community (SLC). Our pseudonym for the institutional units into which City High School was broken. Each SLC included five or six teachers, an SLC coordinator, about 250 students, and several non-teaching assistants (NTAs) responsible for maintaining discipline in the hallways.

Spielraum. Practitioners who act in situations where there is no time-out for reflection still have a range of actions available. They have, in other words, room to maneuver or *Spielraum*. As practitioners gain experience, the range of actions available to them at any one moment in time increases, that is, they have more *Spielraum*.

REFERENCES

Anderson, E. (1999). *Code of the street: Decency, violence, and the moral life of the inner city*. New York: W.W. Norton.

Anyon, J. (1997). *Ghetto schooling: A political economy of urban educational reform*. New York: Teachers College Press.

Apple, M. (1979). *Ideology and the curriculum*. London: Routledge & Kegan Paul.

Bakhtin, M. (1981). *The dialogic imagination*. Austin: University of Texas.

Bannon, L. J., & Bødker, S. (1991). Beyond the interface: Encountering artifacts in use. In J. M. Carroll (Ed.), *Designing interaction: Psychology at the human–computer interface* (pp. 227–253). Cambridge: Cambridge University Press.

Barton, A. C. (1997). Liberatory science education: Weaving connections between feminist theory and science education. *Curriculum Inquiry, 27*, 141–163.

Barton, A. C. (1998a). Reframing 'science for all' through the politics of poverty. *Educational Policy, 12*, 525–541.

Barton, A. C. (1998b). Teaching science with homeless children: Pedagogy, representation, and identity. *Journal of Research in Science Teaching, 35*, 379–394.

Barton, A. C. (1998c). Examining the social and scientific roles of intervention in science education. *Research in Science Education, 28*, 133–151.

Bateson, G. (1980). *Mind and nature: A necessary unity*. Toronto: Bantam Books.

Becker, H. S. (1972). A school is a lousy place to learn anything in. *American Behavioral Scientist, 16*, 85–105.

Billig, M. (1994). Repopulating the depopulated pages of social psychology. *Theory & Psychology, 4*, 307–335.

Black, P., & William D. (1998). Inside the black box: Raising standards through classroom assessment. *Phi Delta Kappan*, October, 1–14.

Bourdieu, P. (1990). *The logic of practice*. Cambridge, UK: Polity Press.

Bourdieu, P. (1992a). *Language and symbolic power*. Cambridge, MA: Harvard University Press.

Bourdieu, P. (1992b). The practice of reflexive sociology (The Paris workshop). In P. Bourdieu & L. J. D. Wacquant, *An invitation to reflexive sociology* (pp. 216–260). Chicago: University of Chicago Press.

Bourdieu, P. (1997). *Méditations pascaliennes* [Pascalian meditations]. Paris: Seuil.

Bourdieu, P., & Passeron, J.-C. (1979). *Reproduction in education, society and culture* (Trans. by Richard Nice). Thousand Oaks, CA: Sage.

Bourdieu, P., & Wacquant, L. J. D. (1992). *An invitation to reflexive sociology*. Chicago: University of Chicago Press.

Boykin, A. W. (1986). The triple quandary and the schooling of Afro-American Children. In U. Neisser (Ed.), *The school achievement of minority children: New perspectives* (pp. 57–92). Hillsdale, NJ: Lawrence Erlbaum Associates.

Cookson, P. W., Jr., & Shroff, S. M. (1997). *School choice and urban school reform*. Retrieved June 14, 2000, from the World Wide Web at http://eric-web.tc.comumbia.edu/monographs/-uds110/

Dewey, J. (1933). *How we think*. Boston: Heath.

Dreier, O. (1991). Client interests and possibilities in psychotherapy. In C. W. Tolman & W. Maiers (Eds.), *Critical psychology: Contributions to an historical science of the subject* (pp. 196–211). Cambridge: Cambridge University Press.

Dreier, O. (1993). Re-searching psychotherapeutic practice. In S. Chaiklin & J. Lave (Eds.), *Understanding practice: Perspectives on activity and context* (pp. 105–124). Cambridge: Cambridge University Press.

Dreyfus, H. L. (1991). *Being-in-the-world: A commentary on Heidegger's 'Being and Time,' division I*. Cambridge, MA: MIT Press.

Du Bois, W. E. B. (1903). *Souls of Black folk*. Chicago: McClurg.

Eckert, P. (1989). *Jocks and burnouts: Social categories and identity in the high school*. New York: Teachers College Press.

Ehn, P. (1992). Scandinavian design: On participation and skill. In P. S. Adler & T. A. Winograd (Eds.), *Usability: Turning technologies into tools* (pp. 96–132). New York: Oxford University Press.

Eldon, M., & Levin, M. (1991). Cogenerative learning: Bringing participation into action research. In W. F. Whyte (Ed.), *Participatory action research* (pp. 127–142). Newbury Park, CA: Sage.

Engeström, Y. (1987). *Learning by expanding: An activity-theoretical approach to developmental research.* Helsinki: Orienta-Konsultit.

Engeström, Y. (1994). *Learning for change: New approach to learning and training in companies.* Geneva: ILO.

Engeström, Y. (1999). Activity theory and individual and social transformation. In Y. Engeström, R. Miettinen, & R.-L. Punamäki (Eds.), *Perspectives on activity theory* (pp. 19–38). Cambridge, England: Cambridge University Press.

Engeström, Y., & Engeström, R. (2000, April). *An activity–theoretical study of expansive learning among middle school teachers.* Paper presented at the annual meeting of the American Educational Research Association, New Orleans, LA.

Epstein, S. (1997). Activism, drug regulation, and the politics of therapeutic evaluation in the AIDS era: A case study of ddC and the 'Surrogate Markers' debate. *Social Studies of Science, 27,* 691–726.

Erickson, F. (1986). Qualitative research on teaching. In M. C. Wittrock (Ed.), *Handbook for research on teaching* (3rd ed., pp. 119–161). New York: Macmillan.

Foucault, M. (1979). *Discipline and punish: The birth of the prison.* New York: Vintage Books.

Fraser, B. J. (1998). Science learning environments: Assessment, effects and determinants. In B. J. Fraser & K. G. Tobin (Eds.), *International handbook of science education* (pp. 527–564). Dordrecht, Netherlands: Kluwer Academic Publishing.

Freire, P. (1972). *Pedagogy of the oppressed.* Harmondsworth, England: Penguin.

Fullan, M. (1993). *Change forces: Probing the depths of educational reform.* New York: Falmer Press.

Gadamer, H.-G. (1975). *Truth and method.* London: Sheed Ward.

Garfinkel, H. (1967). *Studies in ethnomethodology*. Englewood Cliffs, NJ: Prentice-Hall.

Giddens, A. (1991). *Modernity and self-identity: Self and society in the late modern age*. Stanford, CA: Stanford University Press.

Gilbert, G. N., & Mulkay, M. (1984). *Opening Pandora's box: A sociological analysis of scientists' discourse*. Cambridge: Cambridge University Press.

Giroux, H. (1992). *Border crossings: Cultural workers and the politics of education*. New York: Routledge.

Gramsci, A. (1971). *Selections from the prison notebooks*. New York: International Publishers.

Grimmett, P. P. (1996). The struggles of teacher research in a context of education reform: Implications for instructional supervision. *Journal of Curriculum and Supervision, 12*, 37–65.

Grimmett, P. P. (1998). How do teachers learn to improve their practice?: Issues, challenges, and strategies for the future of supervision. *Wingspan, 12*, 12–17.

Grundy, S. (1987). *Curriculum: Product or praxis?* London: Falmer Press.

Guba, E., & Lincoln, Y. (1989). *Fourth generation evaluation*. Beverly Hills, CA: Sage.

Harris, L. (1992). Agency and the concept of the underclass. In B. E. Lawson (Ed.), *The underclass question* (pp. 33–54). Philadelphia: Temple University Press.

Heidegger, M. (1977). *Sein und zeit* [Being and time]. Tübingen, Germany: Max Niemeyer.

Henderson, A., & Kyng, M. (1991). There's no place like home: Continuing design in use. In J. Greenbaum & M. Kyng (Eds.), *Design at work: Cooperative design of computer systems* (pp. 219–240). Hillsdale, NJ: Lawrence Erlbaum Associates.

Holzkamp, K. (1983a). Der Mensch als Subjekt wissenschaftlicher Methodik [Man as subject of scientific method]. In K.-H. Braun, W. Hollitscher, K. Holzkamp, & K. Wetzel (Eds.), *Karl Marx und die Wissenschaft vom Individuum* (pp. 120–166). Marburg: Verlag Arbeiter-bewegung und Gesellschaftswissenschaften.

Holzkamp, K. (1983b). *Grundlegung der Psychologie* [Foundations of psychology]. Frankfurt: Campus.

Holzkamp, K. (1984). Zum Verhältnis zwischen gesamtgesellschaft-lichem Prozeß und individuellem Lebensprozeß [On the relation between whole-society and individual life process]. *Konsequent, 6,* 29–40.

Holzkamp, K. (1991a). Experience of self and scientific objectivity. In C. W. Tolman & W. Maiers (Eds.), *Critical psychology: Contributions to an historical science of the subject* (pp. 65–80). Cambridge: Cambridge University Press.

Holzkamp, K. (1991b). Societal and individual life processes. In C. W. Tolman & W. Maiers (Eds.), *Critical psychology: Contributions to an historical science of the subject* (pp. 50–64). Cambridge: Cambridge University Press.

Hutchins, E. (1995). *Cognition in the wild.* Cambridge, MA: MIT Press.

Il'enkov, E. V. (1977). *Dialectical logic: Essays in its history and theory.* Moscow: Progress.

Il'enkov, E. V. (1982). *Dialectics of the abstract and the concrete in Marx's Capital* (Transl. Sergei Kuzyakov). Moscow: Progress.

Kuhn, T. S. (1970). *The structure of scientific revolutions* (2nd ed.). Chicago: University of Chicago Press.

Kuutti, K. (1999). Activity theory, transformation of work, and information systems design. In Y. Engeström, R. Miettinen, & R.-L. Punamäki (Eds.), *Perspectives on activity theory* (pp. 360–376). Cambridge, England: Cambridge University Press.

Lakoff, G., & Johnson, M. (1999). *Philosophy in the flesh: The embodied mind and its challenge to western thought.* New York: Basic Books.

Lau, E. (1995). *Runaway: Diary of a street kid.* Toronto: Coach House Press.

Lave, J. (1988). *Cognition in practice: Mind, mathematics and culture in everyday life.* Cambridge: Cambridge University Press.

Lave, J., & Wenger, E. (1991). *Situated learning: Legitimate peripheral participation.* Cambridge: Cambridge University Press.

Lee, C. (1992). Literacy, cultural diversity, and instruction. *Education and Urban Society, 24,* 279–291.

Lee, O. (1999). Equity implications based on the conceptions of science achievement in major reform documents. *Review of Educational Research, 69,* 83–115.

Lemke, J. L. (1990). *Talking science: Language, learning and values.* Norwood, NJ: Ablex Publishing.

Leont'ev, A. N. (1978). *Activity, consciousness and personality.* Englewood Cliffs, NJ: Prentice-Hall.

Manning, K. R. (1993). Race, science and identity. In G. Early (Ed.), *Lure and loathing: Essays on race, identity, and the ambivalence of assimilation* (pp. 317–336). New York: Penguin Books.

Markard, M. (1984). SUFKI—theoretische Grundlage und methodische Entwicklung [SUFKI—theoretical foundations and methodological developments]. *Forum Kritische Psychologie, 14,* 56–81.

Markard, M. (1993). Kann es in einer Psychologie vom Standpunkt des Subjekts verallgemeinerbare Aussagen geben? [Can there be generalizations in a subject-centered psychology?] *Forum Kritische Psychologie, 31,* 29–51.

Marx, K., & Engels, F. (1970). *The German ideology* (C. J. Arthur, Ed.; W. Lough, C. Dutt, & C. P. Magill, Trans.). New York: International.

McRobbie, C. J., Roth, W.-M., & Lucas, K. B. (1997). Multiple learning environments in a physics classroom. *International Journal of Educational Research, 27,* 333–342.

McRobbie, C. J., & Tobin, K. (1995). Restraints to reform: The congruence of teacher and student actions in a chemistry classroom. *Journal of Research in Science Teaching, 32,* 373–385.

Mehan, H. (1993). Beneath the skin and between the ears: A case study in the politics of representation. In S. Chaiklin & J. Lave (Eds.), *Understanding practice: Perspectives on activity and context* (pp. 241–268). Cambridge, England: Cambridge University Press.

Munby, H., & Russell, T. (1992). Transforming chemistry research into chemistry teaching: The complexities of adopting new frames for experience. In T. Russell & H. Munby (Eds.), *Teachers and teaching: From classroom to reflection* (pp. 90–108). London, England: Falmer Press.

New London Group (1996). A pedagogy of multiliteracies: Designing social futures. *Harvard Educational Review, 66,* 60–92.

Newman, D., Griffin, P., & Cole, M. (1989). *The construction zone: Working for cognitive change in school.* Cambridge: Cambridge University Press.

Nissen, M. (1997). *Ideologies and developments in practical dealings with addiction.* Paper presented at the Fourth International Congres of Critical Psychology, Berlin, Germany. [http://lehmann.psl.ku.dk/~mnissen.lab/krips.htm]

Onstenk, J. (1999, February). *Enhancing the self-directed learning potential of jobs.* Paper presented at the European Conference 'Lifelong Learning—Inside and Outside Schools', Bremen, Germany.
[http://www-user.uni-bremen.de/~erill/lios/contrib/s7–06.html]

Orr, J. (1998). Images of work. *Science, Technology, & Human Values, 23,* 439–455.

Piaget, J. (1966). *The psychology of intelligence.* Patterson, New Jersey: Littlefield Adams & Co.

Pinar, W. F., & Bowers, C. A. (1992). Politics of the curriculum: Origins, controversies, and significance of critical perspectives. *Review of Research in Education, 18,* 163–190.

Pollner, M. (1987). *Mundane reason: Reality in everyday and sociological discourse.* Cambridge: Cambridge University Press.

Rabeharisoa, V., & Callon, M. (1999). *Le pouvoir des malades* [The power of the ill]. Paris: Écoles de Mines.

Ricœur, P. (1991). *From text to action: Essays in hermeneutics, II.* Evanston, IL: Northwestern University Press.

Roth, W.-M. (1993). Metaphors and conversational analysis as tools in reflection on teaching practice: Two perspectives on teacher-student interactions in open-inquiry science. *Science Education, 77,* 351–373.

Roth, W.-M. (1994). Student views of collaborative concept mapping: An emancipatory research project. *Science Education, 78,* 1–34.

Roth, W.-M. (1998a). Science teaching as knowledgeability: A case study of knowing and learning during coteaching. *Science Education, 82,* 357–377.

Roth, W.-M. (1998b). Teaching and learning as everyday activity. In K. Tobin & B. Fraser (Eds.), *International handbook of science education* (pp. 169–181). Dordrecht, Netherlands: Kluwer Academic Publishing.

Roth, W.-M. (2000). Learning environments research, lifeworld analysis, and solidarity in practice. *Learning Environments Research, 2,* 225–247.

Roth, W.-M., Bowen, G. M., Boyd, N., & Boutonné, S. (1998). Coparticipation as mode for learning to teach science. In S. L. Gibbons & J. O. Anderson (Eds.), *Connections 98* (pp. 80–88). Victoria, BC: University of Victoria.

Roth, W.-M., & Boyd, N. (1999). Coteaching, as colearning, in practice. *Research in Science Education, 29,* 51–67.

Roth, W.-M., & Harama, H. (2000). (Standard) English as second language: Tribulations of self. *Journal of Curriculum Studies, 32,* 757–775.

Roth, W.-M., Lawless, D., & Masciotra, D. (2000). Relationality, an alternative to reflectivity. *Submitted for publication.*

Roth, W.-M., Lawless, D., & Masciotra, D. (2001). Spielraum and teaching. *Curriculum Inquiry, 31*(2), 183–207.

Roth, W.-M., Lawless, D., & Tobin, K. (2000). Time to teach: Towards a praxeology of teaching. *Canadian Journal of Education, 25,* 1–15. (Copyright 2001)

Roth, W.-M., Masciotra, D., & Boyd, N. (1999). Becoming-in-the-class-room: A case study of teacher development through coteaching. *Teaching and Teacher Education, 15,* 771–784.

Roth, W.-M., & McGinn, M. K. (1997). Deinstitutionalizing school science: Implications of a strong view of situated cognition. *Research in Science Education, 27,* 497–513.

Roth, W.-M., & McRobbie, C. (1999). Lifeworlds and the 'w/ri(gh)ting' of classroom research. *Journal of Curriculum Studies, 31,* 501–522.

Roth, W.-M., McRobbie, C., Lucas, K. B., & Boutonné, S. (1997). Why do students fail to learn from demonstrations? A social practice perspective on learning in physics. *Journal of Research in Science Teaching, 34,* 509–533.

Roth, W.-M., & Roychoudhury, A. (1994). Science discourse through collaborative concept mapping: New perspectives for the teacher. *International Journal of Science Education, 16,* 437–455.

Roth, W.-M., & Tobin, K. (1996). Aristotle and natural observation versus Galileo and scientific experiment: An analysis of lectures in physics for elementary teachers in terms of discourse and inscriptions. *Journal of Research in Science Teaching, 33,* 135–157.

Roth, W.-M., & Tobin, K. (in press). Learning to teach science as praxis. *Teaching and Teacher Education.*

Roth, W.-M., Tobin, K., & Ritchie, S. (2001). *Re/Constructing elementary science.* New York: Peter Lang.

Schoenfeld, A. (1985). *Mathematical problem solving.* Orlando, FL: Academic Press.

Schoenfeld, A. (1998). Toward a theory of teaching-in-context. *Issues in Education, 4,* 1-94.

Schön, D. A. (1987). *Educating the reflective practitioner.* San Francisco: Jossey-Bass.

Seiler, G. (in press). Reversing the 'standard' direction: Science emerging from the lives of African American students. *Journal of Research in Science Teaching.*

Shulman, L. S. (1987). Knowledge and teaching: Foundations of the new reform. *Harvard Educational Review, 57,* 1–22.

Star, S. L. (1989). Layered space, formal representations and long-distance conrol: The politics of information. *Fundamenta Scientiae, 10,* 125–154.

Stepan, N. L., & Gilman, S. L. (1993). Appropriating the idioms of science: The rejection of scientific racism. In S. Harding (Ed.), *The 'Racial' economy of science: Toward a democratic future* (pp. 72–103). Bloomington: Indiana University Press.

Stern, D. (2000). Practicing social justice in the high school classroom. In W. Ayers, M. Klonsky, & G. Lyon (Eds.), *Small schools and simple justice: The unfinished fight for fairness* (pp. 110–124) New York: Teachers College Press.

Suchman, L. A. (1987). *Plans and situated actions: The problem of human-machine communication.* Cambridge: Cambridge University Press.

Suchman, L. A., & Jordan, B. (1990). Interactional troubles in face-to-face survey interviews. *Journal of the American Statistical Association, 85,* 232–244.

Tobin, K. (1982). A four phase model for activity oriented science: K–10. *Australian Science Teachers Journal, 28*(3), 63–71.

Tobin, K. (1985). Teaching strategy analysis models in middle school science education courses. *Science Education, 69*, 69–82.

Tobin, K. (1986). Effects of teacher wait time on discourse characteristics in mathematics and language arts classes. *American Educational Research Journal, 23*, 191–200.

Tobin, K. (1987). The role of wait time in higher cognitive level learning. *Review of Educational Research, 57*, 69–95.

Tobin, K. (1990). Changing metaphors and beliefs: A master switch for teaching. *Theory into Practice, 29*, 122–127.

Tobin, K. (Ed.). (1993). *The practice of constructivism in science education.* Hillsdale, NJ: Lawrence Erlbaum Associates.

Tobin, K., & Capie, W. (1980). Teaching process skills in the middle school. *School Science and Mathematics, 80*, 590–600.

Tobin, K., & Fraser, B. J. (1998). Qualitative and quantitative landscapes of classroom learning environments. In B. J. Fraser & K. G. Tobin (Eds.), *International handbook of science education* (pp. 623–640). Dordrecht, Netherlands: Kluwer Academic Publishing.

Tobin, K., Kahle, J. B., & Fraser, B. J. (Eds.). (1990). *Windows into science classrooms: Problems associated with high level cognitive learning in science.* London: Falmer Press.

Tobin, K., & LaMaster, S. (1995). Relationships between metaphors, beliefs and actions in a context of science curriculum change. *Journal of Research in Science Teaching, 32*, 225–242.

Tobin, K., Roth, W.-M., & Zimmerman, A. (in press). Learning to teach science in urban schools. *Journal of Research in Science Teaching.*

Tobin, K., Seiler, G., & Smith, M. W. (1999). Educating science teachers for the sociocultural diversity of urban schools. *Research in Science Education, 29*, 68–88.

Tobin, K., Seiler, G., & Walls, E. (1999). Reproduction of social class in the teaching and learning of science in urban high schools. *Research in Science Education, 29*, 171–187.

Tolman, C. W. (1994). *Psychology, society, and subjectivity.* London: Routledge.

Tolman, C. W., & Maiers, W. (Eds.). (1991). *Critical psychology: Contributions to an historical science of the subject.* Cambridge: Cambridge University Press.

van Manen, M. (1995). On the epistemology of reflective practice. *Teachers and Teaching: Theory and Practice, 1*, 33–50.

Varela, F. (1996). Neurophenomenology: A methodological remedy for the hard problem. *Journal of Consciousness Studies, 3*, 330–350.

von Glasersfeld, E. (1995). *Radical constructivism: A way of knowing and learning.* Washington, DC: Falmer Press.

Wertsch, J. V. (1984). The zone of proximal development: Some conceptual issues. In B. Rogoff & J. V. Wertsch (Eds.), Children's learning in the "zone of proximal development" (pp. 7–18). San Francisco: Jossey Bass.

Willis, P. (1977). *Learning to labor: How working class lads get working class jobs.* New York: Columbia University Press.

Wilson, J. W. (1987). *The truly disadvantaged.* Chicago: University of Chicago Press.

Woolgar, S. (Ed.). (1988). *Knowledge and reflexivity: New frontiers in the sociology of knowledge.* London: Sage.

AUTHOR INDEX

A

Anderson, E., xiv, 288
Anyon, J., 200
Apple, M., 179

B

Bakhtin, M., xviii, 214
Bannon, L., 274
Barton, A., 25, 57, 70, 76, 77, 78, 181
Bateson, G.,, xxiii
Becker, H., 180, 266
Billig, M., 276
Black, P., 290
Bødker, S., 274
Bourdieu, P., xix, 10–11, 75, 80, 84, 100, 103, 115, 148, 179, 180, 181, 207, 252, 278, 279, 296, 298
Boutonné, S., 30, 34
Bowen, M., 30
Bowers, C., 178, 200, 288
Boyd, N., xiv, 30, 136

Boykin, A., 179, 182–186, 187, 196, 262

C

Callon, M., 75
Capie, W., 132
Cole, M., 143, 227
Cookson, P., 178

D

Dewey, J., 278, 289, 296
Dreier, O., 201, 213, 272, 276
Dreyfus, H., 10
Du Bois, W., 182

E

Eckert, P., 21, 78, 181
Ehn, P., 206, 266, 289
Eldon, M., 206, 251, 265, 289
Engels, F., 254
Engeström, R., 75

Engeström, Y., 75, 248–250, 274
Epstein, S., 77
Erickson, F., xxi

F

Foucault, M., 77, 104, 125
Fraser, B., 136, 243, 244, 261
Freire, P., 178, 210, 253
Fullan, M., 9

G

Gadamer, H.-G., 297
Gagné, R., 132
Garfinkel, H., 109, 296
Giddens, A., 10
Gilbert, G., 108
Gilman, S., 183
Giroux, H., 25, 180
Gramsci, A., 277
Griffin, P., 133, 227
Grimmett, P., xvii, 45, 114, 307
Grundy, S., xvii
Guba, E., xviii

H

Harama, H., 180
Harris, L., 178
Heidegger, M., 299
Henderson, A., 206, 289
Holzkamp, K., xvii, 201, 244, 253, 273, 296, 306

Hutchins, E., 309

I

Il'enkov, E., 249, 264, 306

J

Johnson, M., 278
Jordan, B., 144
Joyce, B., 133

K

Kahle, J., 136
Kuhn, T., 244
Kuutti, K., 267
Kyng, M., 206, 289

L

Lakoff, G., 278
LaMaster, S., 136
Lau, E., xxi
Lave, J., 108, 144, 247
Lawless, D., 1, 28, 30, 87, 213
Lee, C., 183
Lee, O., 181
Lemke, J., 180, 260
Leont'ev, A., 276
Levin, M., 206, 251, 266, 289
Lincoln, Y., xviii
Lucas, K., 34, 243

M

Maiers, W., 253
Manning, K., 184
Markard, M., 207, 245, 252
Marx, K., 254
Masciotra, D., xiv, 28, 30, 87, 146
McGinn, M., 77
McRobbie, C., xix, 34, 140, 243
Mehan, H., 276
Mulkay, M., 108
Munby, H., 147

N

New London Group, 179
Newman, D., 144, 228
Nissen, M., 289

O

Onstenk, J., 275, 289
Orr, J., 274

P

Passeron, J.-C., 75, 80, 84, 103, 115, 179, 180
Piaget, J., 130
Pinar, W., 178, 200
Pollner, M., 111

R

Rabeharisoa, V., 77
Ricœur, P., xvii, 298
Ritchie, S., xxiii
Roth, W.-M., xiv, ix, xxiii, 19–2, 28, 30, 34, 77, 87, 110, 145–146, 148, 180, 213, 238, 243, 246, 269, 279
Rowe, M., 135
Roychoudhury, A., 145
Russell, T., 147

S

Schoenfeld, A., 192
Schön, D., 138
Seiler, G., xxiv, 78, 135, 158, 163, 202
Showers, B., 133
Shroff, S., 178
Shulman, L., 147
Smith, M., xxiv, 135, 158
Star, S., 144
Stepan, N., 183
Stern, D., 70
Suchman, L., 144, 148

T

Tobin, K., xxiii, xxiv, 1, 132–133, 135, 136, 140, 158, 212, 213, 238, 244, 261, 279
Tolman, C., 253

V

Varela, F., 148
von Glasersfeld, E., 133

W

Wacquant, L., xix, 11, 298
Walls, E., xxiv, 202

Weil, M., 133
Wenger, E., 106, 144
Wertsch, J., 250
William, D., 290
Willis, P., 201
Wilson, J., 178
Woolgar, S., xix

SUBJECT INDEX

A

Action, 139–140, 143, 147, 148, 189, 244, 246, 266, 279; conscious, xvii, 10, 149; non-conscious, 277, 289, 295, 296

Activity theory, xv, 75–77, 201, 245–253, 266f, 285, 273–275, 278, 286, 289, 290, 302, 303, 306, 310, 312

African American psychology, 182–184, 187–188, 196, 237, 263

Agency, 19f, 24f, 53, 59–60, 68, 74, 76, 81, 88, 177, 244, 246, 311, 313

Autobiography, xx–xxii, xxv, 89, 129–147

Autonomy, 63, 67, 139

B

Being-in/being-with, xvii, 1–2, 8–12, 17, 19, 24, 27–28, 44, 106–107, 109, 115, 119, 146–147, 155, 166–173, 299–301

Beliefs, 179–182

Both/and, 182–184, 309

C

Change, 23, 75–77, 79, 137f, 208, 210, 254, 301, 302, 307, 308; institutional support, 22, 24; systemic issues, 202, 301, 302

Cogenerative dialogue, xi, xiv–xvi, xix, 2, 44, 120, 160, 164, 177, 194ff, 204–210, 213ff, 218–225, 236, 237, 241, 243, 245, 246, 251ff, 257ff, 271, 277, 282–292, 295–307

Collective responsibility, 285, 312, 313

Community, 56, 108, 119, 187, 248, 249, 256; of learners, 66, 79, 86–90; partnerships, 154; of practice, 155

Constructivism, xxiv, 20, 134–135, 139–140, 143ff, 262, 264

Contradictions, 75f, 83ff, 249, 250, 252, 253, 274, 276, 277, 286, 287, 301, 302, 305, 310, 312

Coparticipation, xix, 7, 9, 11, 15, 23, 27, 33, 35, 37–38, 74, 86, 107, 159, 163–168, 173–175, 189, 244, 245, 268, 273, 278, 281, 286, 288, 291

Coteaching, xi, xii, xv, xvi, xxiii, xxv, 1–2, 7, 9, 18, 24, 30–32, 34–46, 57, 72–75, 77, 79, 85–99, 104–111, 115ff, 122ff, 146, 164, 149, 151, 153–177, 186, 189, 190, 193f, 199, 203, 204, 207–210, 213–215, 221ff, 235, 236, 241, 243, 245, 246, 250, 251, 252, 254ff, 265, 268–270, 271, 273, 277ff, 286–293, 295, 296, 298, 300, 304, 307–313

Critical perspectives, xvii, 1, 46, 297, 298, 302

Critical psychology, xvii, 201, 253, 276, 305, 306, 312

Cultural issues, 50, 73, 81f, 89, 124, 177–178; cultural capital, 86, 181, 184–187, 277; cultural practice, 103, 106; cultural production, 200, 300, 311; cultural relevance, 78, 109, 120, 177, 184–188, 262

Curriculum; design, 130f; enacted, 8, 12, 14–17, 20–21, 23, 25, 58–60, 68–69, 185; goals, 20–24; student interests, 284, 285, 299

D

Deep structure, 220, 221, 235, 237, 261

Dialectic, xiv, 248–251, 295, 296, 305, 306, 311

Discourse, 179, 180

Dispositions of African Americans, 196, 263

E

Emancipation, 20, 70, 90, 210

Epistemology, xi, xiii, xix, 1, 8, 20, 29, 43f, 269, 271, 272, 277, 291

Equity, 49, 69, 104, 276, 297

Expectations; high, 61, 63, 69; low, 53, 58, 68, 79

F

Field experience, 131f, 150–153, 162, 166–175

First person perspective, xi, 241, 245–246, 289, 299

H

Habitus, xiii, 1, 4, 7, 9ff, 17, 20, 27–28, 31, 44–46, 74, 78, 81, 85–89, 102–106, 109–117, 140, 150–153, 163, 166, 168, 173, 179, 183, 185, 188, 194, 196, 199, 206, 207, 210, 263, 269, 290, 295, 296, 298, 300, 303

Hermeneutic; analysis, xv–xvii, 298, 302; phenomenology, xvii–xviii, 1, 9, 46

High school students; absence from school, 16, 76, 202; attendance, 62–63, 64; disruption, 66, 82–83, 274; interests, 69, 78–77; motivation to learn, 66–67, 82; parent involvement, 90, 153; as researchers, xxiv, 304; roles as learners, 8, 14–17, 39; suspension, 54–55, 63, 76; as teacher educators, 26–27, 154, 158, 161, 304; sleeping, 16, 58, 63, 198, 257, 279

Home resources, 14, 19, 101

I

Identity, 10, 12, 19, 20, 71, 103, 180

Ideology, xvii, 207, 297

Inquiry, 141, 143–146, 180, 244, 287

L

Learning, 107, 191, 192, 211, 213–215, 223–231; environment, xv, xix, 13, 56, 74f, 85–89, 153, 207, 209, 243–246, 248, 251ff, 264ff, 275, 283, 287, 291, 299, 300, 304, 306, 311; life long, 214, 308, 309; resources to support, 4, 286, 287, 298; to teach, ix, xi, xii, xiv, xv, 4, 42, 44f, 49, 71, 74, 88–90, 115–119, 123f, 131, 133, 140, 143–146, 149f, 153ff, 158–177, 200, 203, 208, 214, 215, 243, 245, 253ff, 263, 265, 277, 287, 292, 295, 296, 309, 310; by teaching, 214, 215, 223

M

Material resources, 14f, 20f, 23f, 62f, 67

Mediation, 248, 249, 301, 303, 312

Metalogue, xxiii, xxiv, 235, 262, 280, 284

Metaphor, 135–138, 143, 174

Modeling, 34–35, 73

Models of teaching, 148, 149

O

Objectivism, 249, 275, 277
Ontology, 148, 266

P

Participation, 25, 58–60, 65f, 79, 195, 310
Peer teaching, 95f, 126, 154, 197
Performance standards, 273, 275
Peripheral participation, 162, 306
Personality clashes, 98, 164f
Perspectives; deficit, 50f, 71, 79, 14, 179, 182, 184, 187, 201, 271; insider, x, xii, 7, 46, 107, 271, 277; macro, 300, 312; micro, 300, 312; outsider, x, xii, xv, 27, 46, 82, 91, 107–108, 110, 268, 270, 272, 273, 277, 278
Planning, 14, 17, 20–22, 27, 30, 35, 37, 66
Power, 104, 110, 115, 126, 139, 206, 240, 248, 259, 276, 288, 291, 293, 297, 306
Praxeology, xv–xviii, 1, 28, 44, 46, 148, 160–161, 169, 177–178, 194, 197, 198, 204, 205, 214, 225, 231, 236, 238, 240, 290, 295, 296, 305

Praxis, xv–xviii, xxii, 2, 5, 8–9, 24, 28, 46f, 50f, 139, 146–149, 177, 205–209, 213–215, 241, 243–246, 253, 254, 264, 265, 268, 273, 278, 280, 290, 295, 296, 299, 305
Professional development, 273, 276, 289, 293, 310

R

Radical doubt, 207, 297, 308
Rapport, 100–101, 103, 115, 126, 189, 195, 297
Rational thinking, 11, 28
Referent, 134, 139
Reflection, 5, 8–11, 41, 47, 89, 113, 136, 138, 143ff, 146–147, 149, 220, 222, 229, 230, 231, 236, 237
Reflexivity, xix, xx, xxiii, 12
Reform, 79
Relevance, 23, 25f, 36, 47, 57, 59, 61, 69, 77f, 81, 188, 262, 268, 283ff, 299
Reproduction, xiv, xvi, 15, 74f, 78f, 85, 104-105, 109, 111, 117, 126, 179, 200, 271, 300, 311
Research, x, xi, xv–xxiv, 177, 213, 269, 299, 309
Resistance, 15–19, 25, 68, 202, 210, 276, 307
Resources; home, 14, 19, 101; material 14–16, 20f, 23f, 62f, 67; to support learning,

4, 286, 287, 298; to teach, ix, xi, xii, xiv, xv, 4, 42, 44, 49, 71, 74, 88–90, 113–119, 123–124, 131, 133, 140, 143–146, 149f, 143–145, 158–177, 200, 203, 208, 214, 215, 243, 245, 253–256, 263, 265, 277, 287, 292, 295, 296, 309, 310

Respect, 19, 56, 71f, 81f, 90, 100–101, 103, 115, 122, 129, 137, 152–153, 189, 195, 270, 288, 289, 297

Roles, 190–196, 199, 200, 202, 204–209, 214, 224, 235, 240, 241, 248, 255, 257–259, 279, 280, 281, 298, 299, 304, 306, 308–312; coop teacher, 6, 25, 27–29, 43, 47, 91, 104, 108–111, 162–177; new teachers, 96–97, 112, 162–177; researchers, 243, 246, 255–257, 265; supervisor, 6–7, 29, 43, 47, 91, 108–111, 162–177

S

Scaffolding, 31, 33, 38, 74
Science methods course, 51, 112–114, 158–162, 200, 202–205, 306, 307
Situated practices, 112
Social; capital, 277, 306; class, 69, 73, 75, 80,

83–88, 103f, 106, 151, 178–181, 201, 287; issues, 124, 311; justice, xxi, 70, 297; processes, 139, 177f, 275–277; structure, 302, 303; transformation, 70; underclass, xiv, 178
Spielraum, 28, 87f, 147, 148, 163, 168, 173, 204, 279, 291
Stereotyping, 58, 68
Strategy analysis, 132f
Street; code, xiv, 73; science, 21, 24–25, 27, 57, 71
Stress, 304
Symbolic; mastery, 113–114; violence, 21, 103, 126f

T

Teacher; classroom management, 26, 55f, 63, 66f, 74, 82, 152, 166, 174; cooperating, 132, 205ff, 306, 310, 312, 313; education as a transformative activity 49, 155–156, 167, 178, 188, 210, 310; evaluation, ix, x, xv, xvi, xxv, 7, 16, 23, 27–29, 43, 46; field placement, 157, 164f; knowledge, 120; morale, 276; new, xi, xii, 43, 51, 69, 149–150, 205–207, 267, 312, 313; pedagogical content knowledge, 235, 238, 240, 241; as researcher, 205; roles, 8,

14–17, 39; supervision, 47, 207, 299, 312

Teaching, x, xii, 13–17, 30–36, 42, 121, 130, 131, 275, 276, 287, 289, 291–293; difficulties, 93, 102, 105–106; evaluation, x, 146–147, 210, 244, 271–293, 299, 307, 309, 310; workaround strategies, 274, 275

Temporality, 5, 10, 29, 41, 46f, 79f, 148

Theory, 149–150, 250, 275; and research, 243, 244; theory practice gap, xii, xviii, 2, 46, 149, 213, 244–246, 254

Time, 278, 280, 284–287

U

Urban schools, xxi, 2, 17, 26, 49, 68f, 72, 75, 86, 89, 149–150, 165, 177, 178, 181, 183–187, 199, 200, 210, 274, 286, 298, 302–305, 312; non-teaching assistants 54f, 72, 106, 109; small learning communities, 155, 157, 165, 169–175

V

Values, 179–182

Studies in the Postmodern Theory of Education

General Editors
Joe L. Kincheloe & Shirley R. Steinberg

Counterpoints publishes the most compelling and imaginative books being written in education today. Grounded on the theoretical advances in criticalism, feminism, and postmodernism in the last two decades of the twentieth century, Counterpoints engages the meaning of these innovations in various forms of educational expression. Committed to the proposition that theoretical literature should be accessible to a variety of audiences, the series insists that its authors avoid esoteric and jargonistic languages that transform educational scholarship into an elite discourse for the initiated. Scholarly work matters only to the degree it affects consciousness and practice at multiple sites. Counterpoints' editorial policy is based on these principles and the ability of scholars to break new ground, to open new conversations, to go where educators have never gone before.

For additional information about this series or for the submission of manuscripts, please contact:

Joe L. Kincheloe & Shirley R. Steinberg
c/o Peter Lang Publishing, Inc.
275 Seventh Avenue, 28th floor
New York, New York 10001

To order other books in this series, please contact our Customer Service Department:

(800) 770-LANG (within the U.S.)
(212) 647-7706 (outside the U.S.)
(212) 647-7707 FAX

Or browse online by series:
www.peterlangusa.com